YOUTH PARTICIPATION AND DEMOCRACY

Cultures of Doing Society

Eeva Luhtakallio and Veikko Eranti

with Georg Boldt, Maija Jokela, Lotta Junnilainen,
Taina Meriluoto and Tuukka Ylä-Anttila

First published in Great Britain in 2024 by

Bristol University Press
University of Bristol
1–9 Old Park Hill
Bristol
BS2 8BB
UK
t: +44 (0)117 374 6645
e: bup-info@bristol.ac.uk

Details of international sales and distribution partners are available at bristoluniversitypress.co.uk

© Bristol University Press 2024

British Library Cataloguing in Publication Data
A catalogue record for this book is available from the British Library

ISBN 978-1-5292-3932-4 hardcover
ISBN 978-1-5292-3934-8 ePub
ISBN 978-1-5292-3935-5 ePdf

The right of Eeva Luhtakallio and Veikko Eranti to be identified as authors of this work has been asserted by them in accordance with the Copyright, Designs and Patents Act 1988.

All rights reserved: no part of this publication may be reproduced, stored in a retrieval system, or transmitted in any form or by any means, electronic, mechanical, photocopying, recording, or otherwise without the prior permission of Bristol University Press.

Every reasonable effort has been made to obtain permission to reproduce copyrighted material. If, however, anyone knows of an oversight, please contact the publisher.

The statements and opinions contained within this publication are solely those of the authors and not of the University of Bristol or Bristol University Press. The University of Bristol and Bristol University Press disclaim responsibility for any injury to persons or property resulting from any material published in this publication.

Bristol University Press works to counter discrimination on grounds of gender, race, disability, age and sexuality.

Cover design: Lyn Davies Design
Front cover image: Stocksy/nomad studio

Dedicated to Risto Alapuro (1944–2022),
our teacher and friend

Contents

Notes on Collaborators		vi
Acknowledgements		viii
Preface		ix
1	Introduction: Doing Society *Veikko Eranti and Eeva Luhtakallio*	1
2	Institutional Participation: Youth Councils and Participatory Budgeting Fostering Better Citizens *Georg Boldt*	26
3	Aspiring Politicians: From Amateur Engagements to Problem Solving *Veikko Eranti and Eeva Luhtakallio*	49
4	Voicing Ideas: Participation through E-democracy *Veikko Eranti and Georg Boldt*	68
5	Imagining Alone: The Necessity of the Atomized Self among Stigmatized Youth *Taina Meriluoto and Lotta Junnilainen*	85
6	Online Transgressions: Imageboards and Cultural Practices of Anonymous Citizenship *Tuukka Ylä-Anttila and Veikko Eranti*	105
7	Street Party: Urban Individualism and the Culture of Commitment *Maija Jokela*	118
8	Reluctant Rebels: The New Climate Movement and the Individual Activists *Maija Jokela, Jenni Kettunen and Eeva Luhtakallio*	138
9	Conclusions: Cultures of Doing Society *Eeva Luhtakallio and Veikko Eranti*	159
Appendix: Mixed Distance Methods and Data *Tuukka Ylä-Anttila, Lotta Junnilainen and Taina Meriluoto*		172
Notes		183
References		186
Index		206

Notes on Collaborators

Georg Boldt (PhD) is a postdoctoral researcher in sociology at the University of Helsinki. His work examines political participation and cultures of engagement. His ethnographic lens pans across a range of civil society practices from institutional forms of participation to direct action. He has published work on institutional youth participation, church democracy and activism.

Veikko Eranti (PhD, MA) is Assistant Professor of Urban Sociology at the University of Helsinki. His research sits at the intersection of political and urban sociology. He has written about urban conflicts, NIMBY and participation, and political participation in online settings, among many other topics. His work has been published in the *Sociological Review*, *International Journal of Urban and Regional Research*, *Acta Sociologica* and *Food, Culture & Society*.

Maija Jokela (PhD) is a postdoctoral researcher in sociology at the University of Helsinki. Her doctoral thesis (2024) deals with network activism and the use of urban space in Helsinki, and she has also done research on climate activism. Her work has been published in *Sosiologia* and *Sociological Review*.

Lotta Junnilainen (PhD) is Senior Lecturer and Academy Researcher in Human Geography at the University of Helsinki. Her research focuses on spatial and cultural dimensions of inequalities, belonging and community, and ethnography. She is particularly known for her ethnographic research on stigmatized social housing estates, describing how communities are experienced and practised locally.

Eeva Luhtakallio (PhD) is Professor of Sociology at the University of Helsinki. Her research is situated in political and cultural sociology, and has the overarching theme of studying the mundane, everyday practices constituting democracy. She has recently written about the public sphere in the social media age, state–civil society relations in climate activism, and the development of methods for studying visual politics. Her work has been published in, for example, the *British Journal of Sociology*, *Distinktion*, *Ethnography* and *Theory and Society*.

Taina Meriluoto (PhD) is Senior Researcher in Sociology at the University of Helsinki. She works on (visual) politicization, democratic theory and practice, and focuses especially on the interrelations between the self and political action among marginalized people. Her work has been published in, for example, the *British Journal of Sociology*, *International Journal of Urban and Regional Research*, *Ethnography* and *Social Movement Studies*.

Tuukka Ylä-Anttila (PhD) is Senior Researcher in Sociology at University of Helsinki. His research deals with empirical morality in social interactions, including politics and markets. His work has been published in journals such as *Social Media + Society*, *Discourse, Context & Media* and *European Journal of Cultural and Political Sociology*.

How to cite this book:

You can cite the whole book using all the authors:
Luhtakallio E. and Eranti V., with Boldt, G., Jokela, M., Junnilainen, L., Meriluoto, T. and Ylä-Anttila, T. (2024) *Youth Participation and Democracy: Cultures of Doing Society*. Bristol University Press.

Please cite individual chapters with their authors:
Jokela, M. (2024) Street Party: Urban Individualism and the Culture of Commitment. In Luhtakallio and Eranti et al, *Youth Participation and Democracy: Cultures of Doing Society*. Bristol University Press.

Acknowledgements

We are deeply grateful for years-long collegial friendships and sustainable work environments to everybody at the Centre for Sociology of Democracy (CSD), especially participants of the CSD seminar, as well as our colleagues at the sociology disciplines and more broadly at the faculties of social sciences of Tampere University and the University of Helsinki, many of whom have contributed to this book by their insightful comments, advice, inspiring research and, most importantly, their warm and steadfast collegiality throughout the years of conducting this research. You know who you are – thank you for being the loyal and trustworthy home team in the turbulent academia.

We thank our research assistants Liban Sheikh, Minja Sormunen, Roosa Tuukkanen and Josefin Westermarck, and our more senior colleagues Sam Hardwick, Jenni Kettunen and Tomi Lehtimäki, who directly contributed to data collection, analysis and translation.

To Gianpaolo Baiocchi, Anders Blok, Nina Eliasoph, Monika Krause, Isaac Ariail Reed and Iddo Tavory, we are grateful for comments on theory, and their friendship and faith in us. The lovely people in the Nordic Network for New Social Pragmatism contributed to our work with many inspiring discussions.

Laurent Thévenot has been the most reliable colleague and friend who has helped us along on our journey in manifold ways and provided his always fruitful comments on our theoretical efforts at countless occasions.

We thank Tommi Laitio and other officials of the City of Helsinki, especially all the youth workers and professionals we met during our fieldwork, and Kalle Korhonen from the Kone Foundation for his interest in and respect for our work.

This project would not have been possible without the sustained funding from the Kone Foundation and the Academy of Finland, for which we are grateful. This project has also received funding from the European Research Council (ERC) under the European Union's Horizon 2020 research and innovation programme (Grant agreement No 804024).

Preface

In this book, we ask how societies are made possible and how will democracy look in the future. We look for answers in the doings of young members participating in society: what kind of actions they take, which political practices they follow and how they tread the path towards the future by walking it. In a world marked by polarization, sustainability crises and fast-paced transformation of media environments, how do young people dream, imagine and engage in action to reach towards our common future?

We start responding these questions with two vignettes of talking with young societally active people. First, Lucy. She was under 20 years old and had just been elected as a city councillor in municipal elections. She was from an affluent neighbourhood and studied in a prestigious programme at a top university. When asked about how her party affiliation started, she painted a picture of her hobbies:

> 'Well, often people are into sports or exercising or those kinds of things, and I was never into group sports. I was getting bored with my art classes and thus not having any hobbies that I would've been interested in anymore. I started, naturally, pondering the things I am good at, and then it just happened that I joined the [centre-right] national Coalition Party Youth organization without knowing anyone there previously.'

She was good at talking to people and had strong opinions on society, and was in need of a hobby to spice up her spare time. Youth politics presented itself as a natural option, which then led to standing up in a local election – the leap from a pastime into a serious commitment to political activism was aided by impressive merits in official youth participation channels, such as the local youth council.

The second scene takes place in a local bar. A couple of slightly older activists are having a discussion over a beer on how to recruit new volunteers to organize the DIY urban activism street party they have been running for a few years:

Alex: Three questions to be discussed with the potential volunteers: Why are we doing Kallio Block Party? Why are you doing

	it? How do you connect it to your greatest dream, and what is that dream?
Leena:	What is the dream you want to fulfil through Block Party?

The block party in question is an annually recurring hallmark of a once-working-class-now-hipster neighbourhood close to the centre of Helsinki. It runs entirely on volunteers and eschews traditional organization structures in favour of a more free-wheeling culture of commitment: people come to do one thing one year, and then move on to something else. Thus, recruiting volunteers is the key to getting the festival up and running, and to this end, the long-term activists reckon that potential volunteers need to feel like the street party is actually their project, a dream they are realizing.

This book is about different ways in which young people interact with society: how they participate in structures created for participation, how they do politics and how they run volunteer projects. We aim at capturing the gamut of ways in which young people engage with broader society: pursuing change in the world, both from the left and from the right, from the stable and organized to the fleeting and the ephemeral. In this book, we do not separate between party politics, activism, online trolling and participating in dedicated participatory programmes, despite their obvious differences. All these activities share a common nucleus we call *doing society*. Even if the trappings change, the core of these activities remains the same: young people draw from what they have learned, organize together or even by themselves, and produce and reproduce the culture and the society in which they live.

For Lucy, her upbringing led her to identify with the right side of the political spectrum: standing for election was easier since a relative of hers was active in the same party. Rose, in contrast, had moved to Finland more recently and was active in many projects of the green and left-wing civil society, most notably Extinction Rebellion (XR). Her take on political identification and belonging was quite different:

> 'I'm not really just involved with XR. That's part of it, but ... I've also been protesting every week by myself outside my library ... And then being involved in many different campaigns. But I don't know, I wouldn't say that I'm particularly affiliated with any group. *I'm more like a personal entity for climate justice* is how I've always described it.'

The dramatic way in which Rose describes her (non)affiliation with XR is not just an individual anomaly. The recent wave of climate movements – Fridays for Future, XR and others – have been built on a sturdy individualistic foundation. The activists are committed to fight climate change rather than being committed to any organization or other affiliation as such.

In this book, we will repeatedly encounter this kind of individualism and individual commitment, defining even the most collectivist projects and colouring all kinds of societal activities. Individual commitment is not limited to political careers starting out as hobbies, or the climate movement providing a platform for individual action: it is also reflected in how Alex and Leena above recruited people to run street parties by making them a vehicle for the volunteers' own dreams. Following these dreams, having something meaningful to do, getting one's voice heard, having a hobby that is fulfilling – these define the engagement with the world, whether in politics or in other things. Individualism, and *doing* instead of *being* are the double tenets of how young people in the 2020s engage with the world. Being a member of a collective can be a source of many meaningful things, such as power in numbers for the politician or psychological healing through globally modelled debriefing sessions for the XR activists. Nonetheless, the collectives do not get to define their members – they are first and foremost individuals, and adhere to collectives in their own terms, often only momentarily.

This is a book about *doing* that is studied based on extensive data collection. We have followed young people in participatory budgeting negotiations and in street demonstrations, we have read the right-wing rants they wrote online alone late at night, we have interviewed committed and professional young political operatives, and committed and desperate climate activists, and have pored over social media feeds and surveys. All this action is doing society, and creating the actual practices of our democracy as it goes along.

Yet, not all young people are actively participating in democratic processes, even if the vast variation described above is counted. Hanna (aged 15) lives in a relatively deprived neighbourhood. We met her, participating in a cooking course in her neighbourhood during ethnographic fieldwork, and she told us the following about what living a good life means for her:

> 'I would love if my life were like this: A husband, perhaps a child, two children – and I'd like to have them when I'm still kinda young. I want to have a nice home, decorated by myself. I want it to be in light colours, in beige, that everything is light-toned, with a few contrasts in black or in brown. I would have a good job that pays a good amount of money, or enough that I can get by, and have something left after all the bills.'

She then clarified that a 'good amount of money' means around €2,000 a month, near the poverty line for a family in the Finnish context, making the dream portrayed here relatively modest by any standard.

One central argument of this book is that *this also is doing society*: the dreams that we have and things we think the future can hold for us set the backdrop for all action. Everybody dreams, not just the segment of people that is traditionally thought of as 'politically active'. In this book, we explore the imagined futures of politically active youth, but we equally listen to those more like Hanna, and others in between. This way, we argue, a fuller picture regarding democracy's future unfolds: one not exclusively describing the story of a certain group of young people, but one that catches the societal understandings of a broad spectrum of young actors.

Interpreting what politics *is* or what *the political* means is a crucial part of grasping the cultures of doing society portrayed by the young actors' engagements. We did not impose these definitions on the young people, but followed their own answers and reflections to these questions. When looking at the right-wing anonymous online communities, we computationally followed the participants' own interpretation of what politics means. Similarly, this was a central question we asked from young people active in youth councils and in the climate movement. In all other chapters, this perspective served as a starting point for the researchers, giving the actors of this study primacy in defining their respective relationships with the political.

The main empirical division in the book is between formal and informal participation. We start with youth councils, youth politicians and e-participation: the institutional channels and political arenas through which young people aspire to get their voices heard. We then contrast these with a chapter introducing young people who feel completely marginalized, outside of society. The rest of the book deals with informal yet organized participation that ranges from online political talk on imageboards to DIY street parties and social movements organizing climate demonstrations.

Hence, the dominating ethos of this book is to eschew siloed thinking and to embrace a more holistic way of seeing participation, politics, civicness – ways of engaging with the world and, through that, creating societies. This holistic ethos is reflected both in the theoretical contribution the book puts forward, the data collection in which we engaged in and, finally, also the writing process. Even though the individual chapters – detailed in the introductory chapter that follows this preface – were written by the people whose names appear in each of the chapters, they were all conceived in the same research project, using the same theoretical tools. Thus, this is not a traditional academic edited volume: the chapters all follow the theoretical groundwork presented in Chapter 1, which was born out of hours of collective intellectual labour, including everyone in the project. While you can of course cherrypick the chapters that interest you, we have edited the book with the intention of making it rewarding to read it like ... a normal book. Just keep turning pages from here and you'll be good!

If you do keep turning the pages, next comes the introductory Chapter 1, in which we explain in detail what we mean when we say that Lucy, Alex, Leena, Rose and Hanna are *doing society*, each in their own way. We also delve deeper into the meaning of context: the empirical data in this book is from Finland between 2014 and 2022. Yet, the big picture emerging is recognizable in multiple other contexts and connects with sociological debates about intensifying individualization.

★ ★ ★

This book would not have been possible without the hundreds of young people who let us in their lives and offered us a window to observe their political engagements, whether formal, informal, active, withdrawing, angry or full of hope. Without them, and without their reasoning, sense making and imagination, there would not be a future to democracy as we know it (or do not yet know). We are deeply grateful to them for letting us in.

Veikko and Eeva
Copenhagen and Helsinki, 29 January 2024

1

Introduction: Doing Society

Veikko Eranti and Eeva Luhtakallio

In this book, we argue that in order to better understand the future directions of democracies, we need a more holistic conceptualization of *doing society*. This concept denotes both the range of actions that constitute the manifold cultural bases of current societies, and the range of actions that direct the future by way of dreams, imagination and aspirations. To offer a view to what such a conceptualization entails, this book presents a multisited, mixed-distance data study (see the Appendix) of young people in Finland engaged in a variety of actions, ranging from social movement mobilization to private dreams of a better social position, from youth party activism to online forum discussions and to top-down participation cultures. The study compiles a multilevel understanding of cultures of doing society, what they mean to a wide variety of young citizens, and what these meanings teach us about the interlocking interpretations of individualism and collectivism in 21st-century citizens' actions.

The hundreds of young people we met during this study were doing society at different levels of publicity, with different stakes and ambitions, engaging with others in different terms, and with different degrees of individualism and collectivism. Yet, their actions are connected by the unavoidable building of the common, and thus of society. While they are trying to forge a place for themselves, they also forge the meanings and understandings that form the society in the making around them. This connection point and constant building site is the object of the analytical gaze of our study: the imagining, engaging and acting done by young people.

Hence, we suggest in this book to not to look at either or, but to offer a view, even if empirically connected to one context, of the full gamut: from activists to young people drafted into participatory projects, from politically doubtful or apathetic citizens to ambitious and career-minded young politicians, and from all the respective actors' range of actions to the accounts of their dreams and imagined futures. Doing so, we acknowledge, and argue that all these perspectives are needed to avoid overemphasizing some interpretation over another: the future of democracy might not be this *or* that, but instead this *and* that, and the conclusions drawn should reflect the multitude of landscapes that have fed the analysis. We draw a continuum on the axis of active citizenship and apathy, of collective mobilization for justice and adherence to anti-democratic worldviews, and, perhaps most comprehensively, of individualistic and collective stances, arranged into a scenery that may have contradicting colours and features, but that also forms patterned cultures of doing society to follow in future research.

Doing society is an analytical and descriptive term that is built on both empirical and theoretical development. First, it builds on a practical observation from both previous research and the empirical fields our study covered: that defining politics and the political, and sticking rigidly with these definitions, often leads to analytical dead ends. It is well documented that all over the world, a good deal of the people social scientists meet, for instance, in activist or participatory settings, firmly refuse to call their activities politics and to describe themselves as politically active, or 'political people' – those 'others' mixed in this dirty game full of dangers of conflict and betrayal. Instead, people prefer to be 'concerned' or 'interested' or 'care' about a particular matter. Researchers have spent a good deal of time and effort in defining politics and the political, and explaining the widespread aversion to politics, as well as in opening up lay definitions of what, actually, is political (previous critical approaches – see, for example, Bennett et al 2012). While we inscribe to a wide notion of the political (see, for example, Warren 1999), and agree with many of the analyses concerning people's ways and reasons of avoiding politics (see, for example, Eliasoph 1998), we wanted to find a way to talk about citizen engagements without running into the necessity of defining, on each occasion, what may or may not 'count' as political action.

This desire emerged, first, from our empirical findings: many of the activities we followed oscillated – also sometimes in the participants' views – from 'less' political to 'more' and back, while often remaining the same meaningful, commonality-building activity to the participants all along. Sometimes these engagements included aversion to politics, sometimes not, and sometimes there emerged a process from apolitical to political. Clearly, however, there was something else than politics as such that the activities had in common: *they were about the common* (see Thévenot 2014, 2015). So instead of looking for political engagements as such, we followed young citizens doing and expressing all kinds of things in relation to the common, to the public, to being part, to belonging, from small-scale and local to national and transnational societies. On occasions, these engagements indeed were explicitly political, while at other times they were at most proto-political, yet they were certainly always in some relation to politics in the widest sense. As for the latter, this sense is rarely shared in lay definitions of politics, and thus it becomes analytically somewhat unhelpful, whereas the *common* and the *society* were terms that were fathomable and also useful to the participants of this study: they did get the common and talked about it with ease.

Second, the idea of doing society is theoretically grounded in pragmatist and cultural sociology. While the contributions in this book build on empirical findings, they have been achieved by adhering to a joint conceptual framework. Thinking from within this framework has allowed us to construct the idea of doing society that serves as the common thread through the different empirical approaches. The framework is based, on the one hand, on so-called French pragmatist thought, in particular Luc Boltanski's and Laurent Thévenot's (2006) initial work on competing moral evaluations as the grounds for problem solving in complex societies, and Thévenot's (2006, 2007, 2014, 2015) further work on the programme of sociology of engagements, in which the idea of people's obligations of building the common from essentially pluralist starting points – from individuals to groups and societies – sets the stage for mundane, everyday operations of engaging in communicating and composing the potential common. On the other hand, we draw on developments in American cultural sociology, and introduce to the pragmatist thinking the metaphors of the cultural toolkit, civic imagination and group styles (Swidler 1986; Eliasoph and Lichterman 2003; Baiocchi et al 2013), all part of a 'family' of theorizing that helps us understand both how groups, cultures and societies function at the level of everyday action, and how they change through small shifts and slow transformations of tools, imaginations and styles. Together these provide a robust set of analytical lenses to concretize 'the common' that often remains relatively abstract in the pragmatist framework.

What *is* the society being done? What are political belonging, membership, participation, and joint action? Doing society is the combination of all these aspects, and these aspects constitute the ways in which people forge the common. Through a particular mix of these activities, patterned cultures of doing society come into being. So instead of mapping definitions of society, we suggest taking the constant becoming-of-society as the vantage point: when doing society, people make up, negotiate and redefine what society is. To make sense of this, we need to follow the action (Lichterman 2020) and approach the resulting concept of society as an adverb rather than a noun (Luhtakallio 2012): as a 'how question' on meanings-in-the-making, the answers to which are constantly subject to change. This conceptual strategy has family resemblance to the *emic* approach in, for example, linguistic anthropology, suggesting observation from within the actions' and actors' own logic and parameters (on the emic/etic distinction, see Pike 1967; Harris 1976).

So, if doing society is what people do, and the resulting society is the common entity-in-the-making in different contexts, what can we say about it in general or about the big questions concerning its future? Where are democratic societies heading? What do we dream about as citizens? How will future politics unfold? In social scientific scholarship, there are numerous takes on the direction: illiberalism and populism are gaining further ground, inclusiveness is reaching new depths due to wider participation, globalization dismantles representative democracy, inequality affects participation and makes democracy increasingly the rule of the few everywhere. Whichever thesis is put forward depends on the perspective: studies on the populist turn emphasize inequality and bubblefication of the public sphere; studies on participative democracy highlight participation, whether critically or wishfully; social movement studies look at mobilizations and deem their importance to be crucial. Posing the question of what are the future directions for the actions constituting human societies requires taking over a vertiginous pile of perspectives and readings. Instead, we suggest it would be more fruitful to approach the question from a new perspective. This new perspective is our objective in this book, an objective we address with the combination of the wide scale of activities we have followed empirically, and the overarching conceptual idea of the common-reaching cultures of doing society.

In the following sections, we first lay out the elements joined in our conceptualization by revisiting the intersection of pragmatic and cultural sociology. In the subsequent sections, we describe the three different contexts of the study on which the book is based. First, we detail both its 'zeitdiagnostic' and empirical contexts: namely, the current trends of individualism and collectivism, and their emergence and manifestation in the current Nordic societies. Second, we take a brief detour on the social scientific field of youth studies to situate the book's contribution, and return to the dynamics of individualism and collectivism among the Finnish youth in particular. The introduction ends with an overview of the contents of the book.

Theoretical grounds for doing society

This book is an exploration on how the doing of society is done: what are the tools and repertoires that are used – either knowingly or unconsciously – to guide young people's civic, political and societal engagements. In the project behind this book, we followed the pragmatist idea of situated action: instead of adhering to traditions of research that are marked by emphasis on group memberships or identities (youth studies, social movement studies and participatory democracy studies), we based our choice of empirical objects on a map of different modes of engagement (Thévenot 2007): formal and informal, more and less active. Conceptually, our point of departure was anchored in the idea that it is impossible to discuss participation in society in terms detached from action (for example, Schudson 1998; Neveu 2003; Rosanvallon 2006; Eliasoph 2011; Talpin 2011; Luhtakallio 2012). Acting in today's societies, citizens[1] rely on a set of practices and repertoires that require learning, imagining, engaging, and doing. This dynamic process of interaction between individuals, societal and state institutions, and social life, is crucial for democracy, in the sense of democracy as a 'form of society' as we know it (Rosanvallon 2011). Our conceptual suggestion of 'doing society' thus addresses the cultural patterns that form the bases of actions constantly building and rebuilding democracy.

Understanding action in this multifaceted way demands conceptual tools capable of addressing different levels and forms of engaging with society. Recent developments in pragmatic political sociology provide such tools by exploring people's capacities to sustain life together in a complex society (Boltanski and Thévenot 2006 [1991]; Thévenot 2007, 2014, 2015; Archer and Maccarini 2013). Extending the conception of political action from traditional public-sphere-bound forms towards non-conventional, singular, personal, even non-verbal forms, provides a more comprehensive and effective research strategy to understanding changes in current political cultures (see Eranti 2018; Luhtakallio 2019; Luhtakallio 2020; Luhtakallio and Meriluoto 2023; Eranti et al 2024).

New pragmatic sociology with French roots (for example, Boltanski and Thévenot 1999, 2006; Thévenot 2011; Ylä-Anttila and Luhtakallio 2016; Eranti 2018) provides a resonant starting point for addressing the building blocks of the cultures of 'doing society'. Within this theoretical approach, Laurent Thévenot's work suggests three modes of communicating and composing the shared and acknowledging differences: three grammars of 'commonality in the plural' that format the processes of working the shared and the common that people engage in (Thévenot 2007, 2014, 2015). These perspectives have proven useful to analyse (and compare) different cultural contexts as well as the instances in which 'democracy' as a form of governance is forged into being, and, as we argue in this book, society is constantly 'being done' (on urban planning and participation, see Eranti 2017; Blok et al 2018; on local activism, see Luhtakallio 2012; on populist politics, see Ylä-Anttila 2017, on politics more generally, Eranti and Meriluoto 2023; Luhtakallio and Meriluoto 2023).

In addition to the theoretical groundwork of pragmatic sociology, the key metaphor that guides our work is the idea of culture as a set of tools – a toolkit – by Ann Swidler (1986, 2001). To quote Swidler: 'Culture influences action not by providing the ultimate values toward which action is oriented, but by shaping a repertoire or "tool kit" of habits, skills, and styles from which people construct "strategies of action"' (1986: 273). From Swidler – who originally treated 'culture' on a relatively macroscopic level, namely an entity that as a whole went through turbulent and settled times – we zoom in to look at cultures in plural that coexist within a societal setting. These cultures that the different engagements in doing society form and format, require varying sets of skills, habits and styles. Our approach is based on the dual idea of *doing society* and the cultural tools that are used by actors in their engagements. We therefore understand our empirical materials through the sets of cultural tools to *imagine, engage* and *act*. Thus, in our conceptual kit, cultural tools are ways of looking into future and dreaming of change (civic imaginations), ways of belonging to a group and being in our common world (modes of engagements; group and scene styles), and ways of acting out moral positions in terms of shared values and common life (justifications and modes of valuation). In the next section, we take a closer look at these three sets of analytical tools.

Aspects of doing society: civic imaginations, group styles and regimes of engagement

For young people, participation in society is always conditional in some sense. Many of the subjects of this book are underage and thus devoid of democratic rights. But even those legally of age often lack the resources and connections more established people have at their disposal when trying to change things in a society. One way of categorizing and understanding different strategies of action, or sets of cultural practices and repertoires, is by looking at how the young people in this book are *imagining* a better future – analysing their *civic imaginations*.

The concept of civic imagination comes from Baiocchi et al (2014: 55–56), who use it to describe the imaginative capacity through which citizens attempt to build a better world. All the active ways of doing society, be they civic or political action, start out, in one way or the other, from the idea that things could be otherwise. Civic imagination is the structure that guides the conceptions actors have on, first, which things could be otherwise and, second, *how* they could be otherwise. Civic imagination refers to the totality of what is seen as meaningful and how can things be changed – to 'acts of inventive, prospective thinking about a better society' (Baiocchi et al 2014: 21).

Baiocchi and his co-authors distilled the concept out of an ethnographic project among activist groups, describing the types of imagination they saw in the field. In their work, civic imagination is essentially a personal quality, a way of making sense of the world. Despite this individualistic flavour, Baiocchi et al (2014: 56, 117) name three 'conglomerations', or relatively stable types of civic imagination they found by observing activists and associational life in a mid-sized US city. These types are structured around redistributing power and privilege, building solidarity and community, and advancing problem-solving and technical solutions. For a civic imagination focused on power and societal structures, the most important task for citizens (and therefore the civil society) is to rectify structural inequalities in the world. Civic imagination valuing solidarity and community see communities themselves as vehicles of changing the world for the better, and therefore the task is to enhance the possibilities of these communities which then lead to positive outcomes. Finally, civic imagination emphasizing technical solutions sees politics and societal life as a series of problems which require new innovative solutions.

In addition to civic imagination, our analysis uses conceptions that address *engaging* with others. Nina Eliasoph and Paul Lichterman (2003) call *group styles* the 'recurrent patterns of interaction that arise from a group's shared assumptions about what constitutes good or adequate participation in the group setting' (Eliasoph and Lichterman 2003: 737). They divide these assumptions into three dimensions – group bonds, boundaries, and speech and action norms – thus building a grid of constitutive features for understanding what groups do and why (Eliasoph and Lichterman 2003: 737–738, 785–786). How do group members relate to each other and how do they collectively define the relations they have with each other? How do they decide on the ways of dealing with outsiders, or on who to recruit and why? What kinds of topics are appropriate to discuss in the group and how can they be talked about, and which action repertoires does the group choose to use?

Responding to the critique received from their previous work on group styles, suggesting that a 'group' is too narrow a starting point to be the object of analysis for studying interaction and the consequences to the cultures thus created, Lichterman and Eliasoph (2014) redirected the theory to address *scene styles*. This shift allows for analysis of the many different styles emerging among, for instance, one and a same group of people, depending on what they are doing, where and with whom. The theoretical tools provided by Lichterman and Eliasoph perfected, for their part, the (operationally rather hazy – however, see Inglis and Thorpe 2023) Goffmanian toolkit, and proved, to us, initially very helpful especially in analysing ethnographic data about engagements towards the common we detected on our research fields.

Engaging also has a second, more defined theoretical meaning. Laurent Thévenot has suggested that three grammars of 'commonality in the plural' format the processes of constituting the shared and the common. These are the grammar of public justifications, based on the actions of justifying and on competing yet recognized and legitimate conceptions of the common good (Boltanski and Thévenot 2006); the liberal grammar, or that of individual interests (for terminology, see Eranti 2018) based on stakeholder interests, negotiations and deals and interacting with the world through well-laid plans; and the grammar of familiarity based on intimate attachments to shared 'common-places', recognized yet often non-verbalized loci of comfort and ease (Thévenot 2007, 2014, 2015).

These three grammars give us tools to analyse the acting out of moral positions in the world. They enable exploring how actors solve conflicts in situations that require them to justify their aspirations and decisions in ways that are understandable for others engaged in the same situation. This process is called justification. We all have the capacity for situational justification and critique (Boltanski and Thévenot 1999; Boltanski 2011), and therefore it is meaningful to approach participation by examining the arguments, justifications and participation of 'ordinary people'. While, within this research tradition, justification usually refers only to public acts in reference to a common good, negotiating over individual interests within a liberal public (Thévenot 2015; Eranti 2018), and extending – or denying – solidarity through the grammar of familiarity, are comparable (even if fundamentally different) ways of acting on moral positions. Following Silber (2003), we approach these justifications as specific sets of cultural tools that are readily available for everyone in specific cultures.

Taken together, these tools – civic imaginations, group and scene styles, ways of engaging, justifications and other grammars of commonality – form a sort of meta-toolkit, a toolkit of toolkits. With this toolkit we can understand the cultural grounds of doing society. The toolkit allows us to analyse *cultures of doing society* in the plural, in a way that is sensitive enough to help us understand everyday practices, even the shyest expressions of dreams, as well as macroconnections between movements and participatory systems. It allows us to analyse micro-interactions as well as to compare different settings and time periods. Finally, it is comprehensive enough to address issues ranging from the self-analysis of nonparticipating youngsters, activists and politicians, to the analysis of the nature of political talk in the public sphere.

Expanding the boundaries of 'the civic'

Since our aim is to look at the gamut of action and nonaction that keeps the societies and communities whirring, changing – or stable, for that matter – the current conceptual repertoire available for describing the actual object of our study in sociology and political science is insufficient. We are not interested in detailed arguments over what action can precisely be called *civic* or *political*, nor do we want to be limited by the framework or perspective of either youth, participation, marginalization or social movement studies. Rather, we are interested in the actions of the young people *interpreted as ways of doing society*.

In their book on civic imagination, Baiocchi and his co-authors (2014) focus exclusively on activists, yet some kind of imagination can be said to guide everybody's participation in civic issues, closer to what Adams et al (2015) call social imaginaries. We do not confine ourselves only to sustained civic projects of the type emphasized by Lichterman and Eliasoph as a prerequisite of civic action (2014), nor to people who are committed to 'making a difference in political life' (Baiocchi et al 2014). While Lichterman and Eliasoph point out that civic action can take place in settings that are not 'obviously civic', such as for-profit enterprises – as long as a civic scene opens up – and that not everything civic activists do is civic either (see also Lichterman 2020), we take the argument further. First, we argue that all kinds of people in all kinds of settings act in ways that at least implicitly outline a civic imagination of sorts. It might be conventional, more focused on maintaining status quo and keeping the cogs of the machine turning – but this is also an important aspect of the life of societies, and therefore should be considered and analysed. Hence, and second, doing society is not a speciality domain of activists, and neither should civic imagination be seen as something that only guides the thinking of activists or otherwise 'prelabelled' civic actors.

This perspective is key to our analysis of the *cultures of doing society*: if politics, or civic participation for that matter, is done through a predefined set of cultural tools, symbols, scripts and so on, the formation and development of these tools is as such also crucial for the analysis of doing society. Thus, while our principal focus lies in forms of active political participation, and therefore in forms of civic action, we argue that a complete picture will not emerge without taking a look, equally, at more tokenistic participation efforts, top-down structures of participatory democracy, and even nonpolitical nonparticipation. These engagements also contribute to the development of the culture that all politics happens in, and define in their respective ways engaging with – and doing – society.

While the concept of *civic action* (Lichterman and Eliasoph 2014) has been a powerful inspiration for us, it is not sufficient by itself to describe the ways of *doing society* that this book presents. According to Lichterman (2020: 22–23): 'Civic action is flexibly organized, collective, social problem solving. Participants are coordinating action to improve some condition of common life that they think should matter to members of a larger imagined society, however they envision it.' Lichterman goes on to show how the concern about civic action traverses Western social thought from de Tocqueville to Durkheim and from American pragmatists to German critical theory (Lichterman 2020: 24). In this book, we follow the action, detect scene styles and analyse the coordination of action aimed at common life. Yet, grounded by the objective to understand political engagements and action of young citizens as widely as possible – to recognize and analyse the different cultural scenes in which civic imaginations were put forward and acted upon, regardless of the effectiveness and visibility of their outcomes, for instance – we gave up on the idea of studying exclusively 'flexibly organized social problem solving'. Instead, we looked for coordination of common life – the forming of the cultures of doing society – on a wider spectrum. The underlying idea to begin with, and also the rationale of the entire study, was to include *both* the kind of political action and talk that fits well with the definition of civic action given earlier, *and* the kind of action (and nonaction) that studies on social movements, for instance, usually disregard, and that ends up as object of other fields of research: studies on formal participation, on marginalized youth, on extreme-right internet groups, on party politics, and so on. However, these latter fields of study touch on a wide range of activities that are undeniably part of the composition of our common life, and our societies in the making.

Over the years of conducting the studies compiled in this book, we sat in numerous seminars and conferences listening to social scientists struggle with the signs of the times: the rise of right-wing populism, to be sure, and all the phenomena around it, but also political marginalization as well as hyperindividualistic societal attitudes encountered increasingly among young actors. We received comments and questions doubting whether the materials we were collecting merited being under the title of civil society, or that of political action altogether. Over the years we came to realize that social scientists are uneasy with coordination of the common that is 'not civic', first, when the noncivicness is grounded on inaction, like an apparent disinterest towards common affairs, or, second, when it is screamingly obvious, like in racist and fascist actions on right-wing online fora. The latter is understandable through the distaste social scientists most often have for the traditions of thought where radical right-wing action finds its base – a distaste we, self-evidently, very much share. The unease regarding inaction and 'passiveness' is a bit trickier to trace, but perhaps finds explanations in the difficulty and uncertainty that a student of such vague forms of action is forced to overcome, and the risks one runs of being tempted to go 'inside people's heads' when otherwise all seems blank – we share this uneasiness as well. Nonetheless, both aspects are crucial. This is not to say, of course, that the empirical fields indicated earlier would be left uncovered in the social sciences, but they are mainly left out of studies that cover civic and political-action-as-we-know-it.

The most relevant contribution we suggest to make with this conceptual and empirical package is an analysis that recognizes human action (and interaction) as moral, and reaching towards commonality – as *doing society* – and thus *always potentially political*, while *not necessarily* 'morally' civic, political by definition, or oriented towards social problems to begin with.

Moreover, the reason why we have felt it insurmountable to include in our analyses both the usual and the unusual 'suspects' of political engagement is empirically and contextually grounded. When approaching the young with the hope of understanding the future directions of democracy and political culture(s), we quickly encountered the consequences of ripened individualization processes. Collectivism and collective thinking at the heart of civic action are not dead – far from it – but are, on the one hand, altered and coloured by varying, yet often significant, degrees of individualist modes (and motivations) of action, and, on the other hand, accompanied with action that also has implications towards the common, but with very little or no collective content at all. This trend is not exclusively connected to the Nordic context, but frames its sociohistorical characteristics particularly well. In the following discussion, we plunge into these characteristics, hoping to show both the general interest provided by this loop, and the features that make the empirical context of the study particularly relevant and potential material for further comparisons. In the next two sections, we look at the context from two different angles: the 'zeitgeist' angle of the dynamics of individualism and collectivism, and the 'empirical' angle of the current societal dynamics in the Nordic countries, particularly Finland.

The 'zeitgeist' context: blurring individualism and collectivism

In this section, we take a closer look at what can be called a 'zeitgeist' context of this book, urging us to revisit the tensions between individualism and collectivism in current societies. The examples blurring the individualistic/collective prerequisites of action – which are multiplied in this book – portray well the core argument we put forward. Doing society may resemble many things either on a continuum from entirely self-interested to highly collective or built from varying elements and degrees of both. These aspects can be part of the same type of activity, or the same person's different engagements, while the goals and effects of these actions all contribute to the common. This argument brings to light the types of tensions between individualism and collectivism that are characteristic of current societies and help us understand the many ambivalent, even contrasting trends in political participation.

The thesis of increasing individualization has been the bread and butter in social sciences for decades. Much of this discussion has been about change, or even about an ongoing crisis due to a shift from collective to a more individualized approach. Putnam (2000, especially 177–182) famously defined individualism as a decline in social capital, leading to the decline in collective and civic activities. This claim is in line with Inglehart (1997), for whom the ascent of the individual and the descent of the collective were connected to overall postmaterialistic values. Beck and Beck-Gernsheim (2002) attached individualism with the withering away of strong, dominant social institutions, such as classes, families and religion, and Giddens (1991) emphasized the construction of individual choices and the importance of lifestyles as the core of contemporary life. Furthermore, Micheletti (2003) continued this thought further by positing that individualized actions, such as shopping, become carriers of civic virtues. Dalton (2008), for his part, conceptualized the change in terms of citizenship: from *citizen duty* to *engaged citizenship*, from voting, paying taxes and obeying the law to being independent, assertive and concerned. Finally, Schudson (1998) suggested that we have entered the age of right-bearing citizens, an age in which politics often takes the life-political turn that Giddens envisioned, and in which these citizens also find new ways of doing politics.

The literature and diagnoses concerning individualization have, while generally accepted as the correct interpretation of the 'zeitgeist' of the past few decades, also received criticism from multiple directions. For example, Putnam's theses have been criticized for overly romanticizing the 'collective lost' and for basing his argument too strongly on contexts that are hardly comparable – an Italian village and a relatively general analysis of US suburban life – and carry many other features that are obscured in the analysis and potentially change the picture (see, for example, Navarro 2002). Beck, Beck-Gernsheim and Giddens have been challenged if not directly, then at least through an increasing disregard of sorts by the expanding field of new research and theorizing on class and inequality, claiming rightfully that while the old class demarcation lines have certainly shifted, social classes and their impact on people's lives have not disappeared (Skeggs 1997, 2001; Sayer 2005; Savage 2015). Our task in this book is not to take part in this debate to any substantive degree, but to further investigate what kind of interpretive scenery these zeitgeist theses are surrounded by in our empirical study.

However, the change narrative is not the only tradition of writing about individualism. In the *Habits of the Heart* project by Bellah et al (2007 [1985]), even the most collective forms of civic life in the US were recognized to be imbued with a deep-running spirit of individualism. The conclusion was that individualism is in no way a recent phenomenon or a particular crisis. One essential takeaway from this seminal study in cultural sociology was that we did not become individualistic at the turn of the millennium; to a certain extent, we always were. This conclusion results, we argue, from a few choices relatively similar to our project. First, not making clear distinctions between people's 'private' and 'public' lives – namely their political and civic activities as not separate from 'the rest', but as part of a continuum of engagements – leads to a more manifold understanding of their stakes towards the common and their own place in relation to it. Second, taking the actors' definitions and their situational emphases at the microlevel seriously broadens the scope of analysis regarding individualism and collectivism. We take this aspect even further than Bellah et al (2007 [1985]) by refraining from classifying the actors we met in a particular way, and rather acknowledging them all as doing society in their own terms. In this way, the research participants provide us with a set of situational potentialities of imaginations, tools and engagements rather than a typology of actors.

That said, the situational potentialities are, necessarily, also situated. Imaginations, styles and engagements we have traced are part of a cultural toolkit or, in Charles Tilly's (1979) words, part of the repertoires of action characteristic of a time and a place that constrain actors. Lichterman and Cefaï (2006: 1) define political cultures as 'the sets of symbols and meanings or styles of action that organize political claims-making and opinion-forming, by individuals or collectivities'. Looking at styles of action in a range of empirical settings, we indeed explore the contemporary Finnish political culture. However, the analysis does not stop there. For example, the particular repertoire of school strikes builds on earlier actions of the climate movement: school strikes started in Sweden, then travelled around the world, and proved to be an easily copyable and applicable, indeed a memetic tool of participation (De Moor et al 2020; Haugseth and Smeplass 2023 – for a similar argument concerning the Extinction Rebellion protests, see Malafaia et al 2024). Similar paths can be drawn to describe engagement in imageboard discussion styles (see Siltala 2020; Tuters and Hagen 2020; Ylä-Anttila et al 2020), civic imaginations emerging among participants of participatory programmes (see Baiocchi and Ganuza 2017; Boldt 2021), individualized tools of urban activism (see Iveson 2013; Finn 2014; Mäenpää and Faehnle 2021; Jokela 2024) and middle-class-aspiring engagements to the society in poor urban areas (see Anderson 1999; Blokland 2008; Junniainen 2019). In our connected age, cultural tools are never *sui generis*. This book provides numerous local variations of global themes similar to the ones described earlier, providing a way of also looking into the global themes themselves (Juris 2008; Bennett and Segerberg 2012; Luhtakallio 2012). Next, we zoom in on the setting of the local variations: the context of contemporary Nordic societies and Finland.

The Nordic context for individualistic cultural tools

The second level of context opens a window onto the Nordic welfare societies with, in principle, heavily collective cultural building blocks – and yet increasingly also individualized, even polarized, and anti-collective contemporary features. We argue that this empirical context, and that of Finland in particular, provides an especially topical setting for the purposes of investigating the questions at stake in this book: questions concerning the futures of democracy, political action, citizen engagement, and the (new) tensions between individualism and collectivism therein.

In historical studies of the Nordic political cultures, one particularly noteworthy feature emerges, which differs from most other parts of Europe in the formative period of the 'birth' of the class society and the emergence of less limited political rights (for male citizens) therein. It is the *smoothness* of the organization of the working classes into movements and, consequently, labour unions, gaining the right to strike and collective bargaining (Stenius 2010). This smoothness resulted from the fact that such a novel organization of society was introduced, for an important part, from above: the bourgeoisie and the representatives of the middle classes, not the working class alone, as was generally the case elsewhere (Stenius 2010). Indeed, the democratic principle of mass organization met with very little resistance in the Nordic context. Mass movements in the Nordic countries were an inherent part of, and played a crucial role in, the state project (Alapuro and Stenius 1987). According to conceptual historian Henrik Stenius (2010), this project, which was thus very differently grounded compared to other parts of Europe, provided the basis for the *universalistic principle* by which the Nordic societies are profoundly marked: according to it, both politics and popular mass movements had the task of building society as a whole, not just their particular segment of interests, and thus everybody – reformists and opposers alike – were part of the state rather than being outsiders to it. In the period before the French Revolution, the political culture in the Nordic societies was characterized by loyalty, obedience and legalism. After the Revolution, these grounds enabled the emergence of particularly strong popular movements that were defined by 'an abiding loyalty to the state and authorities and a commonly felt responsibility for contributing to the necessary division of labour' (Stenius 2010: 51).

Ever since these early developments in the Nordic countries, civil society has been fundamental to the societal stability, and the basis of the political culture can be described as collective to the bone (Alapuro 1994, 2005; Stenius 2003; Kettunen 2004).

According to Risto Alapuro (2005), the strong organizational networks of civil society have created, on the one hand, a political culture grounded in mediation and mediating structures, and, on the other hand, a conception of political representation that is essentially transparent and 'descriptive'. Descriptive representation indicates that the comprehensiveness of civil society membership renders the 'people' and its interests visible and known as a collective entity.

Civil society's role in this constellation has been to communicate the people's mindset to the government. This, in turn, has gradually translated into a system that has granted a wide inclusion of civil society organizations in decision-making bodies, which has also ensured that political parties are strongly anchored in civil society groups. The result has been a highly organized society, in which an overwhelming majority of people are members in voluntary associations. The breadth and depth of this feature are particularly thorough in Finland, to the degree that the country has been said to suffer from an 'organization syndrome' (Selle 1996; see also Wollebæk and Selle 2002): a civil society in which it is almost impossible to tackle a new problem – to politicize something – without ending up, usually sooner than later, founding a new association with a formal status and structures. This tendency has led to an association-dense society discouraging mobilization, and instead encouraging passive association memberships (Woellebæk and Selle 2002, 2003). Yet, a slow but steady decline of these memberships has been recorded in recent years (Toikkanen 2020). In particular, younger generations are less inclined to sign into the traditional adherence to civil society. Instead, a general withdrawal, as well as looser forms of adherence have become popular from social media-based, often relatively short-term engagements to informal modes of organizing in, for instance, urban activism.

Another historically shared feature in the Nordic political cultures is a traditionally weak notion of contentious political opposition. Thus, associations and popular movements have been widely accepted by powerholders and, conversely, movements have abided by the idea of a one-norm society instead of strong polarizing implications, 'transforming the ideal of conformity into a universalistic figure of thought' (Stenius 2010: 31). Indeed, this figure of thought is manifest in the concept of 'society' in all the Nordic languages that with only slight variation has the meaning of 'what we have in common'. As Stenius (2010: 54) further notes, there is a shared understanding in the Nordic countries about a matter being in good and trustworthy hands once 'society takes the responsibility for it'.

These historical foundations are only part of the story, and in different historical phases, the balancing of similarities and differences between the Nordic countries has varied significantly. Notably, the groundings of the Finnish political culture cannot be understood without considering one of the bloodiest civil wars in European history, in which, over a few months in 1918, 1 per cent of the entire population was killed. Causing a long-lasting societal trauma, this tragedy, nonetheless, also had collectivist roots. Alapuro (2019) has argued that the civil war, also dubbed the Finnish revolution, was only made possible by the high level of organization of the workers' movement. So, while the low level of opposition thesis fits this grim moment in Finnish history poorly and, compared to the other Nordic countries, it exemplifies the Finnish singularity in its position between the East and the West, strong collectivism holds its own even here.

Since the horrors of the civil war and the divided nation trauma, Finland has gradually become known for quite a different set of characteristics. The Finlandization years – providing world politics with the hitherto lacking concept to describe domestic and foreign policy of a country heavily affected and directed by a strong undemocratic influence of a neighbouring state – forged Finland into a mediating player between Western and Eastern superpowers. Finland embraced a neutral status and became visible to the world as such in manoeuvres like providing a venue to the Conference on Security and Cooperation in Europe (CSCE) in 1975. After the collapse of the Soviet Union, the neutral status began to lose its power and became an increasingly empty signifier, especially since Finland joined the European Union in 1995. The country's Western affiliation reached its completion in 2023 when Finland joined the North Atlantic Treaty Organization (NATO) in a fast-paced process, heavily accelerated by Russia's attack against Ukraine.

Alongside the aforementioned development, Finland has followed the path taken by the other Nordic countries in its societal development, first to a somewhat stripped-down version of the Nordic Welfare state and, consequently, to its partial dismantlement through new public management and its market-driven efficiency projects (see, for example, Kettunen 2001; Moisio and Leppänen 2007). Simultaneously, it has had its share of the 'Nordic magic' in international comparisons, and perhaps even some extra attention due to a certain distinctiveness among the Nordic countries. Thus, in large-scale comparisons, Finland 'excels' in terms of citizens' equality measured from almost any perspective, and scores extremely high on a variety of measures of democratization; politically, the country is peaceful and deemed 'the most stable country in the world', and citizens' trust towards society's institutions, including politicians, is at a record high compared to nearly any other country (for links to all these statistics, see Statistic Finland 2018). Furthermore, Finland has even been nominated the number one country in the World Happiness Report (Helliwell et al 2023) for the sixth consecutive year at the time of writing (there is a lot to be said about the methodology of producing this report, and it should be noted that this nomination is often received by Finns with a dose of sarcastic humour).

The well-established talk about the crisis of democracy – whether based on decreasing voter turnouts and systemic distrust (see, for example, Dalton 2004) or on record-breaking indicators of increase in economic and social inequality (see, for example, Wilkinson and Pickett 2009) – has been in the headlines in Finland as well as elsewhere for the past few decades. Therefore, the excellence measures mentioned in the previous paragraph do not give the whole picture and should be reviewed with caution and a critical eye, but they nonetheless position Finland in an interesting spotlight internationally. For the agenda of this book, we argue that the general perception of a relatively stable, well-governed Nordic empirical context offers an unparalleled perspective to understand currently ongoing changes in the dynamics of individualism and collectivism, civic imaginations, styles and forms of engaging, and cultural tools forging political cultures. This is not to say that change is not contextual, but by looking at changes in doing society in one, relatively small context marked by a strong presumption of stability, we find overarching themes that resonate widely beyond the immediate empirical contexts of this study.

Taking a closer look at recent changes in Finnish political culture reveals several aspects that follow the development in many other European countries. Whereas the Finnish party structure has been highly stable ever since the birth of the Finnish representative system, and Finns have been relatively loyal voters, voting generation after generation more or less as their socioeconomic background would predict, the system has shown signs of unprecedented turbulence in recent decades. One of the big changes in the party structure system was the founding of the environmental movement-based Green Party in the late 1980s, the first direct consequence of the new social movements of the time. Even more so, as elsewhere, since the turn of the millennium, right-wing populism has rendered the Finnish political arena more shaky and less predictable than it used to be. The first landslide victory of the Finns party in 2011 was not foreseen, in the same way that right-wing populists have surprised pollsters everywhere.

Furthermore, the equality of political participation has become a question mark, recently even in statistically significant terms: since the parliamentary elections of 2015, it has been established that nonvoting is significantly and increasingly the choice of the least well-to-do citizens (Grönlund and Wass 2016). In the subsequent elections, the multipolarization of the party field has been further confirmed, and thus the old stability is deemed to have ended in this respect (Borg et al 2020): Finns are no longer loyal to parties, and they have to some extent stopped voting based on their background. Also, the younger one is, the less one votes in contemporary Finland (Statistics Finland 2023).

How intact, then, are the collectivist Nordic foundations of civil society–state relations in the face of such locally specific changes, and more generally in today's world of turbulence and crises? In a bold attempt to shed light on the big picture in the current Nordic societies, Alexander et al (2019) explored the 'Nordic civil sphere', concluding that while the old basis for trust and efficacious organization continues to exist, the Nordic societies are heavily conditioned by newly increased tensions of exclusion and inclusion. Their focus is on the Scandinavian side and the topics of multiculturalism and immigration dominate the discussion – quite legitimately. Tognato (2019), in an enlightening commentary in the aforementioned volume, suggests that the developments in recent decades are tearing the state and civil society apart in the Nordic countries. However, he suggests that the root cause of the troubles is in the welfare state that was, through its universalizing interventions, the all-encompassing force promoting civil society and that then, gradually, deteriorated with the 'neoliberal turn' of governance and the consecutive economic crises since the 1990s (Tognato 2019; see also Enroth and Henriksson 2019; Keskinen et al 2019). While we acknowledge and share the importance of these themes, in this book our gaze is directed differently in search for answers to what indeed seems like an ongoing transformation of civil society, in which the collectivist foundations tremble and new formations appear.

In the next section, we further contextualize this study in relation to yet another perspective: the young Nordic generation this book is about, and the scholarship in youth studies.

Studying young people's engagements

The field of youth studies has for a long time had as its primary research object studying the young as a particular group of actors in societies. Thus, the first candid questions we posed in the preface of this book about what the future of democracy will be like exposes us: our primary interest is not in the young as a particular segment in a given society. While the empirical subjects of this study are young, their youth was not our primary interest, but instead their ways of using the cultural tools of making the common and, hence, forging the future of democracy while carrying on with their activities. We could have conducted this study among adults just the same; it was the future orientation that directed us to the young. Young people are the ones using, *en masse*, cultural tools in their most recent development, such as the tools of intensified individualism, as well as the concrete means and affordances of engagement, such as social media. Furthermore, quite concretely, the young have, in principle, the most time ahead of them to affect the future of democracy. In sum, the authors of this book are political and cultural sociologists empirically piggybacking on the field of youth research. In this section, we approach contemporary youth studies by mapping some family resemblances and some differences to the project of this book. Our focus here is mainly on youth studies about political participation, with Chapters 2 and 4 especially providing more context-dependent views to specific aspects on young people and democratic participation. At the end of this section, we provide a broad view of results from our own survey into young people's participation, which then sets up the theme of individualization that will be one of our core viewpoints in the analysis.

Many studies from the field of youth research note that the contemporary youth as a generation has been the group most affected by global transformations in, for example, the labour market, education or living conditions due to digital technologies and, especially, the sustainability and climate crises (see, for example, Woodman and Wyn, 2014; Pickard and Bessant 2020; Honkatukia and Rättilä 2023). Political apathy on the one hand, and direct and revolutionary action on the other hand, facilitated and heavily conditioned by online communication (such as the Arab Spring, and in the West, the Occupy movement),[2] have both been expressions of the grievances of a generation to whom promises have not been honoured: who, for instance, did 'all they were supposed to' and graduated, but did not get jobs or good positions, and thus were the victims of the 'neoliberal bargain' (Woodman and Wyn, 2014: 2). More recently, it is the future itself the current young generation feels deprived of. The intensifying climate crisis has affected young people's perception of the future horizons grimly, and a general feeling of being betrayed by governments and the political system are found in studies from various contexts (for example, Knops 2021; Honkatukia and Rättilä, 2023). For us, these points have served as important background knowledge, while of course the reality is versatile. Not studying specific groups of young, but instead a wide range of actors engaging in society as we have done, puts the preceding situation into perspective: not all are either apathetic or revolutionary, or even disappointed or anxious to begin with. Some of the young we met were all of these, of course, but some were other things. Our interpretation of the use of cultural tools of individualism cutting across the spectrum of actors we followed doing society is this study's response to 'generational' descriptions. The latter are bound to always be partial (on the troubles of generationalism, see Purhonen 2016), while taking a more abstracted conceptual perspective has been helpful for the analysis of this book in terms of finding interpretations that can cover the range of actors without the danger of forcing round features into rectangular moulds.

As for arguments about individualism, in youth studies, there has been a tendency to see the theory of individualization guilty of obscuring the continuities in structural inequalities (see Woodman and Wyn 2014). Patterns of inequality within youth persist and perhaps even deepen. We join Woodman and Wyn (2014), as well as many influential youth researchers before and after them (for example, Furlong and Cartmel 2006), in the concern that as transformations and changes in the world hit young people in the most visible ways, what is sometimes obscured is how, nonetheless, extant inequalities tend to persist and be reproduced. Nonetheless, these also change and gain new forms in a transforming world. In other words, young people's lives are indeed probably the most in flux at any given time, and the structural inequalities that mark differences in terms of how they experience the change are marked by both continuity and the emergence of new risks and precarities (see Woodman and Wyn 2014).

In our approach and the empirical studies we have conducted, it is indeed evident that inequalities – both old and new – are massively intersected with the individualized cultural tools that the young have at their disposal. The 'promise' of individualization – everybody's unique individual path and chances – is all but equally available to the young we have met. Much like Woodman and Wyn (2014), we use the idea of individualization as a feature overlapping with many other conceptual aspects, serving as an umbrella concept of sorts, instead of a uniform descriptive tool of young people's life situations.

The perspective of studying the young by predefined *groups* marks many of the recent hallmark studies in the field of research on youth. Pickard and Bessant's edited volume (2018), for instance, sets out to explore an abundance of visible political processes taking groups of youth as starting points, from famous cases like the Gezi Park protests and the Occupy movement to local cases of student activism and regional activism. This kind of analysis is valuable in its own right, but it departs from ready-made definitions of groups of actors and, eventually, politics, and therefore serves a different purpose from this book. Similarly, reporting on a wide European comparative research project, Giugni and Grasso (2021) note the lack of subgroup analyses in investigating differences in the political participation of youth cross-nationally. With their survey results from nine European countries, they looked at a variety of themes that are similar to the questions posed in this book. For instance, what is the role of political socialization gained in a variety of activities – the participation patterns – in which the young engage, especially for their attitudes towards institutional forms of politics? The results of the survey show, for example, that youth who had gained experience of democracy on school councils, and the like, tended to vote more often, have higher levels of trust in political institutions and participate in contentious forms of politics more often than youth without such experiences. This is one example in which our study offers 'similar' results (see Chapter 3), but the differences are important: instead of subgroup analysis, we have focused on young in a variety of (situational) engagements. Furthermore, with dominantly qualitative data analysis, we concentrate on how such socialization takes place, which cultural tools the young have at their disposal and which ones they end up using, and, finally, what kind of qualities the socialization may possess.

At a more conceptual level, Walther et al (2019) take cue of the critique towards research on youth participation, and address the question of how the concept of *participation* should be broadened. With this goal, they share our objective in part. In their study on formal, nonformal and informal participation of youth in European cities, the authors propose a perspective combining the 'openness' of grounded theory – basically, actors' definitions of participation – with a constructivist approach to sensitize the concept of participation by unpacking its meanings into a sixfold conceptual spectrum. With this relatively prolific set of tools, the authors engage with the question of how, in concrete participation processes, the youth re-signify the extant participatory practices. Walther et al's analyses point partly in the same direction as ours: first, with the Bourdieusian language used, the authors conclude that those who already possess capital that benefits the sense making of a participative process are prone to both making the best out of the processes and making them 'theirs'. Those without adequate capital to begin with are less able to play the game set within certain institutional limits. Using ethnographic and biographical methods, the authors illustrate different forms of participatory potential among the young, and the evolving of participation practices within the everyday citizenship acts of the young. In so doing, they problematize the top-down practices and policy, and eventually the very notion of citizenship education. In this step forward, the authors find the direction for rethinking youth participation from a relational perspective. Similarly, Honkatukia and Rättilä (2023) have taken a wider – and also relational – perspective to participation and politics, in their case expanding it to questions of wellbeing among the young. They highlight the constraints and labels 'the adult world' forces upon youth participation and, individually, on the young trapped in what they call the 'transition machinery' (Honkatukia and Rättilä 2023). This, and the grievances and resistances they have found emerging among the young as a consequence, are similar to the features we discovered in numerous analyses in this book. We join these authors in arguing that wellbeing is and should be taken seriously as a political question in today's often extremely demanding environments of participation.

However, our primary contribution to the literature reviewed in the preceding paragraph has a different focus: the dynamics of individualism and collectivism apparent in youth's engagements with society. To prepare our investigation of the different aspects of doing society at a more macro level, we conducted a representative survey on political participation of the youth in the Helsinki region (see the Appendix). Two findings emerged that are seemingly in sharp contrast with one another, but are well in line with those of Bellah et al (2007 [1985]) to which we referred earlier. The first is that Finnish youth are definitely not 'bowling alone'. Only 0.2 per cent of respondents report never doing any kind of participation at all, with 85 per cent reporting participation in two or more 'societal' things in recent years, and 26 per cent in five or more (with three as the median). The potential activities listed included everything from church summer camps to squatting buildings, from participatory budgeting to boy and girl scouts, with school student councils, church-related activities and student organizations being the most popular activities. The second notable finding is that 70 per cent of responders say that a good citizen *acts themself to make their life better*. It is, after voting in elections, the second most popular claim altogether. Moreover, traditional collective ways of using political power, such as joining a party, participating in civil society activities, activist groups or community organizations score behind the choice of the response option *you don't have to do anything if you don't want* (11 per cent of respondents).

In effect, all the youngsters have participated in one way or another, most often by rather traditional collective ways of participation. Yet, at the same time, they think that a good citizen is primarily responsible themself for making their life better.

This is our route to studying the youth in Finland. As the survey results indicate, the youth portray the general trends of transformation, yet perhaps in a sharper way than can be detected in the analyses of the political culture at large.

Nonetheless, it remains at least in part unclear what the arrangements of Finnish civil society will look like in the future: how strong the currently building polarization between participating and withdrawing citizens will be, what the role of the 'old' associative base and structures will be, and what the most prominent new forms of organizing will be. Yet, something in the general ways of organizing is changing, in Finland, as in the Nordic countries more broadly. There is a growing heterogeneity of civil society participation from new social movements to spontaneous project-based individuals participating online, as well as new, pronounced forms of inequalities and marginality marking a withdrawal from participation, connected to many tensions in these societies from polarization of income differences to immigration-related creation of (unofficial but culturally effective) differentiated and discriminating citizen categories.

We argue that these changes are at the heart of understanding the current tensions of individualism and collectivism. If individualism was a 'first language' through the vocabulary of which all aspects of life were fathomable for the Americans Bellah et al (2007 [1985]: 20) met with, the Nordics seem to be turning increasingly 'bilingual'. In contrast to the Americans of the 1980s, their 'first language' – instinctively understandable – is the language of collectives and of building structures that go beyond what we can achieve or experience as individuals.

But the young generation, on whose actions this book is focused, is also increasingly 'fluent' in the language of individualism, and while the ideas expressed in the first language are not alien or at risk of disappearing, some commitments, some rationalization and some actions are more naturally committed in the second language.

In the following section, we provide an overview the forthcoming chapters of this book.

Overview of this book

How does *doing society* – reaching towards the common, be it at the level of imagining, engaging or styles of action – work in the contexts of this study?

How do people alternate between, mix and merge cultural tools marked by collectivism and individualism when imagining their futures, engaging in affective communities or organizing political action? These are the questions this book sets out to investigate. In the following, we give an overview of how and in which order.

This book is based on a multisite, multimethod study conducted between 2014 and 2022. We ask the following questions: what cultural repertoires are guiding the action of the young people studied and how are they changing these repertoires? To answer these, we utilize path-breaking methodological triangulation. The book includes long-term ethnographic research on both marginalized and engaged youths, computational text analysis of anonymous internet imageboards, hundreds of interviews, textual analysis of policy and other documents, and a representative survey of young people in the capital region of Finland (details of all the methods and data used can be found in the Appendix). A common theoretical framework keeps the analysis focused on common themes.

In Chapter 2, Georg Boldt opens the book's empirical content by a multisited ethnographic study on formal youth participation. Through his rich, longitudinal fieldwork in a youth council, on the one hand, and two sites of a participatory budgeting processes targeted at young people, on the other hand, unfolds a picture of youth participation that treats young people unequally, both by chance and by unfinalized planning, and thus gives them very different takeaways, from a sturdy set of tools to further pursue political engagements, to deep disappointments and experiences of disillusionment and exclusion.

Veikko Eranti and Eeva Luhtakallio continue the theme of formal political participation in Chapter 3 by introducing the world of (rarely studied) young electoral candidates, many of whom turn out to be among those who have benefited from the participatory-industrial arrangements presented in Chapter 2. The young candidates draw, through their accounts in interviews with the authors, a picture of individualistic actors building their path forward with politics that for many is only one of the building blocks of future success. Party choice is rarely self-evident, nor is the commitment to long-term political work for most – and yet, in the political party context, the candidates enjoy the support of a collective environment that is mostly missing in the other settings of young people's engagements of this book.

Chapter 4 is the last one to address the more 'formal' sides of participation. In this chapter, Veikko Eranti and Georg Boldt analyze suggestions young people have submitted to the youthideas.fi online service targeted at youth and promoted at schools. The ideas portray civic imaginations prone to favouring, for the most part, technical solutions to young people's concerns. In these often very concrete proposals unfold an engagement to justify one's ideas mainly by way of showing how efficient or affordable they were. The chapter discusses what kind of cultural tools such e-democracy strengthens and what kind of doing society can be detected in the use of these tools.

In Chapter 5, Taina Meriluoto and Lotta Junnilainen lay out a completely different world of societal imaginations: that of youth with different experiences of marginalization. With their multisited ethnographic fieldwork among such young people, in contexts of urban areas marked by marginalization, substance abuse rehabilitation and mental health struggles, the authors show how those who do not feel they belong to society in the first place forge a distinct culture of doing society. They do it by way of many markedly *active* actions, from (often explicit) withdrawal to disruptive resistance, and, eventually, even to public denounciation of the causes of individual exclusion. These often very private civic imaginations form a cultural pattern of atomistic engagements to a (often far away) common.

Chapter 6 continues the theme of 'informal' politics by a computational analysis of discussions on *Ylilauta*, a 4chan-style online imageboard hugely popular among Finnish youth and known of its often alt-right-leaning features, and discussion styles marked by unruliness and carelessness of norms (and good behaviour). However, in this chapter, Tuukka Ylä-Anttila and Veikko Eranti show that a patterned culture of doing society takes shape in the group styles of the online participants: one with its own peculiar norms and grounded in extreme individualism, yet controlled by collectively negotiated rules of the game.

In Chapter 7, Maija Jokela introduces us to the buzzing urban neighbourhood activism of the Kallio movement. While community-minded in its explicit presentations, the movement unfolds as a prime example of personalized politics, where the volunteers accomplish the movement's goals by carrying out 'solo gigs' and fulfilling their individual desires rather than adhering to the allegedly prefigurative community building promoted by the movement's self-acclamations. The chapter offers a rich discussion on the multiple consequences that intensified individualism of the participants has for commitment, ideological belonging and building political community.

Chapter 8 provides an interpretive counterpart to the enthusiastic street party builders of the previous chapter and ends the book's empirical contribution with a topic that cannot be bypassed in a study of today's young people: climate activism. In this chapter, Maija Jokela, Jenni Kettunen and Eeva Luhtakallio show how local Extinction Rebellion activists all but perish under the heavy burden of the weight of the world placed on their (perhaps surprisingly) solitary shoulders, despite the seemingly collective movement context. It turns out that climate activists, while praising the caring practices of the movement, engage in an extremely lonely and demanding duty of saving the world, marked by instrumentalization of the collective and a standard of optimized and efficient protest action. The movement serves exclusively the (nonprefigurative) goal of urgently changing climate politics, and the activists find themselves facing a future in which they have given up on 'normal life' or potentially have no future at all, should the movement fail to achieve its goals.

The book concludes with Chapter 9, in which Eeva Luhtakallio and Veikko Eranti revisit the theoretical project presented in this introduction. The conclusion completes the conceptual work begun here and further fed throughout the chapters by summarizing the cultures of doing society that the book lays out and proposing ways forward with the toolkit tuned into studying engagements to the common in societies marked by a changing dynamic of individualism and collectivism.

As this summary shows, some of our field sites are marked by formal modes of participation and engaging in society, and some by more informal ones. They also differ in terms of potential collectivism – we go from internet-enabled social movements to individuals in top-down one-off participation events, and from online image board trolling to party politics. Furthermore, there are different expressions of civic imagination: from narrow technical ideas to broad and bold demands of systemic changes. In the empirical material in this book, different engagements reflect expressions of doing society: mundane, everyday action and situational coordination in which the common is forged. In some cases, the action is clearly observable and outright political, while in other cases, it is more introspective, a question of projecting oneself in the future, a way of imagining what one might be, among the others. It is through this action that the young citizens we have studied reflect their civic imaginations – what seems, to them, desirable and feasible in society. This action is their practice of citizenship and, ultimately, democracy by using, reproducing and creating cultural tools that are suitable for their context of action.

2

Institutional Participation: Youth Councils and Participatory Budgeting Fostering Better Citizens

Georg Boldt

Introduction

This chapter describes two types of formal youth participation, organized by municipalities in the Helsinki region: first, a youth council rooted in the tradition of liberal representative democracy; and, second, a process of participatory budgeting that combines participatory and discursive democratic ideals (Ferree et al 2002) with youth work practices. Both formats of participation are framed by the organizing authorities as opportunities for young people to influence things that are significant in their lives, and even to instil them with civic virtues, but the two approaches could not be more dissimilar.

The official Neartown website describes the youth council in the following way:

> The youth council promotes the needs of young people, makes their opinions on current issues known, and gives attention to their wishes ... The objective of the youth council is to increase awareness of civic action and how to participate in politics, inspiring young people to follow political processes and influence them actively.

This institutional framing of the youth council turned out not to reflect the actual experiences that representatives had, particularly in terms of their political influence. In fact, the most salient feature of the youth council that emerged during fieldwork was how many of the representatives lost interest in it. During an interview, two representatives of the youth council commented on how their enthusiasm waned in the first few months of their mandate and was replaced by a sense of responsibility:

Vanessa: I'm not attending these meetings because I can't think of anything more fun to do or because this would be the high point of my life, but because I feel the need for our work to have an impact and turn our youth council into something better.

Antti: When the initial enthusiasm wears off and people realize what it's like, I'm sure many get bored. Enthusiasm is replaced by a sense of responsibility. It lasts longer, but it's not equally strong with all members of the youth council.

While youth councils are largely self-organized and autonomous in terms of deciding what they speak about and how, the Ruuti participatory budget is a youth work practice that aims at empowering participants by promoting civic engagement in a safe, family-like atmosphere of intimacy, transforming the identities of the participants by giving them a sense of competency and confidence (Eliasoph 2011: 2–8). This decreased the threshold for participation, but would also lead to frustration as some participants felt that their capacities were underestimated and misrecognized. During a fieldwork visit to a school, a youth worker was explaining the voting procedure when a student unexpectedly stood up and exclaimed: "Surprise, surprise, the youth understand something, and they know how to read too. Could we just vote?" That the speaker was not afraid to stand up and make his remark – and that none of the others present wished to challenge him or speak in favour of the youth workers – confirms a tension in interactions between youth workers and young people brought about by patronizing attitudes, such as referring to the young as children and expecting them to sit still and keep quiet until they are given permission to act. While somewhat of an edge case in terms of agonistic exchange in the participatory budget, it exemplifies how the participatory budget, with its top-down organization and youth worker-led implementation, was something young people were subjected to rather than engaged in.

Decades of declining election turnouts and the decreasing popularity of traditional civic and political stakeholders, including unions, community organizations and political parties, have cast a shadow of doubt on whether the current model of representative liberal democracy can be sustained (Fung and Wright 2003; Ziblatt and Lewitsky 2018; Mounk 2018). Analyses indicate that young people increasingly engage in individual rather than collective action, and in transient, issue-based engagements, especially those that resonate with self-actualization and lifestyle politics (Harris 2015: 88; see also de Moor 2017). This suggests that representative democracy itself, rather than political apathy, might be the reason why citizens increasingly feel detached from political decision making (Bang 2004; Busse et al 2015). Consequently, public authorities have turned their gaze towards participatory democracy and its promises to strengthen democracy by including marginalized groups, giving participants the skills and means to influence political decision making, and conveying citizens a sense of ownership over political decision-making processes (for example, Pateman 1970, 2012; Habermas 1984; Irvin and Stansbury 2004; Fung 2006; Barber 2009; Talpin 2011; Baiocchi and Ganuza 2017). In an interconnected process, states have been implementing youth participation policies with the objective of recognizing the right of young people to express their views and concerns in decision making and to support their political socialization into engaged democratic citizens (Convention of the Rights of the Child 1989; European Commission 2001; Council of Europe 2015).

Most municipalities in Finland have a youth council. In fact, they are almost mandatory. The Youth Act (Nuorisolaki 1285/2016) expresses a commitment to advance young people's civic engagement and capabilities to function in society. Moreover, the Municipal Law requires that minors are offered opportunities to learn and exercise civic skills (Kuntalaki 510/2015 §26). Not all youth councils are equal in terms of size, resources and procedures, and their format is not regulated, so actual practices differ (Paakkunainen 2004; Gretschel and Kiilakoski 2015). However, they typically follow the practices and procedures of liberal representative democracy.

Research on youth councils in multiple countries has repeatedly raised questions concerning representation, influence, fairness, accessibility and recognition. A recurring criticism has been that youth councils mostly engage those that are already socially integrated and efficacious in their engagement. Partly due to these reasons, the city of Helsinki dragged its feet, establishing a youth council only in 2018, decades after its closest neighbours. In the meantime, starting in two neighbourhoods in 2013, the city successively expanded an annual process of participatory budgeting, a practice rooted in the contemporary trend of participatory democracy and popular inclusion (Baiocchi and Ganuza 2017; Ferree et al 2002; Pateman 2012), reaching citywide implementation in 2016. In brief, the Helsinki youth department participatory budgeting provides youth in lower-secondary schools (13–15 year olds) the chance to deliberate on local needs and develop proposals for how to use youth department funds in their own neighbourhood. The popularity of these proposals is established by school votes, after which a committee decides which proposals will be implemented.

I use the two cases of institutional youth participation to argue that commitment to participate in these practices hinges on the perceived meaningfulness of the process. As the empirical sections demonstrate, participants are quick to discover what is going on when they engage with these processes and to figure out whether they serve their purposes or not.

Young people have different capacities to participate, as well as different objectives for their engagement with the system. Moreover, the various styles of engaging civilly appeal to different groups of people. Styles are relatively durable elements of culture that filter collective representations, consequently generating what Eliasoph and Lichterman (2003: 737) refer to as culture in interaction. Engagement in youth participation processes led participants to develop specific group styles (Eliasoph and Lichterman 2003, 2014), situationally defined, recurrent patterns of interaction based on shared assumptions about what constituted good or adequate participation in the group setting.

Before diving into the empirical descriptions of institutional youth participation, this chapter proceeds with an overview of research on formal youth participation, and the democratic ideals on which institutional youth participation processes build.

Youth participation, participatory democracy and institutional practices

In colloquial speech, participatory democracy is often understood as any form of citizen engagement in a public decision-making process, ranging from consultative gatherings to avenues of direct democracy. In democratic theory, however, participatory democracy is understood as a theoretical model for a democratic public sphere which is normatively distinct from representative modes of democracy. Its perceived benefits and central differences compared to representative democracy are the inclusion of as many as possible in deciding on things concerning them (Ferree et al 2002: 295–297), teaching the skills needed to transform individuals into active citizens (Pateman 1970: 42; Bohman 1997: 324–325), discovering public interest through the convergence of free and equal citizens (Rousseau 1998; Bertram 2018), and using democratic reasoning, rather than voting or the aggregation of preferences, as an alternative political process (Cohen 1997; Ercan 2014).

The oxymoronic term 'representative form of participatory democracy' (Kiilakoski 2020) has been used to describe youth councils, youth parliaments, youth forums and other such means of participation through formal political and governmental institutions where youth representatives are selected to play the role of lay experts or stakeholders. Such structures allow participants to develop their practical skills in doing politics, but a prerequisite to access these opportunities tends to be a capacity for public functioning (Bohman 1997). Consequently, youth participation through representative structures tends to favour the accumulation of social, cultural and political capital among privileged groups instead of deepening democracy by empowering groups that have previously been excluded. Such forms of youth participation arguably reproduce many of the problems that participatory democracy is thought to solve (Boldt 2021). On the other hand, participation that is based on participatory and discursive concepts of democracy, such as participatory budgeting, favours methods that are more inclusive, avoid imposed closure in decision making, offering an alternative to styles of representative decision making that are no longer considered supportive of deep-rooted democratic vitality (Fung and Wright 2003: 3).

Youth councils first started appearing in Finland in the late 1990s (Sundback 2004: 145; Siurala and Turkia 2012) and by now exist in virtually all Finnish municipalities (Suomen Nuorisovaltuustojen liitto 2020). Regardless, the structures necessary for power sharing are still largely missing (Eskelinen et al 2015: 68). Youth councils are often forgotten within public governance structures, members rarely receive training, and municipalities fail to hear youth councils even in decisions that directly affect young people (Feldman-Wojtachnia et al 2010: 38).

Taft and Gordon (2013: 93–97) have found that some politically active youth chose to leave youth councils, or not to join them in the first place, because of their 'distrust of youth councils as potential spaces for meaningful engagement'. They argue that youth councils only offer one 'interpretation of democratic citizenship: participation as a voice, as an elite practice, and as managed by the state'. Consequently, institutional avenues for participation lose meaning for young people who emphasize impact, collective engagement and contentious politics in their engagement. Likewise, Laine (2012: 46) describes a plurality of political repertoires used by youth, ranging from engagement in performative acts that contest power relations to expert citizens using their positions to influence the political system. Moreover, Harinen (2000) and Tomperi and Piattoeva (2005) describe how young people can find it demotivating to participate in societal development in what they perceive as a static and ready-made society. An important lesson emerges from these observations: reaching out to young people in traditional 'political' ways may forestall other, more imaginative ways of doing politics. To engage all kinds of young people through institutional youth participation, a full repertoire of participatory forms that challenge the conventions of adult political structures is necessary (Matthews and Limb 2003: 190).[1]

Moreover, methods and timeframes tend to cause problems when they are designed to suit public officials and politicians rather than the capacities and schedules of participants. When participation requires eloquence, comprehension of institutional language and adapting to cultural codes of interaction, many of the people that have the most to gain from participation, such as migrants, young people or the functionally impaired, become excluded (Hill et al 2004: 86–91).

Studying the Porsgrunn model, a well-known model of 'best practice' from Norway, Ødegård (2007: 274) found that youth councils appear to have a positive effect on the political socialization of those that do participate, but since this opportunity requires fluency in the rules, norms, and style of communication expected by the political elite, any larger social effect is left out. A similar finding from the US (Augsberger et al 2018) indicates that caution is needed to avoid the reproduction of social inequality: regardless of proportional representation, youth council members had mixed understandings of whether they were supposed to represent their neighbourhood, with some feeling out of touch with the diverse needs of youth.

A survey among Finnish youth (Sundback 2004: 150) showed that less than half of the respondents knew whether their city offered youth participation opportunities. Moreover, only 2 per cent of the young Finnish respondents to the International Civic and Citizenship Study in 2009 were 'very interested' in local political issues, and 79 per cent answered they were either 'not very' or 'not at all' interested in these issues (Suoninen et al 2010: 49). Contesting this result, a 2018 Finnish Youth Barometer survey on political participation (Pekkarinen and Myllyniemi 2018) reports a relatively high interest in politics among Finnish youth, in contrast to other recent surveys. The authors suggest that the disparity is due to how informants interpret the intention behind the word 'politics'. Responses indicate that young people considered voting, consumer choices, signing initiatives and giving feedback on services to be central forms of civic participation.[2] This seems to confirm a demand for participatory rather than representative democracy.

Participatory budgeting is a process that enables non-elected citizens to take part in allocating public funds. The method was conceived in Porto Alegre, Brazil in the late 1980s. Since then, the method has spread across the world and its popularity has increased massively. In Europe, participatory budgets could be counted on the fingers of one hand in 1999, but by 2012 there were well over 1,000 examples, the largest of them involving the 700,000 inhabitants of Seville, Spain (Sintomer et al 2016: 20).

By involving laypeople in deliberating on their own everyday needs, experiences of participatory budgeting in Brazil led to a reversal of spending priorities in favour of the poor and disadvantaged (Gret and Sintomer 2005). This method introduces a new approach to political participation by offering a low-threshold opportunity for civic engagement without the need for the formality, communicative competence and burden of preconceptions associated with formal representative structures.

Much like youth councils are youth-friendly adaptations of civic practices in formal political and governmental institutions, participatory budgeting has also been adapted for the participation of minors (Cabannes 2004: 38).

A mixed bag: multisited observations of institutional youth participation

In Helsinki, an annually recurring process of participatory budgeting is organized for students in lower-secondary school. The process starts with RuBufest, a mass participation event for information gathering. This is followed by locally organized workshops that develop proposals based on input from the previous step. The popularity of these proposals is assessed through school votes. Following the vote, an executive committee meets to discuss how to implement the results of the vote in view of the available budget.

The participatory budget builds on a markedly different conception of democracy than the youth council. Instead of electing a group of representatives, everybody in the age group is invited to take part. Participating in mass events does not require the courage needed to run for public election; reducing the expected length of commitment from years to hours lowers the threshold for engagement; and focusing on tangible, local issues rather than the general and abstract increases the number of people that can envisage a project within the given framework for participation. Most importantly, participatory budgeting in Helsinki has some direct influence over how the youth department budget is allocated.

However, increased influence is coupled with stronger oversight and control by adults. Participants were engaged on the initiative of youth workers and school authorities, and they were invited to work on categories and subjects that had been chosen by adults. Although open participation ensured a pluralism of participants in comparison with the youth council, the process sometimes misrecognized the capacities and interests of the target group. Due to this, there were significant local differences in the perceived utility of the participatory budget and in the commitment shown by participants.

Youth councils and participatory budgets are representative of the cross-pressure between representative and participatory conceptions of democracy on the one hand, and between established political culture and the call for popular inclusion on the other. This contention over how to organize civic participation, in combination with the legal requirement to give minors political influence, makes the Finnish case interesting and enlightening in the wider international context.

Based on nearly three years of ethnographic fieldwork in the greater Helsinki region, this chapter describes two practices of institutional youth participation, offering both a theoretical exploration of top-down participation projects and the possibilities of acting within them, and an empirical narrative on how young people with budding political aspirations navigate procedures and processes, and the limits of their influence.

Institutionally, the Neartown youth council is securely anchored into municipal structures as it is one of the first youth councils to be founded in Finland, and unlike most youth councils in Finland, it has a full-time secretary-general employed by the Neartown youth department. During my fieldwork period, the youth council received regular media visibility and representatives attended events in parliament, other cities and even abroad. In many ways the Neartown youth council represents an ideal type of youth council with its longstanding institutional ties, support structures and multiple alumni who have gone on to assume influential political positions. These traits make it well equipped to live up to the policy objectives stated in the law, and exemplifying what institutional youth participation through a youth council is like.

Second, the two locations for participatory budgeting presented here, Hilldale and Oceanview, are as disparate as two neighbourhoods in Helsinki can be. Hilldale, the site of a positive discrimination programme due to its high levels of migrants, unemployment, poverty and social problems, is a village-like community in which the youth centre and youth workers are key members. Oceanview is a centrally located, well-to-do neighbourhood, sometimes described as the happiest place to live in Helsinki. Its youth centre feels dormant in comparison to the bustle in Hilldale. Youth workers lamented that many young people in Oceanview attend hobbies every day of the week. Their friendships and communities are formed at football practice, band rehearsals, scout groups, protest movements and yacht clubs rather than at the neighbourhood youth centre.

This research is significant because it reveals a recurring source of conflict in the way in which public officials misrecognize the needs of the participants, and in how participants misrecognize what they can achieve within the platform. The two following sections use fieldwork data to describe, first, how participation in a youth council is mostly about engaging in representative democratic structures and procedures without much political influence. Following that, a section detailing the process of participatory budgeting in Helsinki speaks of a willingness within municipal governance to initiate changes in favour of a more inclusive conception of democracy.

Neartown youth council: learning through simulation, instead of participation

The Neartown website describes the youth council as the voice of young people in the municipality. They can influence decision making through statements, motions, consultations and events. Besides promoting the needs of young people, the youth council increases awareness of civic action and how to participate in politics, inspiring young people to follow political processes and influence them actively.

Procedurally speaking, the council and its 40 members enjoy the same standards and democratic procedures as any other part of the city's public administration. Elections for the youth council are held every two years and anyone aged 13–18 is eligible to vote and run for election. The youth council meets in the city hall once a month for its general assembly. A typical agenda starts with a roll call, an announcement that the meeting is quorate and reports on notifiable matters. After these introductory agenda points, there might be guests giving presentations, requests for comments on various issues that concern youth in the municipality, elections for internal positions and the selection of representatives for meetings to which the youth council has been invited. Sometimes the youth council decides to make a declaration and works on it during the meeting, before finishing with reports from committees and any other business. The meetings follow standard parliamentary procedure, and learning its choreography prepares and socializes participants to act in liberal democratic fora, such as a city council meeting (see Chapter 3), the board of a student union, or the national parliament.

The youth council elect a chairperson, vice-chairpersons and board members among themselves. Additionally, representatives are selected to nine committees appointed by the city council. Their membership consists of elected (adult) party representatives, and they deal with day-to-day political decisions on topics such as education, healthcare and city planning. Positions on these committees are sought after by members of the youth council because of the increased influence and the monetary remuneration they offer.

Offering youth councils access to municipal committee meetings is becoming the standard of inclusion and a best practice of municipal youth participation in Finland. These positions are coveted by council members, but their political utility in terms of power and influence is questionable. The following extract from an interview with Risto gives a forthright description:

> 'I've represented the youth council on several different municipal committees, attending these meetings has been totally useless. Most of the issues on the agenda have been decided beforehand by email, in discussions where youth representatives aren't included. Having a youth representative on the committees is just to fulfil the ninth paragraph of the Youth Law, to make it look nice, like they are listening to young people … instead of decreasing the voting age and including young people directly in real decision making.'

Risto's four years on the council may have made him sardonic about institutional youth participation, but he had not abandoned politics. On the contrary, he was about to stand for local elections for the first time.

Despite regularly criticizing the limited influence of the youth council, the representatives that showed sustained commitment, thereby gaining experience, skills and networks, all shared a privileged background. This is a central observation pertaining to the youth council as a field of engagement: its similarity to and integration with formal politics make it an ideal stepping stone for a career in politics, at least for those with the capacity to commit themselves to playing this particular script.

When a former youth council member and rising star of Finnish party politics was invited to speak to the youth council, he started his speech by describing a traditional path through networks of advocacy organizations towards the political elite:

> 'I would never have become interested in politics unless I had been a youth council representative, and after a while I became involved in more things. I was in the union of secondary school students in Finland, I chaired the advocacy organization for conscripts, I worked in parliament, and now I am chair of the youth wing of the National Coalition Party.'

Similar narratives were shared by others during my fieldwork. For some members, the youth council was clearly a comfortable home, nurturing their ambitions to learn and practise politics, while others described a loss of resonance as soon as they became familiar with the day-to-day business of the youth council. In an interview with Sam, a new member in the 2016–2017 term who was not doing very well despite his earnest effort to fit in, I got a glimpse of the other side of the story:

> 'They [information available from the city, school, and former council members at the time of running for election] exaggerated the influence of the youth council. We don't have real influence, only a chance to rehearse political processes. No one spoke about the atmosphere; the impression was very jolly, and they downplayed how much time it takes. They [the city administration] keep us busy so that we don't have time to complain, so that we don't have time to do something [meaningful].'

Sam's comment describes a dissonance with the official framing of the youth council presented at the beginning of this section. In fact, the most salient feature of the youth council that emerged as I was conducting my fieldwork was how many of the representatives lost interest in it. When the empirical credibility of the collective action frame (Benford and Snow 2000: 619–622) endorsed by the municipal officials turned out to be weak, a disengagement of representatives followed as the framing lost its resonance (Benford and Snow 2000: 619). Interviews confirmed that the expectations of new representatives joining the youth council were largely in line with the Neartown authorities' framing of the youth council. Over time, members realized how curtailed their political influence was, and many decided to leave. Those who committed themselves to the council work formed a group within which they honed their skills in the game. Vanessa described this insight in an interview response:

> 'I don't really believe a youth council representative or even the chairperson has any power. I think it's more like you learn certain things that give you a certain air, that people perceive you as someone powerful. You don't get respect for being a youth council representative. It's the ways you learn to speak and act that lead people to respect you.'

As pointed out by Taft and Gordon (2013: 93–97), the political repertoires of youth councils are perceived to be elitist and conservative by some, driving them elsewhere to enact their civic engagement. Consistent with their findings, attendance at the monthly assemblies decreased to a third before stabilizing a few months into the second year of the term (Boldt 2021: 69–71). By the end of this period, those who still made their way to the monthly assemblies and other meetings of the youth council had formed a tight-knit group. They were united by a shared sense of responsibility for the youth council. Some members of this group were political party members; most of them were members of their school student council. Sharing a solid commitment to the youth council through their engagement in municipal committees, the youth council board and other central assignments, their interaction reinforced the understanding of how a youth council member in good standing should behave.

On my first visit to one of the monthly general assemblies of the youth council, late on in the 2014–2015 mandate, 12 (out of 40) members showed up for the meeting. The youngest were still attending lower-secondary school, while some of the outgoing members had started university or entered military service. At the next few meetings, until the end of their incumbency, I would generally see the same handful of people – about a quarter of the members of the youth council – showing up at meeting after meeting, sometimes too few to be quorate. At the start of the following term, meetings were initially well attended, but after the first summer break, only half of the members turned up for the monthly meetings, and attendance continued to decrease. Once more, only a few committed members were taking care of running the youth council. Antti, a new member in 2016, quickly advanced into the leadership of the council, making an impression with his eloquence and knowledge of local governance. He commented on the workload in an interview: "I think power is centred on a few, five to seven persons, and in a way I'm also a victim of this, since I am one of these people burdened with all the work, running from one place to the other."

The first clue to what was causing the decreasing attendance of youth council members came from a chat with some veterans of the youth council at the last meeting of their term in 2015. Olli, Carl and Päivi were discussing the upcoming constitutive meeting of the next youth council. At this meeting, the youth council were going elect among themselves the chairpersons and the board, as well as representatives for the city council committees. They told me that I should expect fierce backstabbing since everybody is trying to be selected for positions on the board, committees and the like. "But at the end of the day we're like one big family", said Olli. "Yeah, everyone that still sticks around", I responded, to which they replied "Yeah, that's the spirit of the game". These speakers were veterans of three consecutive mandates on the youth council. The reference to 'one big family' was not just rhetorical, but an actual reference to their community, a group of people with a shared understanding of what being committed to the youth council means, including loyalty to a specific style of acting. These group bonds give the council stability, but also restrain the possibilities of new members with different agendas from gaining influence on the council.

Another perspective on inclusiveness and the requirements for establishing bonds and a feeling of belonging to the youth council was offered by Peter in an interview conducted a year after he had stopped attending youth council meetings halfway through his term. His reasons also demonstrate how closely the sense of belonging to a scene of civic action is interrelated with its boundaries of action and normative assumptions of acceptable repertoires:

> 'I got interested in a kind of politics that youth council members don't care about. I joined the youth wing of the Finns Party.[3] Already before that my opinions were quite different. I might be prejudiced, but I expected that I wouldn't be welcome any longer. I was a slightly unusual youth councillor; I didn't do too great in school, and I used to get into fights. I feel like everyone on the board, they have perfect grades and so on. That's the kind of people that get involved.'

Peter was not forced out, but he found that his political positions were too distant from those of the established members. Nevertheless, the youth council proved not to be impervious to radical nationalist rhetoric. Two other youth council representatives blew a fuse whenever multiculturalism, celebrating sexual diversity or campaigns against hate speech were mentioned. Later on, they would cause a local scandal as they used racist imagery in their election campaigns for the youth council. A couple of years after finishing my fieldwork, a Finnish anti-fascist watchdog reported that several people active in radical nationalist movements associated with street fights and terrorism charges also held leadership positions in the youth council. In a local newspaper article, the Neartown youth work coordinator brushed it off and noted that many ideologies fit into the youth council, without showing any regard to the groups this attitude might exclude.

In terms of normative repertoires, it is important to note that much of what goes on in meetings of the youth council has nothing to do with youth advocacy. Hours are spent debating the wording and grammar of motions, how to elect or discharge a representative, whether a ballot should be open or closed, or if the general debate on a proposal should precede or succeed the discussion of each paragraph. To take part in these discussions requires a mastery of the internal regulations as well as a working knowledge of parliamentary procedure. These standards are effortlessly navigated by seasoned council members. This unreservedly aesthetic approach to political agency, favouring pedantic procedure and intricacy rather than practicality, resembles a role play with elaborate instructions in its quest for authenticity. As one representative commented at his first meeting of the youth council: "[It's] terribly technical-official, much ado about nothing." Nevertheless, the focus on procedures persists from one mandate to the next because it is used to establish the merit of individual council members and to counter status threats (Blumer 1958) from new representatives on the council. The following excerpt from a group interview with the youth council leadership in early 2018 describes this recurrent pattern of interaction.

Vanessa: [T]hey just pulled out rules and regulations that I had never heard of … I felt like it didn't matter what someone said, there was always someone else saying that we cannot do that because of the rules …

Antti: I'll tell you a secret. They didn't know the regulations any better than you. It's just a strategy of power, because they know that there is no one that knows those regulations so they can just make anything up.

The internal regulations, and all the rules about how to conduct various procedures in the meetings, were a source of power for older youth council members that they used to ensure they would get their wishes granted. Nonetheless, use of power was not limited to rational-legal authority.

Since the political influence of the youth council is small, the attention of its members is turned inwards, towards achieving status within the council – a status that is reached primarily by being a member for a long time and learning to play along, following the norms of speech and repertoires that are imposed by more senior and influential members. This customary authority is the most-wielded power within the youth council, and it grants members a position from which to contest and dispute legal authority (Weber 2009).[4] It is also regularly used by council members in what Goffman (1986: 58) refers to as ceremonial keying. Ceremonies key events by providing a division between the officiators of the ceremony and the officiated. In these performative displays, council members use their authority to epitomize themselves as senior members of the council by aestheticizing mundane procedures, with the objective of generating awe among less experienced members. These performances establish connections and ramifications between the officiators and the officiated, in ways that strengthen individual ties to those ways of engaging, or by weakening the resonance of the scene, leading to individual feelings of indifference towards the council as a site for civic engagement.

The central tool for political action available to the youth council is passing a motion or a resolution to the city government or some other relevant actor within the city governance apparatus. In the years 2014–2016, the youth council passed 15 motions on topics ranging from apprenticeship agreements to school lunch and infrastructure projects. Eleven of the suggestions were dismissed by civil servants. The youth council were not able to initiate a political process within the system and their motions were little more than 'Dear Santa' letters. Following all the trouble of composing these motions, the youth council typically received a multipage letter filled with jargon and bureaucratic detail, outlining why the request was impossible to fulfil. Alternatively, the city would respond with indeterminate promises to introduce gender-neutral toilets whenever a new school building is constructed or to renew their measures against bullying.

The following quotes from a group interview with youth council board members summarize the frustration felt at the lack of power and authority:

> 'For me the most frustrating thing is the extreme inefficiency that is everywhere. It's inefficient to get anything from the youth council to civil servants, it's inefficient to get anything from the youth council to political representatives. It's slow, complicated, difficult, and tiresome to get anything done through the youth council at all. It feels like anytime the youth council wants something; the initial reaction is to oppose it. Of course, the world is like that, and you've got to get used to it, maybe it was just waking up from the innocence of childhood, but it's been infuriating.' (Antti)

> 'People show up on the youth council thinking they are going to improve school lunches but come to realize that all our decisions are part of a bigger picture. You've got to consider budgets, allergies or something. There are so many obstacles that all the enthusiasm disappears when you realize it is so much harder to change anything.' (Hilja)

The inefficiency and obstacles described by the informants is conveyed by one of the motions accepted by the Neartown city officials: to erect walls for the painting of legal graffiti. The youth council submitted two proposals on this: the first in 2012, followed by another in 2014. Two years later, in 2016, the first graffiti wall was constructed in Neartown. Since then, several more have been built, but in the meantime the originators of these motions have become older and have perhaps moved on to other things.

Youth participation based on a model of representative liberal democracy reproduces both existing privileges and negative and cynical attitudes towards engagement in public decision-making processes. In other words, it fuels the legitimacy deficit associated with representative democracy rather than solving it. Establishing a youth council makes it easy to tick the checkbox of youth participation, since youth councils fit well into the existing bureaucratic practices. This was nicely demonstrated when the Ministry of Social Affairs and Health consulted Finnish youth councils on a health and social affairs reform by requesting comments on hundreds of pages of legal text with a short deadline and no clear indication of how this feedback would be utilized. While youth councils are great learning opportunities for some young people, they can hardly be applauded for making decision making more accessible or inclusive.

Next, I turn to the participatory budgeting process in Helsinki and its attempt to engage youth through participatory and discursive democratic practices.

RuutiBudjetti: a youth work approach to democracy

At the start of most events, a short video (Ruuti Munstadi 2015) explaining the RuutiBudjetti (participatory budgeting) process was shown to the participants. A professionally produced animation outlined the steps in the process, with a voiceover stating that the objective of participatory budgeting was to engage young people in planning free-time activities and developing the city. Young people were encouraged to suggest anything: "Sometimes crazy ideas will become reality" and "[the] suggestions that gain the most votes will be realized in the following year".

As the next section shows, a few proposals did sound a little crazy, but most of them were predictable reflections of known issues. They dealt with needs and desires that have been articulated through youth engagement processes across Europe for a long time (Borland et al 2001; Morrow 2001; Hill et al 2004; Autio et al 2008; Boldt 2018): for instance, establishing places where young people can mingle and interact without feeling threatened or bothered, changing the public perception of young people as an unpredictable nuisance into something more positive, preventing bullying and getting help with everyday problems. Unfortunately, the participatory budget often turned out to be a blunt tool for these purposes.

Besides the shared features, there were distinct differences between the two neighbourhoods in terms of the dreams formulated, the commitment shown and interpretations of what the participatory budget could be used for. This difference in interpretation turned out to be one of the bigger tensions within the process. While many participants were enthusiastic about developing their neighbourhood and the city, what was being offered was an annually recurring opportunity to suggest changes in how local youth work was organized. Apart from projects within the institutional boundaries of the youth department that could be achieved for less than €3,000, the influence of the participants was small and mostly communicative. Ideas that were more costly or related to the competencies of other departments of the city could receive institutional support from the youth department, but their chances of becoming reality proved to be slim.

Commitment to the participatory budgeting process was strong among participants, youth workers and school staff in Hilldale. However, dedication to the budgeting process in Oceanview was fleeting, without much expression of shared responsibility for the realization of mutual interests. Consequently, decisions in each subsequent stage of the process were made by people who had not previously been involved in discussing the suggestions. They would often arbitrarily, without reasoned discussion, decide against something that participants in a previous step had prepared.

Weak bonds to the scene of participation led to events which were not always in agreement with the normative values that characterize participatory and discursive democratic practices, namely the avoidance of imposed, nonconsensus-based closure, dialogue and mutual respect. The ways in which the public is involved in decision making affects the perceived legitimacy and justice of participation (Fung 2006: 70–72), and when differences in access to participatory opportunities exist, they lead to unequal power relations and the promotion of self-interest rather than the common good (Ercan 2014). Youth workers in Hilldale repeatedly reminded participants to represent Hilldale, not only their own interests. This attitude was not shared in Oceanview. When the executive committee meeting in Oceanview was discussing the results of the 2016 school vote and the desire for youth spaces in shopping centres. Joonas, a visitor at the youth centre who was co-opted to participate, posed the question "Should I think of the common good or myself?", arguing that "I don't see how youth spaces in shopping centres improve the situation of young people". The response from the youth workers was confused head-scratching and silence, although the proposal had received a quarter of all the votes in the district. Since no one argued against him, Joonas decided to stick to his personal principles and preferences rather than reason on behalf of ideas that had fared well in the school vote.

The accountability that goes hand in hand with pluralistic participation is an important safeguard in democratic decision making. In a process where each stage builds on the previous work of others, respectful consideration of that input should be the norm. The lack of direct accountability was a feature of the participatory budgeting, due to the self-selection of participants and the lack of public reporting throughout the process. This atomization of the participants counteracted the formation of strategic collective action. This was never an issue where participation was high. However, when inclusion was traded off against efficiency and easy implementation, the process shifted style, from democratic participation in support of civic renewal and increased trust in public institutions (Fung 2004) to a fun day with the local youth workers.

Regardless of the strong initial support for the process in Hilldale, the commitment of participants showed signs of foundering as the process kept going without any tangible signs of progress on some of the projects after the school vote. Over time, participants dropped out as it became obvious that, unlike the promise in the introductory video, dreams would not be instantly fulfilled. This loss of resonance came about as the group bonds and shared assumptions about obligations among group members (Lichterman and Eliasoph 2014) were challenged by youth workers asking participants to commit themselves to the realization of the project. Prior to these gatherings, all parts of the participatory budgeting process had been carried out during school time, and participants had not been expected to commit themselves to more than actively participating in the meeting they were attending. By underlining the responsibility of the participants for achieving their goal, youth workers shifted the scene style from a collective endeavour into one of individual duty.

At the executive meeting a youth worker said: "The trouble with this Ruuti thing is that these ideas might not be accomplished before you are a lot older." Then she told the young participants that "the role of the executive committee, that's you guys, is to further these initiatives", switching from the culture of engagement at the introductory event and workshops, where participants could express their wishes without committing themselves to further action, to one in which the group members were faced with the responsibility for achieving the collective aspirations of the neighbourhood.

When the discussion turned to the youth café, the most popular suggestion in the neighbourhood, everybody sat in quiet anticipation. The participants were no better equipped to turn their dream into reality than the youth workers who were assigned to the participatory budget. The district director summarized what had been said about the youth café so far and suggested it might be easier to start the café in the youth centre, a suggestion to which participants had already objected before. Everyone remained quiet, looking away. Nothing was decided except for continuing to work towards the café.

Next up was a proposal to improve the ice-skating field and to build a rink for hockey. Considering that Hilldale is the neighbourhood of Helsinki with the lowest levels of political engagement defined by voter turnout, the fact that a group of disorderly boys who could hardly sit still at the workshop had managed to formulate the proposal, present it with reasonable arguments and gather enough votes to make their suggestion the second most popular was quite extraordinary. Clearly, as a format of participation, there was a potential to meet the policy objectives of increasing engagement and developing civic skills. Taking the floor, a representative from the sports department gave a briefing on how to advocate for the proposal within the city bureaucracy: "The rink will not happen unless you make some noise. The message that locals want this must come from here [not from me]." This seemed strange, considering the popularity of the suggestion. The sports department representative encouraged the initiators to frame a proposal for the sports department around safety aspects: a rink would protect children and other skaters from those playing hockey. A handful of participants were enthusiastic, promising to continue working on this with the youth workers: "We will aim directly at the leadership level in the sports department"; "Should we write an address?"; "Everyone will help, if we start now, we might have it by next winter".

Nevertheless, the promise of turning dreams into reality proved to be empty. Instead, the participants received a lesson in advocacy. Both the youth workers and the sports department official told the boys that the future of their proposal was in their own hands, implying that all their work would be in vain unless they did some more. As of September 2023, there is still no hockey rink in Hilldale.

The same story was repeated in 2017, when Hilldale youth once again proposed a youth café in the participatory budget. The youth workers kept worrying that the relevance of participatory budgeting would be questioned by participants unless the proposals were realized. As school students participating in the school vote were leaving the room, a youth worker asked them how it felt to vote, reminding them that in a few years' time they could vote in real elections just as easily. As she was walking out of the door, a student said, "The café proposal was already there last year, and it didn't lead to anything", as if reminding the youth workers that although no one else had brought this up, it did not mean they were not aware of it.

The events that unfolded in Oceanview in 2017 were quite different. One of the workshops took place in a small classroom, stuffed to capacity with participants. A particularly rowdy boy was constantly interrupting and disturbing the others by conversing with the persons next to him while the youth workers were talking. The restless atmosphere increased when the youth workers got annoyed and shouted at everyone to stay calm and focus. Leino, the unruly boy, managed to disrupt the scene together with his friends. The workshop failed to establish the mutual respect between participants and organizers that was the norm at other events. The boys made a joke of suggesting a *Scooby-Doo*-themed bouncy castle, and it ended up as one of the ideas from the workshop. One of the boys turned to Leino: "Did anyone even vote for that, weren't these supposed to be the ideas of the youth and not your ideas? It's such a stupid suggestion." Leino simply responded: "That's the point." While he recognized that the bouncy castle was not a representation of the type of idea that should be suggested within the participatory budgeting process, he took the opportunity to ridicule the process, thus breaking with the expected norms of action and switching the scene style as an act of counterconduct.

What started out as a skilful act of disruption (Isin 2008), turning the process upside down while still staying within it, eventually became the second most popular initiative in the school vote, just behind reduced-price summer events and tickets for young people. Although some of the participants at the workshop were trying to develop ideas based on the aggregate results from RuBufest, the workshop disintegrated because Leino rejected all responsibility for working for a common good through the budgeting process. Nevertheless, he did not leave or refuse to participate; instead, he managed to subvert the process. When a scene style is dissonant, a participant has the three options: playing along, questioning the script through scene-breaking acts (Goffman 1986; Isin 2008) or leaving. Although Leino's actions could simply be dismissed as bad behaviour, they can also be interpreted as acts of citizenship. Consciously breaking the script by making a fuss was a tactic repeatedly resorted to when the scene of engagement forced participants to consider whether they were losing their dignity by playing along. The timing and formulation of such acts require skill in identifying situations where the tension in interaction is strong and the risk of losing face because of others taking sides with the organizers is small. Berger (2015) describes how participants in scenes of asymmetrical interaction resist the ways of being that are imposed upon them. Institutional criticism can be more convincingly delivered by participating according to the instructions, down to the last detail. This lets participants use their attentiveness to the process as a cognitive and moral resource, forcing officials to maintain the mutual commitment. Lastly, by subverting the order of visibility, participants can turn themselves into the protagonists of the scene (Berger 2015: 17–18). On the other hand, in this case, the use of the arts of resistance (Scott 1990) was not for the benefit of all the participants. One of them continuously but unsuccessfully tried to propose "that adults would react to harassment, that they would come to ask if everything's OK". The attempt by the youth workers to control the chaotic workshop through authority failed, at the cost of excluding the weak voices in the room.

At the Oceanview executive committee meeting, none of the three participants had been involved in preparing proposals or voting for them. The *Scooby-Doo* bouncy castle proposal confused them, and when they asked about it, the local youth worker sighed and responded: "This is what it's like when you do participatory budgeting with young people."

The youth worker asked whether the participants would like to remove some of the suggestions immediately in order to make it easier to focus on the suggestions that seem possible to implement. The boys agreed, and the bouncy castle was the first idea to be removed, without any further discussion, regardless of its popularity in the vote. Next, Joonas took the lead on a suggestion to host an exhibition of young artists in the contemporary art museum: "This could cause a lot of problems with professional artists; they have worked a long time to get their art into the museums, and suddenly young people get there just like that. It sounds very hard to execute. Maybe I'm too strict, do others have any opinions on this?" Since no one had anything to reply, he exclaimed: "Remove it!"

The youth worker in charge of the meeting took notes, and the meeting moved through the proposals. Joonas continued: "Is there some kind of trend with outdoor cinema?" The youth worker explained that the workshop participants had identified it as one of the most popular suggestions at the introductory event. "I would get rid of it", said Joonas, and it was off the table.

Suggestions that had received plenty of support in the school vote were discarded in a matter of seconds. At the end of the meeting, Joonas said: "Those who came up with these ideas should have been here." While the executive committee participants in Hilldale had attended the meeting in order to further shared goals, Joonas curated the initiatives in Oceanview according to his own tastes, engaging in self-actualization instead of speaking on behalf of a collective of local youth.

Since none of the initiators of the proposals was present, there was no one to speak in favour of them, but even more crucially, participants were not expected to commit themselves in any way to the projects and ideas they were discussing. Therefore, the motivator for the rationalistic, informed and in some ways pessimistic rhetoric was not the avoidance of commitment, but the lack of bonds to the groups behind the initiatives, and the absence of transparency, accountability and respect for the work previously done by other youth during the process.

Widely disseminating information about the possibility to participate can force participants to consider the public good in addition to their own self-interest, since more people are bound to know about the process and be curious to know who decided what. Transparency builds trust (Irvin and Stansbury 2004: 61) and educates the public (Beierle 1999: 82) about the mechanics of the decision-making process and the trade-offs involved. On the other hand, a lack of transparency and predictability can also cause a loss of commitment.

The observations that have been described so far are examples of recurring attributes and characteristics of the fieldwork locations, most of which were influenced by the empowerment style of promoting civic engagement in a safe, family-like atmosphere (Eliasoph 2011: 2–8). While this style resonated well with the youth in Hilldale, who were accustomed to positive discrimination strategies and the presence of municipal youth workers in their free time, it could not have been less appropriate for the students in Oceanview. The low turnout of participants speaks of the poor local relevance of the participatory budgeting process, and when young people did participate, their desires were often a mismatch with what the youth department could offer.

Discussion

This chapter has described two kinds of institutional youth participation processes in Finland: a municipal youth council and neighbourhood-level participatory budgeting. Both of these approaches to youth participation are born out of the same policy objective of strengthening democracy by instilling cohorts of young people with civic virtues, while letting them decide on things that are important in their lives.

Observation of these institutional youth participation policies reveals that the ways in which young people want to imagine, engage and act in common do not always agree with municipal youth participation initiatives. For some participants, participation was an important and meaningful experience, while others found the situated action meaningless in terms of furthering their goals and purposes.

Centrally, both empirical cases show that playing along to a preconceived script, whether it follows the normative standards of liberal democracy or the ethos of empowering youth work, can help some young people figure out who they are, what they want to work on and how they want to do it. Conversely, for others, engaging in ready-made scenes of participation is stifling. These participants fail to find reasons to commit themselves to institutional youth participation, either dropping out or manifesting their dissatisfaction through script-breaking acts. It also became apparent that the success of a youth participation policy often hinges on the capacities of individual youth workers to communicate and translate the procedure in ways that appeal to the participants.

Despite its constrained political influence, the youth council efficiently served the function of socializing and preparing participants for acting in other publics with a family resemblance to liberal democratic parliamentary procedure. In three consecutive terms, about a third of those elected found reasons to commit themselves to the youth council, while the rest dropped out due to various reasons, mainly because the ways of forging the common in the youth council did not resonate with their sense of values, belonging and ways of imagining a better world.

In a similar manner, the Helsinki youth department approach to participatory budgeting was initially well received in Hilldale. Defining common goals was easy there compared to the socioeconomically fragmented but generally better-off Oceanview. Without competing free-time interests and with fewer opportunities to spend their free time away from teachers, youth workers and parents, Hilldale youth were quick to identify both small and big projects for the benefit of young people in their neighbourhood. Notably, these proposals were largely related to tangible improvements such as a youth café, a hockey rink or the necessary equipment to host a movie night at the youth centre. In Oceanview, on the other hand, mobilizing participants was a struggle, and finding people committed to participate in multiple steps of the process seemed impossible. However, in contrast to Hilldale, participants from Oceanview also formulated abstract political proposals dealing with community, nondiscrimination and solidarity. Unfortunately, the participatory budgeting process was neither well adapted for furthering this type of initiative nor for making infrastructure investments or launching youth led businesses. While several neighbourhood projects were funded through the participatory budget, the process itself spoke of a misrecognition of the interests of young people as well as a misunderstanding of the level of influence one could wield through the process.

Analysing these cultures of engagement, the youth council plays host to tightly controlled events with limited access and defined roles, while the participatory budget is a mix of events with varying levels of access – for instance, the introductory event and school votes are open to anyone, but participants self-select to attend workshops and the executive committee. While both methods of youth participation are cyclical, the youth council members get selected for a two-year mandate, compared to the six months or so that the participatory budgeting takes. Additionally, the participatory budget is porous in the sense that participants keep flowing into and out of the process, contrasting with the closedness and high density of commitment on the youth council. In terms of resources, as both the youth council and the participatory budget are organized by youth departments, they have the potential to operationalize similar physical assets. What sets them apart is that the participatory budget does have direct influence over some share of budgetary allocations, while the youth council, due to its history and the type of young people engaged in it, has access to a larger gamut of human, social and symbolic resources, although this seemed not to translate into increased influence.

Despite all the talk about how to engage young people, the fieldwork clearly showed that commitment really depended on whether a participant managed to engage in a meaningful project of their own. For core members of the youth council, the council itself was their project. While they would submit motions from time to time, the actual day-to-day grind was mostly about going to meetings. This also explains why representatives with specific desires to initiate changes with an impact in the lives of people beyond the youth council so quickly lost interest. Conversely, young people realized a range of projects from movie nights and LAN parties to school cafés and poetry slam events through the participatory budgeting. However, the desires of the participants often went beyond what was possible to achieve or influence through the youth department. They expressed a determination to improve wellbeing through the improvement of urban infrastructure, establishing safe spaces for hanging out, helping refugees and campaigning for the rights of sexual minorities. Unfortunately, these aspirations could not be satisfied through these avenues for youth participation.

To sum up, the youth council was more likely to thrust participants into experiences with a potential to transform their capacities for public functioning, but the noninclusive nature of its events, and its failure to acknowledge and celebrate the intersectionality of its members, caused a mainstreaming of the core activists, most of whom had already been competent in their capacity to engage in the public sphere before becoming members. On the other hand, the empowerment narrative, youth work approach and familiarity of the participatory budget engaged youth who would probably not have a voice or choose to participate under other circumstances. On the other hand, it failed to accommodate aspirations to affect decisions beyond the authority of the youth department. That being the case, both methods of institutional youth participation turned out to be inclusive of some groups and exclusive of others.

In the next chapter, we turn to the group of young people for whom the empowerment narrative became lived experience: young candidates in municipal elections, many of whom have literally grown up in youth councils and participatory budgeting projects.

3

Aspiring Politicians: From Amateur Engagements to Problem Solving

Veikko Eranti and Eeva Luhtakallio

Introduction

In this chapter, we move from participatory democracy to the most formal level of youth political participation: that of party politics and running in a local election. In Finland, the characteristics of the electoral system make candidacy particularly open for young people. The multiparty elections using party-list proportional representation, combined with a great number of small municipalities, together create a situation where municipal elections in large cities include over 1,000 candidates who all have a chance of getting elected. In order for the political parties to maximize their chances, they need to recruit a great variety of candidates, and hence, at every election, there are a considerable number of young and inexperienced newcomers hopping into the political stage. Because of the large number of parties involved in municipal elections, and the relatively large size of municipal councils (ranging from ten members in a typical small municipality to 85 in Helsinki, the capital), in every municipal election there are, nation-wide, tens of thousands of candidates with potential of achieving a position of some influence in municipal decision-making. During the 2017 municipal elections, this translated to almost 1 per cent of the voting age population of Finland running for a seat in the city or municipal council. Such a huge number of candidates has two consequences for the analysis in this chapter: first, it possibly makes candidacy a more relevant form of political action for young people in Finland than in many other contexts;[1] and, second, it provides this book with a significant viewpoint to party-political engagement among young people.

Perhaps because in many other countries, electoral systems are not as open to newcomers, the empirical focus on young candidates in elections is relatively rare in youth studies, let alone more generally in political research. However, some recent studies have explored youth engagement as party members, as well as members of party youth organizations. It has often been shown in large-scale comparative studies that young people are a heterogeneous and somewhat more volatile group of party members than adults, and have both varying motivations for their membership and dilemmas about their commitment (Bruter and Harrison 2009; Weber 2020). Often being a party member at young age is, nonetheless, a signal predicting political careers in adulthood (Fjellman and Rosén Sundström 2021). While the studies acknowledge that youth organization membership is more diversely motivated and more fluctuating than membership in 'mother' parties tends to be, the party's resources and attention tend to impact youth organization members' commitment: the more integrated the youth organization, the more committed its members (see, for example, Hooghe et al 2004; Bolin et al 2023).

While these studies provide background for this chapter's analysis, it is nonetheless noteworthy that they do not consider young candidates per se. Joshi (2012) noted both the scarcity and the need of such research a decade ago in his study on the impact of electoral systems to the election of young Members of Parliament (MPs). Still, ten years later, Chou et al (2021: 428) lament the fact that 'only a scattering of scholarship exists on the demographics, motivations, and experiences of young political candidates and politicians' (see also Stockemer and Sundström 2019). It is noteworthy that in the rather small body of research that does address the topic, the great majority looks at voting patterns, and is survey-based (for example, Kumar 2014; Sevi 2021; Stockemer and Sundström 2021; Belschner 2023). These studies examine young candidates as a potential drawing factor for young voters, and young candidates' electoral success in relation to a variety of factors in the respective parties and electoral systems: the extant literature is for the most part political scientific electoral research and tells us little about the ways of doing society that participating in elections as a candidate entails.

From the starting point of our research interest, instead, we wanted to know how the youth engaging in representative politics reflect on their choice, make meaning of such participation and forge a patterned culture of doing society through their actions. With this research problem, we partly share the approach of Chou et al (2021), who examined the motivations and political content that young Australian candidates emphasized. In their survey-based research, the principal motivations for running in local elections were serving the local community, personal political convictions and dissatisfaction with the way in which local council was being run (Chou et al 2021). The most important political topics for the young candidates were: climate change, local environment, 'youth issues', LGBTIQ+ issues, affordable housing and planning, all with around 10 per cent of mentions.[2] While the formulations of questions in our survey that we presented briefly in Chapter 1 of this book were not directly comparable, the results point to broadly similar trends: the issues with which most young people in Helsinki metropolitan area agreed upon and regarded as important were LGBTIQ+ issues, welfare state issues, eradication of poverty and entrepreneurship. However, even though both surveys show some interesting indications of the motivations and topics that potentially draw young people towards representative political engagement, in order to grasp the cultural patterns of such engagements, we need to get closer to the meaning making of young candidates. How did they come to the decision to stand in an election and what is characteristic – in comparison to their peers engaging in very different kinds of action in participatory programmes, online fora or street activism – of the young aspiring politicians' culture of doing society?

This chapter is based on thematic interviews of 32 candidates who were standing in the elections for the first time in 2017 and who were under 30 years old (the majority of the interviewees were under 25) during the time of the interview. They were chosen at random from the candidate lists presented in the Helsinki metropolitan area (including the electoral districts of Helsinki, Espoo and Vantaa), yet sampled in a way to ensure a representation across the political spectrum.[3] In the interviews, we asked about the candidates' backgrounds and paths to candidature, as well as motivations both to run in elections and to be active in politics in a party context more generally. To understand the civic imagination of the young candidates, we formulated questions from Baiocchi et al's (2014) definitions of civic imagination (see Chapter 1 for an in-depth description of the concept). We asked which approach the candidates saw as having primacy in their own perspective to doing local politics: dismantling unequal structures, finding solutions to societal problems or enhancing community and participation. To understand the ways in which they engage with communities through plans and in justification (see Chapter 1), we invited the candidates to talk about their future plans and aspirations, as well as how and through which kind of engagements they ended up as candidates in the first place.

The young politicians' accounts of their paths to electoral politics draw a general picture of opportunities that seems to present themselves as having arrived in that position by chance. Many follow an invitation – often a surprising one, in an event they have 'ended up in' – while some volunteer themselves to a party organization, both with similar lightness. Party choice is hardly a matter of life and death – with the exception of the candidates of the youngest party, the right-wing populist Finns Party – and many have pondered between several parties, albeit mostly within one side of the left-right divide (there also are those who have considered, more or less, all of the parties). While the degree of determination and commitment varies greatly among the interviewed, we can distinguish three separate paths to candidacy. Often the paths intertwine, but one path usually stands out as the most salient one. We call the first one 'the participatory-industry path', the second 'the youth organization veteran path' and the third 'the hobby-collector path'. The three also call for different repertoires of engaging: the participatory-industry path and the youth organization veteran path mainly evoke engagements in a plan (Thévenot 2007), be it a plan partly dictated by the constraints of a participatory project, or an individual plan connected to career development, and sometimes also civic valuation of a collective cause, or even a familiar aspect of sharing. The hobby-collector path, in turn, builds on a hybrid between the former and an engagement in exploration, in which a future self is experimented with (Auray 2007; Thévenot 2014). We will return to these perspectives later on, looking at how each path unfolded in the interviews.

In the following, we focus first on the paths to candidature, along with accounts of what motivates the young. We then look at how they envision the political action in which they are about to engage and what kind of common they imagine building – also in terms of the civic imagination their responses portray. Finally, we explore the future orientations and aspirations the interviews highlight, and reflect on the patterns of doing society emerging therein.

The participatory-industry path to politics

Chapter 2 presented projects and structures aimed at getting young people to participate in political decision making: youth councils and participatory budgeting. The young people in these contexts had serious reservations about whether they had any actual influence over issues: while there were wins, the processes were often lost in the weeds, abandoned outright or succumbed to something resembling tokenistic participation. Nonetheless, as Chapter 2 also concludes to be the case regarding some of the young participants, the young electoral candidates stress how important these structures and projects sometimes are to the kind of personal capacity building (public speaking, understanding of structures) that is advertised to take place in youth councils. Quite naturally, this makes such structures even disproportionally relevant to some young people's trajectories into politics. In a strong sense, political candidacy is often a natural continuum from various participatory projects. In the following, Risto, whom we met in Chapter 2, describes his first steps towards a political engagement in a way that clearly shows that he, despite some discouraging experiences, eventually felt like he could actually influence some things in the world through the youth council:

'(Chuckles) My whole spark was lit when I was 15 and I was lured into the local youth council. I got excited: even if I'm only 15, I can actually influence things happening near me. There, bit by bit, the level of my influence grew onto NGOs [nongovernmental organizations], and into party politics. And in the municipal elections I want to have power over even larger issues and areas.' (Risto, The Greens)

A majority (over two thirds) of the young candidates we interviewed had come through the participatory-industrial path like Risto. They had backgrounds in school councils, youth councils, or participatory budgeting projects, and, later on in their trajectory, frequently in student politics. They had tried many things and engaged on different levels and systems of participation, and thus found their way into party politics. Even if the young people did not feel particularly influential, they at least got a sense of personal growth or grew familiar with party politics. Gitta, who chose her party because it was 'neutral and for a lot of good things', states the following about her history with party politics:

'I studied political science, and was active in various student organizations, but I wasn't part of any political organization as such … Except yes, yes, I was a youth councillor in my hometown back in the day, but even that's a little, there are no parties in that sense … Because of the youth council, I sat at the board of education as the representative of the youth, as well as in the land use and planning board, but as a 15–16-year-old, all that was pretty abstract to me. But I got a lot out of sitting in and listening to debates over whether we should close a particular school and so on, in the board of education.' (Gitta, Swedish People's Party)

For Gitta, back when she was younger, planning issues felt abstract, but matters concerning education gave a glimpse into the actual world of politics. Maria also grew up in various participatory structures and youth organizations, including a two-year stint as a chairperson of her hometown's youth council. For her, the same abstractness of discussion that Gitta mentioned had a much more profound effect, and she ended up joining the far-right-leaning Finns Party because of the experience:

'Perhaps the biggest reason why I joined the youth organization of the Finns Party was because, at that time, I had attended a lot of local board meetings, as an observer. Everything was so, well, very difficult to understand, and the structures of politics annoyed me. When you wanted to change something, you had to go through three different levels first. And all those papers documents that were discussed in the various boards, they were completely incomprehensible to me, a young person who had only taken one social studies course in upper secondary school. I kind of realized that I wanted to do something to make it simpler, to be able to talk about these issues in a way that people could actually understand. And because the Finns Party has strongly profiled itself in this matter, it might have been the biggest reason for my choice of party.'

Despite the major differences in these two stories, in some sense the educational function of youth councils was quite clearly fulfilled: having a literal seat at the table had an effect that lowered the barrier for taking a more active party-political path in the future for both Gitta and Maria.

On this same path, many of our respondents describe the 'spark' also mentioned by Risto earlier: memorable moments that have laid foundations both for a conviction that participation is meaningful, and, perhaps more importantly, that one as an individual has the capacity to act and make things happen. Leila, while reflecting widely on the possibilities and limitations she encountered in her many engagements within participatory structures, puts the key moment in words as a simple example of individual fulfilment:

'I remember the day I was elected [as the chair of the Youth Council], the only thing spinning in my head was that *I was kind of important*, I'm important ... And it was a really awesome feeling. Of course it's an individualistic feeling only focused on myself, but it was also a great feeling of having accomplished something big.' (Leila, The Greens)

It is noteworthy that while the type of participation experience described in Chapter 2 ends up disappointing most participants in various ways, it nonetheless provides a specific avenue forward to the few selected and interested. They describe a spectrum of important learning processes that are not exclusively tied to positive experiences. Leila, describing her memorable triumphant moment, also noted that she met the boundaries of youth participation structures at numerous occasions, and gradually concluded that these contexts would not offer the influence she was hoping to achieve:

'I was in the Voice of the Youth magazine's [a website run by the local youth services] editorial staff for quite some time where we tried to have a say. And there was always (the acknowledgement that) having an influence was not as efficient as it would have been through the (actual) media, which would have required a career in journalism. And that is, well, pretty much so that in Finland you can't really be a career journalist anymore, the job is so haphazard. So, I gave up on that dream and drifted to the Youth Council. There, in turn, I saw that no matter what, when the gavel is banged in the [Municipal] Council, it's the Council that decides.' (Leila, The Greens)

Even those with much more disappointing experiences often acknowledged the importance of the participatory projects they have gone through, often at quite a young age.

Miriam, who was already a seasoned youth politician before turning 20, for instance, begins her description of her path to electoral candidacy starting from the participatory budgeting for youth in Helsinki. For her, the experience was an eye-opener that led to other positions:

> 'When I was elected to the Ruuti budget core group [see Chapter 2], I was like, what kind of clownery is this, we are in no way taken seriously. In a way, while I was there, I started to pay attention to what is the position and status of young people in our society, or in our city. And the diversity of the youth in Helsinki wasn't present at all … Well, ever since junior high I have been on the governing board and in the ninth grade I was the chairperson of my school's student council. In high school, for the last year I was the chairperson of the student council executive board and sat in all kinds of school-wide bodies and teacher meetings, ranting about student wellbeing. So, that's where I've got some experience from.' (Miriam)[4]

Most of the young people interviewed had at least some experience of the systems designed to make young people participate, and some had followed this path exclusively up until the candidacy. This feature can be interpreted as a win for the participatory system that, to put it bluntly, is designed partly as 'actual' participation and partly as democracy education (see also Chapter 4). Clearly, if the participation aspect may remain vague, the educational function is fulfilled: the young people learning how to step up and read meeting materials find it quite natural to continue to municipal level party politics. These people feel relatively confident in well-lit conference rooms and well-run meetings because they have grown up in these environments. They might be young, but they are already civic veterans.

One clear separation between participatory programmes aimed at young people and municipal politics naturally comes from the inescapably partisan nature of the latter. All the youth participation structures are arranged in a seemingly nonpartisan way: there are no party lists in youth councils, even if many take on party affiliations already there. This fact is reflected in the individualistic nature of the youth participation veterans' talk: they always speak about *my* possibilities for influence, or if they talk about 'us', it is about a quite abstract 'young people' as *us*. What is completely lacking is the sense of a group or a community as a political actor or subject.

However, not all young people come from such individualistic participation backgrounds. Given the traditionally important role associations and various organizations have played in Finland (see Chapter 1), these also work as a route to party politics for many.

The youth organization veteran path to politics

Apart from the meeting rooms of the participatory projects, the young candidates had sat endlessly in youth organization meetings – but they had also marched in demonstrations, planned direct actions and formed entire life contexts in NGOs and social movements. The youth organization path to electoral candidacy takes on different colours according to the party affiliation: in terms of style of engagement, right-wing organizations lean towards the NGO-type structures and action orientation, while left-wing organizations tend to lean towards a social movement style. Nonetheless, we argue that the youth organization path has a similar core to it regardless of these differences. It is that of often long-term involvement in an activity with like-minded people, in contrast to the participatory structures in which projects come and go (like the participatory budgeting rounds), and people come and go (like in the youth councils where the representative turnover is often high; see Chapter 2). The candidates principally following the youth organization path had often multiple strings attaching them to the political community: years of commitment, circles of friends that have evolved gradually around the activities, and many key experiences from their formative years.

The right-leaning organization veterans' sense making of their background was, on the one hand, centred on a narrative of a path paved with making friends and networks and engaging in activities in an organizational environment that was structurally quite determined. Aleksanteri, for instance, gives an account of his years in student politics:

> 'Where I went to university, the student organizations were quite passive and after checking them out for a while, I agreed to be the chair of the Centre Party student organization. That year we got a lot of new members, and it was exciting and nice hustle and bustle, we organized the annual meeting of the national umbrella organization, learned to do all that. This opened the door to the Student Union's board, it was a kind of a victory, we got three people from the Centre Party in. But the main point was that it was really pleasant organizational activity, I got to work and meet people and learn, learning is really important to me.' (Aleksanteri, Centre Party)

On the other hand, some described their path to politics as a strategic series of memberships to achieve one's goals. These were sometimes explicitly political ones, but often also pointing at other directions, namely career success. Jonas, a Swedish Party candidate, described his rather instrumental relation to the party:

> 'I think I became a member of the Swedish Youth at some point during high school without even really thinking about what it is, just because it's some kind of an organization. And then I was a candidate [for their student organization] in some school elections. I thought about [running in the municipal election] and thought, yeah, it's really great visibility. I have a stake in a small business, and the Swedish-speaking circles are quite small, so that's also a contributing factor to getting visibility. It's like, as selfish as it can be.' (Jonas, Swedish People's Party)

Both the preceding paths to political candidacy follow a plan (see Thévenot 2015; Eranti 2018): they portray engagement in interest-based action, be it working for a community of interest, as in the first excerpt, or maximizing self-interest, as in the second one. In both, the instrumentality of engaging in organizations – either as providing valuable experience to potentially achieving further political goals or providing assets for other areas of life – is blatant.

In contrast, some of the left-leaning candidates stood out in terms of their description of a path to politics that can be dubbed the social movement track. These accounts resemble activist biographies, in which candidacy is but one tool among many in a palette of engagements in activities for a better world. Mikael describes the overarching nature of the Left Youth organization: more than a party youth chapter, it is a do-it-all organization connected to an entire network of left-leaning social movements. It has offered him an all-inclusive context for activism:

> 'I've been active in the Left Youth since I was 15. I've been pretty much an insider for a long time before this candidacy. The Left Youth is pretty versatile, there is direct action on streets and in the cabinets. So, it has pretty much taken all my volunteering resource. The Left Youth is involved in many other types of activism, like house squatting and the like … I have participated in demonstrations and have organized all kinds of activities to our members, courses for example.' (Mikael, Left Alliance)

Joonatan, another candidate with similar background, adds a layer of international experiences to a similar praise of the offerings of the youth organization:

> 'I was the chair of the [Left Youth organization's regional chapter], but after beginning my studies, I immediately enrolled to the Left list in

the student union representative council elections and got elected. It has been really meaningful, I've got to do cool stuff through the Left Youth, for instance, during the Paris Climate Summit, I participated the demonstration trip that they sponsored a lot so that it was quite cheap and thus it made it possible for me to take that trip, and it was really a super cool experience. You got to discuss with people from all over the world who were practically involved in the same umbrella movement of climate justice.' (Joonatan, Left Alliance)

While our limited interview material does not allow for representative arguments about the political spectrum's impact on the candidates' differences, there is a dividing line in the youth organization path narratives concerning the goals of political engagement. It spans from an organizational logic or a self-interest on the right-wing side to a general civic engagement from smaller common goods to big issues like climate justice on the left-wing side. Yet, also in the latter accounts, the candidates highlighted their individual experiences – they "got to do cool stuff" – rather than emphasized the causes for the action. Overall, the youth organization veteran path to politics unfolds as instrumentalizing formal politics and candidacy, if not subordinating these entirely to other matters. If the participatory industry clearly pushes aside most seeds and starts of collective thinking by training participants into either representatives (of a group assigned from above) or experts (by trade or by experience) (see Meriluoto 2018), organizations and social movements typically teach people the meaning of doing together.

The hobby-collector path to politics

Although many aspects of the youth organizational path to politics have to do with the young people's leisure – for many, it seemed these activities indeed took up all their spare time – there were also those for whom politics altogether resembled more a hobby[5] than anything else, to the degree that they themselves called it so. The difference compared to some of the previous section's committed and well-aligned activists is remarkable, yet the 'hobby-collectors' take instrumentality even further than the most strategic youth organization members. At the same time, there is a similar incidental feature to this path to the one anchored in the participatory projects, with the difference being that the hobby-collector path is made by the individuals themselves rather than structured by any ready-made context of engagement. The 'hobby-collectors' describe their political involvement either as one hobby among others, without giving it a very special role as such, or as a strategic choice of an activity that they hope will help them forward with other (often more important) goals they have in life. In other words, in their actions of doing society through politics, they engage in exploration, an engagement oriented primarily towards the future, with a characteristic of playfulness and an expectation of serendipity and surprise (see Auray 2007; Meriluoto 2023).

Katja and Lucy, both candidates for the National Coalition, position their party affiliation in a palette of options to fill their spare time with:

> 'I finished my MA thesis and graduated and thought, well damned it, now I have time, so why not run in the municipal elections. Kind of like "what else could one do?" My other reason [for joining the party] is my personal life situation. I mean, the fact that I moved to Helsinki last summer, and I had no real community here, like a study community. It took me some time to find a job, but currently, I actually work from home. Our headquarters are in London, and there are a few of us here in Helsinki. And then, like, to speed up my own adaptation here, to find new social contacts, new activities, new friends, like-minded people ... So, it was one reason, purely based on my personal life situation.' (Katja, National Coalition)

> 'For me, it started from not really having a hobby I would enjoy. Many people do sports and such, I've never been into group sports. And I was kind of getting unmotivated. I was in an art school and I grew bored with it so I was like humph, I could start a new hobby. Then I kind of automatically started thinking about what am I good at, and so it then happened that I went to the National Coalition Party Youth organization without knowing anyone there previously.' (Lucy, National Coalition)

While Katja emphasizes the situational (and somewhat fortuitous) potentials getting into politics opened up in her life, and the hopes she has about the candidacy enriching it, in Lucy's account, politics is somewhat diminished. She downplays the difference between engaging in politics and in a sense, 'any' other leisure activity, in a way that makes her choice of hobby seem quite unexciting. Perhaps, however, the most interesting – and exciting – aspect of her account is her act of choosing. She is not primarily engaged in a community or committed to a cause; she has chosen an activity for herself, among many options, and pursues the activity with due approach, also identifying that her peers do the same. In Chapter 8, we will meet activists who do not want to be activists and who resent quite strongly the idea of adhering to something collectively defined – even though cherishing the aforementioned community spiritedness of their context of engagement. Similarly, the young candidates here rarely talk about committing to the party, or committing to being a politician, with the few exceptions we will address in the last section of this chapter. The 'hobby-collectors' engage in political activities, but reserve the right to choose differently at any point if they so wish, just like when the art school got boring. Lucy continues her explanation of how she meets the same faces everywhere, whether it is a central youth organization or a youth council: "If you look at the people in the National Coalition Youth, I would say that 90 per cent of them are not politicians, it's just a hobby for them."

This relaxed experience is not the one all young people have when taking up a political position. Some parties are viewed as ideological in a way that labels people and requires explanation. The far-right Finns Party is one of them. In the following example, Maria, whom we met earlier and who chose the Finns Party because she felt that they were trying to make politics simpler to understand for the layperson, narrates what kind of an effect publicly representing a party like this can have on your social life:

> 'About my own party, I have to say that you really have to believe in your cause if you want to be a candidate for the Finns Party. Because the consequences might not be only positive in your private life, you might lose friends or get into trouble at work. You have to believe in the ideology if you stand up, we are not the kind of party where you join just to have some fun, or because all of your friends do it. If you compare this, for example, to the Coalition Party, the people there are very much also looking for networks in the private sector. Another thing is that if you move to the left-green sector, I feel like there's quite often a group of friends who share the same values and are motivating each other, and they think that it is nice to do it together and that is awesome in its own regard – and we do not necessarily get that, because being a Finns Party member is not something you necessarily want to say out loud.' (Maria, Finns Party)

It is notable that Maria does not herself bring up the more controversial opinions that quite a few of the Finns Party candidates have, including racist ones, but limits herself to talking about the potential discrimination the party's activists may face from others.

What is politics for? Civic imagination and engagement in a political career

The young people we interviewed had in common the belief that politics was a meaningful way of having an impact in the world. "In addition to learning and all of that, I actually want to make some change. I am a healthcare professional and there are big changes coming in that sector, and the best way to influence those decisions is to be involved", said one Social Democrat. When we asked whether she could influence things as a city councillor, Miriam responded that "it is the easiest place to have an impact on issues in Helsinki, the kinds of issues that are felt in everyday life".

In a way this is natural, since these people have made the conscious choice of becoming involved in elections. But even after choosing formal municipal politics as the avenue, their view on what politics actually is, where influence happens and how to best describe the work a city councillor does can take quite different forms. Municipal councillors have more power than other young people, so it is interesting to become acquainted with their understanding of civic imagination: what do they view as the most important aspects of political action, or what they believe can – and what cannot – be changed through politics.

To capture these views and beliefs, we formulated interview questions that directly cited the three aspects of civic imagination that Baiocchi et al suggested based on their ethnographic work among American civic actors (2014; for more detail, see Chapter 1). We asked the young candidates to choose the most important thing in politics between creating new solutions for problems, fixing structures of inequality, and enabling and representing communities. While these three aspects were originally crafted as ethnography-based findings in a very different setting, following the abductive approach of the study, we wanted to dig deeper into the concept of civic imagination. The concept had proven to be a fruitful tool to make sense of ethnographic fieldwork (see, for example, Chapter 2), and we wanted to approach this different 'distance' data, the interviews, with takeaways from previous analysis. We thus changed the way of using the concept from an analytical tool for understanding actions *of* the research participants to a more practical, hands-on one to be explored *with* our research participants (see the Appendix).

At first, facing the questions laying out the three options of civic imagination – the technical solution-oriented, the social justice-oriented and the community-building-oriented – most of our interviewees were baffled. "I guess the [technical solution-oriented] one kind of solves also the other problems" was a typical comment. Even if with some degree of confusion, the solution orientation was, for most, the first choice. However, most interviewees continued by saying that actually, all three are interlinked and it was not possible to really choose one without also choosing the others. Community enhancement was the least popular option to be on top of the list. Perhaps it was a problem of the initial formulation: the division of different forms of imagination, based on US urban activists' sense making, may have been contextually distant from the world of Finnish youth politicians. Nonetheless, these somewhat hesitant reactions were, in most interviews, followed by more in-depth reflections about what politics was for in the minds of the young candidates. In light of previous research, their emphasis on the technical solution-orientation is, perhaps, quite understandable as the first reaction of people navigating the interview situation with tools from the Finnish political culture. Several analyses of the forms of moral justifications in public conflicts have noted that in the Finnish context, argumentation grounded on efficiency and technical expertise tends to outnumber most other grounds of argumentation (Luhtakallio 2012; Kukkonen et al 2020; Väänänen and Liukko 2023 – for an overview, see Luhtakallio and Ylä-Anttila 2023). Even though our material does not allow for detailed analysis along party lines, it is notable and expected that candidates from leftist parties were more naturally aligned with challenging power structures.

While this interview material does not allow for a more in-depth analysis of moral justifications, it is interesting to mirror the emphasis on (practical and technical) solutions with the candidates' talk about the issues that were important in their electoral campaigns. These issues and themes, as noted in the beginning of this chapter, echo both the responses to our survey about important issues for the youth and, to an extent, the issues prioritized by the respondents of the survey by Chou et al (2021):

> 'Well, I have for instance these [themes]: I think in Helsinki, free-of-charge contraception should be offered to all under 25 years of age, absolutely. Also, I have this sanitary napkin campaign, I think that for instance schools should provide young people free-of-charge sanitary napkins and tampons, this is something I have for the youth [in my campaign]. I would definitely promote an increase in support for urban culture, I think we have a fabulous bunch of these urban activists ... with a huge potential to do things, and we have Kallio Block Party type of super stuff.' (Rita, Left Alliance)

There were those, on the one hand, who framed issues broadly, and talked about a personal responsibility, like Social Democrat candidate Kristiina:

> 'Those who can, must. This is pretty much my mentality in politics that those who can talk in favour of the important things, who have the time and the resources and, they have to do this job. Maybe this is selfish, but I would get a bad conscience if I didn't step up.' (Kristiina, Social Democrats)

On the other hand, many put focus on issues on which they had a personal perspective. The mental health crisis of the young generation (see, for example, Rikala 2020; Rissanen et al 2022) is an example of a theme that emerged recurrently in the interviews with a personal connection or motivation: several candidates talked about the importance of improving mental health services to the young, and many noted that they had a friend or a partner whose struggling they had followed closely. A very personalized, even familiar angle to politics was also apparent in accounts that emphasized the candidate's relationship to the local context. In the following quote, John's description of his process of deciding to become a candidate illustrates the full spectrum of how the candidates spoke about politics: what and why in politics was meaningful and important for them, from a strategic choice of a party to concrete issues of personal expertise and related ambitions, to an intimate, inspired account of a moment of revelation:

> 'Of course, the pragmatic reason [for choosing the National Coalition] is that it's the easiest access to candidacy, they take you, their list is wide. I had been involved in student politics and noticed how much decisions important to students are made at the municipal level, so I saw an opportunity there to have an impact on traffic and zoning stuff very naturally. Of course, first place, Helsinki is a magnificent city and the greatest city in Finland and so it would be excellent to be involved in and developing it. In a way it started when I was jogging in August, and around Kulosaari, I was watching [the new district of] Kalasatama being built there before my eyes, and the evening sun was setting and I'm like yeah, I truly have to run in the election, that was the cinematic moment for me.' (John, National Coalition)

The possibilities of influence the young candidates foresaw for themselves in politics, and their own development and learning possibilities therein, were often closely intertwined. Learning from politics and self-development were paramount to many young candidates, as illustrated in the following answer from Gitta to a question on how she feels about a career in politics:

> 'I think I'm not going to decide (whether to have a career in politics), in a way, I want to keep the door open. Mostly it's for experiences that I see could be useful in many other situations in life. Just things like expressing opinions, being able to articulate well, speaking in front of an audience, you know, these kinds of things.' (Gitta, Swedish People's Party)

As we have seen, for many of the young candidates, the choice between parties often reflected personal ambitions at least as much as stronger ideological undercurrents. Gitta and Jonas respectively found the Swedish People's party 'neutral' and beneficial for their professional careers, John found it easy to become chosen as a candidate in a large party such as the Coalition, and Katja and Lucy found a desired new social scene through the party. This does not mean that ideology is not important, but given the eight to ten possible parties to choose from in Finnish politics, almost everyone had enough ideological flexibility to fit to several different ones. Sometimes, in student politics, social circles can be the defining attribute: Leila from the Greens told us she was signed up for the party by "a guy" she had a crush on, "and then I was just like, well OK, that's that then". Kristiina, for her part, recalled how she ended up in the Social Democrats, a party that was seen as somewhat uncool among young people at the time:[6]

> 'I'm studying political philosophy at the Uni, and I was asked by three different parties to stand up in the student union elections so ... And I'd say that the Greens and the Left Alliance already had preparations well underway for their election manifesto, and I got the feeling that my own voice would not necessarily be heard there. Whereas the Social Democrats wanted me to come and write the manifesto ... and also, Koskenkorva [Finnish vodka] played a part here, *apparently* I had had conversations about this at a student party's afterparty.' (Kristiina, Social Democrats)

She later said that she would see herself in politics, but maybe in a more behind-the-scenes professional role rather than as a candidate or a representative herself. At the time of writing, this describes her later career quite well.

Despite coming to politics through different paths, candidacy and even a potential career in politics requires some amount of engaging in a plan (Thévenot 2007, 2011; see also Chapter 1). Our young candidates conceive the world in terms of projects and plans, and quite concretely project themselves in the future (Thévenot 2007). This may be another reason why the problem-solving civic imagination dominated in their answers. Political careers are plans, and when approached through at least partly individualistic principles, it makes sense to think of the substantial things to be done through the language of solvable problems. Isolated issues that can be 'solved' take away part of the elemental conflicts necessarily involved in political decision making.

The pattern of political commitment strongly conditioned by a *quest for power* also emerged in some of the interviews. The power-hungry young candidates stood out from the material in their explicit determination to pursue a career in politics. Yet, their reasoning did not include any more commitment to a party, or valuations of a more collective or general nature. They talked about their futures in politics in firmly individualistic tones. What is missing is interesting here: there are no accounts of networks, building support, or harnessing the party. Antti, for instance, described his understanding of the way forward in politics:

Antti:	Those who say that power does not interest them are just lying (chuckles). Pretty many people have this thing that they want to influence things in their own municipality, want power for themselves … And even though they say that you shouldn't practise pork barrelling, you notice if there has been nobody there to defend the place.
Interviewer:	Are you particularly interested in notably municipal politics? Or could you see yourself interested more widely in the future?
Antti:	I am indeed [more widely] interested. I mean, in practice how this works is, it is a fact that going to parliamentary elections, it does require the municipal politics background … Just so that one understands stuff sufficiently. That's the way to push through. It's a little … When you get a taste of something, you want more of it and this is a good place to start.

Dreams of the future took more concrete shape for those who had chosen their path. Most of the candidates saw ahead of them a path of learning by doing different things, and doing society by carving their unique individual path through various engagements they deemed meaningful.

Maija, a Social Democrat candidate, had come through the participatory industrial path and was already at her early 20s working as a full-time political staffer. She answered in a composed and restrained way to all the questions, until something clearly touched her in the question about future and power:

Interviewer:	If you could choose, do you see yourself in politics or not in politics in ten years?
Maija:	In politics.
Interviewer:	In what kind of a role? Be brave, you can daydream here.
Maija:	I'm allowed to dream? OK … This isn't something you normally would say … the culture is that you do not say these kinds of things out loud.
Interviewer:	That's true.

She leans closer, visibly excited. There is a sparkle of ambition in her eyes.

Maija:	But I'll say this to you now: a government minister.
Interviewer:	OK! That is good. That's a goal. Or a dream.
Maija:	A dream … A goal is something you set yourself to do meticulously, a dream is something you only think about, you caress it …

Interviewer: Does it matter which portfolio you would have?
Maija: (Excitedly) Something heavy! Like defence ... or foreign trade or law and justice.

Of all our respondents, she has indeed had the most successful political career thus far.

Conclusions

In this chapter, we set out to explore the cultures of doing society of young people whose relationship to politics is the most explicit one of all the young people included in this book. This has been somewhat pioneering research – to our knowledge, there is extremely little prior research on young candidates' own perceptions of their political commitments and visions. While previous studies have conducted surveys on young candidates, a qualitative approach defends its place here: instead of listing what kind of political issues the youth hold as important, we discovered their meaning making of what had brought them to candidacy, their motivations for the commitment and the meanings they gave to politics. As candidates in municipal elections, the young of this chapter were definitely clean of the disinterest and passiveness regarding politics that young people often are suspected of – they were deep in it, although how deep exactly and for what kind of reasons varied significantly, as we have shown.

We named three distinct yet sometimes overlapping 'paths' to electoral candidacy, according to whether the interviewees emphasized their experience in participatory projects or youth organizations, or whether they somewhat more lightly portrayed politics as something that was (or had at least begun as) one hobby among many others. The three paths manifested in different repertoires of engaging: while the first two summoned engagements in a plan, with some composites and variation of course, the third surfaced an engagement in exploration, a clear emphasis on politics as another colour in their palette of self-realization.

The diverse paths that the young people we interviewed had taken to arrive at candidacy all pointed to one general observation: party politics was a natural continuation of a self-project for the youth. Be it the participatory 'machine' they had been trying out, or a committed engagement to youth organization and social movements, or a relatively light-hearted picking up of a new hobby – for all of them, the candidacy was a step on their path to building an individual future. Politics had the function of a vehicle for self-development: you can benefit from previous experiences, and develop skills and networks needed for successful (professional) life.

What kind of a common were the young candidates building and what were their perspectives on doing society? In terms of civic imagination, politics was problem solving for many of the interviewees. It was about rational discussion using expertise – or, more broadly, a variety of industrial justifications – in a civil manner and using creativity to subvert existing problems. However, politics was also about the realization of one's dreams, belonging, having an impact and, for some, gaining power. The view of politics as a conflict was remarkably absent in the interviews, which may have resulted in part from the timing: the interviews were conducted in the middle of campaigning, not during the everyday of a municipal council work.

Nonetheless, the young candidates were doing society by realizing their own dreams, but also by taking part in something they felt was broadly meaningful and important. Many had their hearts in certain issues, some had ambitions for power, and some saw politics as part of a spectrum of things that mattered – for them to succeed, but also for the society to keep rolling. They had a positive drive to things. And however individualistically they envisioned their futures in politics, there was a patterned confidence in a support they would have. Unlike their peers in many other settings in this book, the parties had their back, however much their commitments varied. While few talked about this explicitly, the party hovered around their accounts: they were grateful of concrete support they had received, experienced strong belonging to the party's structures at some level, or felt outright 'at home', protected and safe in a big, powerful structure. In sum, their individual engagements were connected to a collective. In this aspect, the analysis of the young candidates' engagements opens a window to a culture of doing society in which sharp individualism and quite traditional-looking collectivism interlink.

4

Voicing Ideas: Participation through E-democracy

Veikko Eranti and Georg Boldt

Introduction

In the two previous chapters, we showed first what young people drafted to physically participate in participatory programmes think of participation and politics (Chapter 2), and then focused on the outliers, the people who consciously chose to run for local office (Chapter 3). The young people in these two chapters chose a sustained, at least semi-public participation, and literally showed up when asked.

In this chapter, following the research design of the whole book, we broaden the perspective to young people with a much more fleeting, almost minimal, but crucially still existing interaction with official participatory systems and channels. Nuortenideat.fi, translated from now on as 'Youthideas. fi', was an e-democracy service aimed at young people (it was discontinued in 2022). The service tried to provide proactive possibilities for participation: it literally asked young people for their *ideas* in an open-ended way, instead of a more reactive feedback on already planned projects quite commonly used in e-democracy projects. In their typology of e-participation, Aichholzer and Rose (2020) call this kind of service *agenda setting* (see also Juusola and Varsaluoma [2023] for a broader look on youth e-participation in Finland). In this chapter, we also zoom out in terms of analytical distance (see the Appendix) to capture a broader view of the cultural tools used by young people to do society in participatory settings.

The following two examples of ideas presented in the service show their close connection to everyday experiences of young people, as well as the controlled nature of their lives. For context, in most Finnish schools, it is mandatory to go outside during recess, regardless of the weather.

'We should have a freezing limit for outdoor recesses in schools [meaning you should not be forced outside when it is -20°C]. Additionally outdoor recesses should all in all be more voluntary, by having for example two mandatory and two optional per day. We could use the exercise facilities and library during recesses, and the use of phones could be allowed also for the younger students.'

'Jyväskylä should install public graffiti walls, where the youth could paint freely and without needing to be afraid of fines or punishments. The walls could be run as part of a youth centre, where the youth and the staff could take care of the walls. You could paint over the walls on regular intervals, and photograph all the pieces.'

Through looking at the hundreds of ideas submitted, it is possible to gain a broader look of the conceptions of democracy Finnish youth have, and how these ideas are manifested in the political claims they make. By examining what young people are interested in changing, and the justifications they give for their positions, we can paint a picture of their civic imagination (see Chapter 1), and consequently of the political culture to which they adhere. By studying these justifications and means for influencing others, in parallel with the ethnography and interviews of the two previous chapters, we make inferences about Finnish political culture as it is manifested in various formal participatory settings. Definitions for political culture vary (see, for example, Almond and Verba 1963; Chilton 1988), but in this text we follow Lichterman and Cefaï's (2006: 1) definition, according to which: 'Political cultures are the sets of symbols and meanings or styles of action that organize political claims-making and opinion-forming, by individuals or collectivities.'

Do young people base their claims on the common good or on private interest(s)? And if they evoke ideas of common good, how do they define it? And, on the other hand, what kind of civic imagination guides their actions: is decision making seen as a technical process of improving the world, or as a more structural and fundamentally more contested moral conflict (Baiocchi et al 2014; Eranti 2014, 2016, 2017; Thévenot 2015; see also Chapter 1 of this book)?

The Youthideas.fi service was jointly produced by the Development Centre of Youth Information and Counselling nongovernmental organization (NGO) (Koordinaatti ry), the Ministry of Justice, and the Ministry of Education and Culture.[1] Through this service, young people could send in *ideas* and *recommendations* on whatever they felt was important. Ideas could be commented and upvoted by other users, and the service promised that ideas receiving the most support would be passed on to the relevant officials, often at the municipal level. On a practical level, some municipalities and schools had clearly used the service to ask young people for their opinions in local participatory events. The service was mainly used by school-aged young people, although there was no formal age limit. Between 2015, when the service was opened, and 2017, when the data was collected, over 450 ideas had been submitted. These ideas were scraped from the website using a custom application.

As such services directed at young people are always, in one way or another, about democracy education, we can assume that the ways of participation in which young people engage also show what kind of democracy we are teaching them. The description on the website frames the service as *influencing* or having an impact: 'Youthideas.fi is a national influencing service for young people, through which young people can easily make suggestions, participate and influence matters concerning them.'

The service was created as a response to the rather mild interest towards societal issues young people are thought to hold. For example, in the 2009 International Civic and Citizenship Study (ICCS), only 2 per cent of Finnish youth said they were 'very interested' in political issues concerning their local area. Correspondingly, 79 per cent responded to being 'not very interested' or 'not interested at all' in these issues (Suoninen et al 2010: 49). This low level of interest is likely a reflection of how little both young people and officials know about the opportunities youth people have for influencing societal matters (Paakkunainen 2004; Gretschel and Kiilakoski 2015). A survey conducted in 2004 (Paakkunainen 2004), examining the attitudes that 15–30 year olds had on influencing and democracy, showed similar results as the ICCS in terms of attitudes and interest towards politics. According to the survey, young people were most interested in influencing themes relating to leisure time, the environment and commodities. Low interest in politics displayed by young people is not only a current problem, nor is it related solely to the Finnish context. Already at the end of the 1970s, Uusitalo (1979) noted that young people's interest towards politics and participation was low and mainly focused on rather technical issues.

However, the situation is not necessarily that grim. Cammaerts et al (2016) note that even though young people in Europe are the most likely group not to take part in elections, a clear majority of them are still interested in influencing common matters. Cammaerts et al also note that first experiences on voting and participation are central in terms of the person's future political agency. The Youthideas.fi service is therefore not only a channel of influence for young people, but also has a long-term objective of bringing about changes in attitudes, with an implicit promise of strengthening young people's active citizenship.

Using a service like this is voluntary, and the users can freely choose what kind of ideas they wish to present and promote, and how they justify them. Therefore, by examining the ideas and justifications that young people present, we gain knowledge about their civic imagination – what they consider to be important and possible to influence via such a service (Baiocchi et al 2014, also Chapter 1).

The central research question in this chapter is: what kind of political culture is manifested in the justifications a broad group, whom we assume to be rather ordinary young people, present for their ideas? How do people whose days are *not* filled with questions about advancing a political career or gaining power, or even about a personal and political project where private gain and noble goals intertwine, act on grievances and persuade other youth? To answer this question essentially requires finding out what kind of issues young people attempt to influence with their ideas – how they are doing society.

What kind of youth participation is this?

But before we get to the question of the *content* of the service, we have to take a look at what kind of input is *sought* by the system, and what this tells us about the democratic and educational ideas behind it.

In broad strokes, the Youthideas.fi service follows the ideas of participatory democracy outlined in Chapter 2 of this book. The aim of participatory democracy is that as many people as possible would take part in decision making on matters that affect them. The discursive tradition outlined there (and originally in Ferree et al 2002: 316) corresponds closely with aims of the Finnish Youth Act (Nuorisolaki 1285/2016) and its objective to promote young people's involvement and possibilities for influencing.

The preconditions for involvement in public decision making can be roughly divided into views that either focus on the democratic-technical virtues of the participatory process, or those that emphasize the preconditions of substantive involvement, meaning that they focus on the possibilities for equal participation, regardless of one's skills, competence and/or social status (Ercan 2014; Wright 2019: 12–13). When planning young people's participation, emphasis should be placed on the special needs of the group in question (Morrow 2001; Hill et al 2004). However, as participatory practices have become more common, approaches to power sharing have become more nuanced (Fung 2006: 67). Young people get their say in various ways: student boards, youth councils (see Chapter 2), various food opinion panels and the like, and of course freely and with various styles online (see Chapter 6), but the significance of their voice differs according to the issue at hand. In many cases of youth participation the emphasis is on learning citizenship skills. Nevertheless, even if the Youthideas.fi service is not meant to transfer decision-making power to young people, the service has nevertheless aimed at giving them a significant chance to make initiatives.

Instruments for measuring the level of democracy in participation (see, for example, Beierle 1999; Irvin and Stansbury 2004; Fung 2006) generally underline pluralistic and democratic values in both the selection of participants and the ways in which it is possible to participate. In addition, the possibility for deliberation[2] among participants is commonly considered to be important (for example, Fung 2006), with the aim being to ensure that ideas created through the process would develop through dialogue, eventually accounting for various points of view – that is, into compromises and syntheses for the common good.

Considering these points of view, the Youthideas.fi service is inclusive, as it is open for all young people (compared to, for example, a predetermined group of participants), and communication in it is intensive and deliberative (Fung 2006: 69), as users can express their wishes and discuss them (expressing one's will can also be done by liking the ideas). Also, users have, at least potentially, a decent amount of power, since their ideas can eventually end up in the hands of decision makers.

People are usually expected to hold certain skills in order for them to be considered fully fledged citizens (France 2016). Being capable of expressing oneself verbally is likely the most important of these, together with the (expected) competence associated with age. However, it is questionable whether such modes of hearing that promote participation based on a narrow repertoire of skills actually increase young people's active citizenship – or whether they benefit only those who already fit these requirements based on their skills and attitudes. Means for participation that are substantive, and that enforce participation and the vitality of democracy, should therefore make it easier for young people to be heard in a way that does not rely excessively on, for example, previously gained cultural and social capital. The goal should be that everyone has the possibility to participate based on their own starting points (Hill et al 2004). Participatory structures should foster development from a pedagogical standpoint as well, with emphasis placed both on the social connections young people create during participation and the experience or sense of participation they produce. In this way, participatory structures could make possible what James Bohman (1997: 322–343) calls the equal capability for public functioning – that is, deepening the conception of participation from technical tinkering to efficient influencing and conscious political deliberation.

As a channel for influence, Youthideas.fi is rather technical and compels participants to articulate their ideas according to a 'proper' form of participation, verbally, argumentatively and suitably for the presented idea.

Civic imaginations and justifications in Youthideas.fi

Our analysis of the ideas submitted to the service is based on justifications, grammars of commonality, and civic imaginations (see Chapter 1). The most central justifications in Youthideas.fi are the *civic* common good, based on the principles of equality and collective participation, and the *industrial* common good, based on principles of efficiency, measurability and objective improvements (for more on the definitions of common good, see Boltanski and Thévenot 1999, 2006). Previous studies (for example, Luhtakallio 2012; Luhtakallio and Ylä-Anttila 2023) have concluded that justifications based on efficiency are the most prevalent form of common good to which actors tend to resort in the Finnish political culture. Furthermore, it has been noted that resorting to private interests (Thévenot 2015; Eranti 2017, 2018), meaning either the direct interests of the individual or a larger interest group, is an equally legitimate way of making claims in the Finnish context. These two conceptions of politics – common good and private interest-based – are to some extent contradictory: in the former, the actors resort to different forms of common good to solve conflicts, whereas in the latter, political decision making is about crossing interests, and conflicts are solved based on the support for each solution.

Political claims based on either the common good or private interests differ from each other significantly. Where argumentation based on private interests is about making claims, wishes and suggestions grounded in the actor's right to state their opinion, argumentation based on the common good is based on fundamental values. The conflict between these two different registers is at the heart of political culture (for example, Almond and Verba 1963; Lichterman and Cefaï 2006), and is therefore important in regards to young people's participatory services as well.

Our intention here is not to say that either one of these ways to make sense of political discussion would be better than the other as such, or to claim that they would be mutually exclusive. Instead, they provide ways to examine political culture from the actors' point of view. When someone submitting an idea to the service aims to convince other users – and eventually those really making decisions – do they justify their claims based on a repertoire of values and the common good, or do they make claims based on their private interests?

Baiocchi et al propose a typology of civic imaginations where engagements are structured around: (1) power and structural inequality; (2) solidarity and community; and (3) problem solving and technical solutions. When civic imagination is structured around *power and societal structures*, the most important task for citizens (and therefore civil society) is to rectify structural inequalities in the world. In the civic imagination valuing *solidarity and community*, communities themselves are seen to change the world for the better, and therefore the task is to enhance the possibilities of these communities, which then lead to positive outcomes. And, finally, in the civic imagination *emphasizing technical solutions*, politics and societal life is seen as a series of problems which require new innovative solutions. We can assume that the majority of the ideas submitted were considered at least remotely possible and desirable by their authors.

We specifically sought the moral grounds and justifications of the ideas presented in Youthideas.fi: why should a particular claim be accepted and put into practice, and how do young people justify the excellence of a particular idea? To this end, we categorized the materials into different classes according to both the moral justifications and the form of civic imagination presented in them. In addition, we also analysed the ideas by focusing on whether they concerned local or wider disputes, and how they related to central institutions in young people's daily lives, such as schools or youth clubs.

We can assume that the users of the service are likely to be more interested in societal issues than not, and somewhat fluent in either Finnish or Swedish, the languages of the service. The data reveal that some schools have organized special participation days or other events where ideas have been gathered, and that in some cases the ideas have even been submitted by adults. This is one of the intended uses for the service (Junttila-Vitikka and Peitso 2016), also affecting the kind of ideas that have been submitted. Judging by the quality of the ideas, in some of the schools, students have been assigned to submit ideas as part of schoolwork. The lack of ambition in these initiatives gives the impression that students have chosen the easiest solution to a mandatory assignment. All the same, similar circumstances produced some of the most elaborate and best justified texts on the service: they were submitted on behalf of the whole class and their style implied that they were the results of elaborate discussions. In these instances, the political ideas and claims presented by the young people were quite likely the results of a deliberative process – arguably an ideal type for democratic decision making. The following excerpt does a good job of connecting a mundane problem to wider dynamics, ending in a place quite similar to that of the young people active in Helsinki participatory budgeting we saw in Chapter 2:

> Most of Hollola's young people are bored during the wintertime. *Nuokku* is only open twice a week and *Mesta* also has bad opening hours [*both are local youth centres*]. If young people want to hang out indoors, such as at restaurants or shops, they will be pushed out immediately. Lack of activity can lead to substance use or excessive gambling at home. For example, the opening hours of *Nuokku* and *Mesta* could be improved, such as being open on weekends. Some kind of youth cafe could be established in Hollola, where young people could stay and buy products. This would not require much financial effort, but it would do a lot of good! With kind regards, upper secondary school class 9H.

The service is open for all ideas, and those that received support were presented to decision makers. This means that concrete, tangible, easy-to-implement ideas were most fitting to the ethos. They could be easily forwarded to a relevant civil servant for further decision making, again reminiscent of Chapter 2, but without the modicum of direct power.

Let us in from the recess when it is cold: what do young people want?

Previous research tells us that in participatory settings, young people commonly wish for more and better places for leisure, hobbies, school and local residential areas; better possibilities to participate especially in their schools' decision making; actions to reduce bullying; cheaper public transportation for young people; and efforts to create a more favourable public image for young people (Hill et al 2004; Autio et al 2008; Boldt 2017).

Figure 4.1 shows the most popular broad topics from the Youthideas.fi data. Sport facilities and sport clubs were by far the item that was the most commented and the most wished-for, with various school issues coming second, requests for YouTube meetups and other events third, improving the quality of school food (Finland has a free school lunch programme) fourth, and other hobbies and the facilities thereof following. Also, various transportation methods, including mopeds, cars, public transportation and

Figure 4.1: Distribution of the content of the ideas submitted by the young people

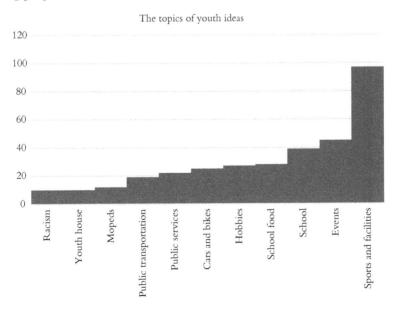

bicycles, are often mentioned. This falls well in line with the previous research cited earlier.

As can be seen from the figure, sports and free time, possibilities for recreational activities, and more pleasant schools were clearly the most popular themes at Youthideas.fi. The ideas are quite often expressed in a rather concise form, such as: 'We need a place to play basketball in Huittinen.'

Ideas related to sports facilities often deal with the rather narrow possibilities for young people in different localities, and at times there are explicit equality arguments presented. Youth who live in small cities and rural municipalities are quite often given little attention, with local resources going to the ageing population (often larger in numbers) instead. Numerous ideas demand possibilities for sporting activities directed at young people, such as opening gyms specifically for the youth. After all, young people are in a subordinate societal position: they are excluded from many events, activities and facilities intended only for adults: 'A gym for young people in Pori. Most gyms have an age limit and young people cannot exercise if they want to', stated one idea.

This subordinate position leads to a weird situation in which the young people seemingly feel that they can ask the city or other officials to arrange for popular Finnish artists to play in commercial venues in their area:

> 'There could be more youth concerts, because there are more concerts for adults than for young people. Preferably pop music. Artists like *Sanni* or *Antti Tuisku* would be nice ... Once in every two months. Venues in the winter when it's cold could be like the youth club in the city centre. In the summertime the venue could be in Pori market square.'

> 'Me and my friends would like to have the rapper *Uniikki* for a gig in Lohja, because the dude hasn't been here a single time. There are not many gigs for young people in Lohja anyway, even though we think there are a lot of good venues. It might actually be that there has never even been a gig without an age limit. Most gigs are commonly quite far away and there are not that many trains going to Lohja, which makes it kind of hard to attend gigs. We've tried contacting everyone about this.'

In some sense, this is natural – the service asks for the ideas of young people. In some sense, it is rather absurd; cities are not often arranging hip-hop gigs for young people in small municipalities (see also Chapter 2 for similar discussion). But this does tell us that the governing structure holds a place in the imagination of young people and that the local government is seen as an organ that can fulfil wishes.

The plight of the youth in smaller communities is exacerbated by the fact that the mobility of underage people is severely limited – no driver's licence, no money for public transportation and poor connections outside big cities. Thus, it is no surprise that transportation is also an important theme in the submitted ideas. Especially for those under the age of 18, public transportation is a prerequisite for their social lives. The existence of bus connections might be the deciding factor in whether a kind of sociality is possible in the first place or not. This is also evident from the large number of ideas dealing with microcars and mopeds, the main modes of mobility for slightly older young people in many rural communities: 'We need heating for microcars so that they start up even if the weather is freezing.'

Ideas relating to schools vary from changing the whole evaluation criteria in the school system to wishing for better school lunches and better recess activities. Many ideas related to the school system were about improving it more widely, instead of mere technical improvements:

'Really a lot of those in lower secondary school want to drink for example coffee and other beverages during school time [not just sodas but healthy snack drinks as well]. Would be refreshing and would help to make it through the school day.'

'[In opposition to a planned new school building]: The Investment should rather be put on the future and pupils. Student don't want a huge new high school building anyway. Transportation from the city centre will get worse. In addition, the teaching and support for students will get worse if there is a huge amount of students in one high school. Renovating a school is expensive, but if one argument for the new huge high school is cutting costs, it makes sense. We would like to hear other good arguments.'

Most of the ideas relating to schools dealt with school lunches, recess and physical failings of the school buildings – things very close to the ideals of grassroots democracy and local participation, focused on improving the everyday.

Figure 4.2 presents the distribution of the most important institutions, the spatial scope, justifications and forms civic imagination used in the submitted ideas. Approximately one third of the ideas dealt with issues related to schools, and almost half with municipal services. The ideas were extremely local in their scope: 79 per cent concerned issues situated at school, its immediate neighbourhood, or the local municipality.

Numerous discussions in both politics and research during the 21st century have emphasized the relevance of the so-called grassroots democracy (for example, Council of Europe 2004; Bäcklund 2007; Eranti 2014; Kuokkanen and Palonen 2018). Quite often in these discussions, it is especially the hyperlocal scale of improvements in people's immediate living environments that is emphasized. As important as that is, if the claims young people are

Figure 4.2: Distribution of idea scales, relevant institutions, civic imaginations and justifications in the data

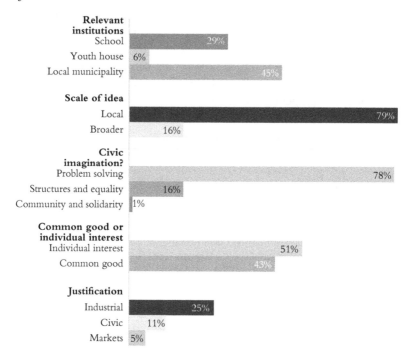

taught to make only concern their local areas and immediate surroundings, the bar for democratic imagination has been set rather low. The usefulness of such exercises for broader democracy then hinges on the capabilities learned and the positive habits picked up.

To put it another way: there is a paradox of grassroots democracy evident in these ideas. It is easier to change one's local environment than to make nationwide structural changes; however, if local issues are considered to be the only ones worth influencing, national and international issues are inevitably left outside of one's imagination. If this is the democracy we teach, we might end up also getting it.

Of course, it is possible that this bias is a reflection of the service users: perhaps those young people who wish to engage in nationwide issues have already found another channel, such as an NGO or a political party, through which they can engage in influencing these issues.

Justifications of youth ideas

As we have already mentioned, a significant portion of the submitted ideas related to, in one way or another, technical improvements for existing things, and were focused more on making claims than presenting moral justifications.

Approximately one quarter of the ideas (see Figure 4.2) referred to the industrial order of worth in one way or another. In these justifications, the common good is based on efficiency, measurability and improving things in an 'engineer-like' fashion. This is the single most common way of making an argument, second only to direct claims without any justification whatsoever. Arguments using industrial justification were presented, for example, in the following way: 'In the course of years and due to heavy use, the old graffiti wall in the park has gotten into pretty bad shape, so a new wall would be needed, preferably already during this Spring/Summer.'

The argumentation in this example goes that because this thing already exists, it should work better, or because such a thing has been built, it needs to be repaired now. The argument appeals to the desire for getting the most out of an investment already made, or it tries to convince decision makers that the claimed issue could be achieved by switching to a smarter solution. It is easy to imagine that the assumption behind this kind of argumentation – which can also quite possibly be accurate – is that new resources will not be available for these ideas anyway. Therefore, the more practical or technically 'reasonable' the ideas sound, the more likely it is that they gain support (this is what the young people in participatory budgeting learned the hard way in Chapter 2). Civic justification is the second most-common moral justification relating to demand for equality. One prominent subject in the ideas using this justification was the aforementioned subordinate status young people under 18 have in society. In this example, mandatory religious education for members of the church is questioned on the basis of equality: 'In Finland, a member of the church is forced to attend religious education in school. Whereas a young person who doesn't belong to a religious community can study ethics, or religion if his or her parents request so. Why is this?'

The data also include alt-right-type use of equality argumentation opposing feminism:

> *Helsingin Sanomat* reported today that during the spring of 2017, all ninth graders will receive the book *We Should All Be Feminists* by Chimamanda Ngozi Adichie. This raises the question of why the authority of the Finnish school system is used to distribute feminist propaganda in the name of equality, as feminism is about promoting the interests of women, not equality.

As in many other internet forums, Youthideas.fi also includes quite a lot of anti-immigration, anti-feminist and misogynist ideas (Keskinen 2013). Only one out of all the hundreds of ideas in the data can actually be considered feminist: one that addressed gendered sporting facilities.[3] It is possible that such an internet-based service that is connected to the school environment but still separate from it provides the opportunity to raise opinions which oppose the actual pedagogic goals of the school system – an opportunity taken up especially by young males. On the other hand, this might also be a quality of internet posting and so-called imageboard culture (Keskinen 2013), as such discourses thrive in various online image- and textboards where people (can) post anonymously (see Chapter 6).

The third most-used moral justification used on Youthideas.fi was market justification, although it was used much less frequently than the other two that were mentioned. These justifications referred to market efficiency and how municipal funds are used, usually either in a rather technical way or in certain cases as an argument for anti-immigration ideas. For example, improving certain bus routes or providing opportunities for certain sports were considered to bring more revenue for the municipality.

When we examine the data using Baiocchi et al's (2014) idea of civic imagination, it becomes clear that the ideas young people have submitted are limited to a certain surface level of democratic participation. Only technical problem solving was strongly present in the young people's ideas (see Figure 4.2), as approximately 78 per cent of the ideas resembled this kind of civic imagination. This stands partly in contrast to the youth politicians we encountered in Chapter 3: even if they often reach for the language of problem solving, they also have other political goals, and place emphasis on structures of inequality and the value of community.

The emphasis on problem solving in youth ideas is connected to the emphasis on private interests present in the ideas: when the ideas emerge straight from the needs of those presenting them and are formulated in a technical-rational way, they hardly reach the level of structural changes. The youth present collective actors in the form of school classes, 'moped riders', 'city youth' and other ad hoc communities.

Technical improvements are suggested for schools, recess programmes, school lunches and traffic arrangements – even to Finland's copyright laws. This is one of the examples where broader structural changes are sought:

> Finland's outdated copyright laws forbid taking pictures of public artwork with the intent of making profit, so for example you can't take a picture of the Sibelius monument or Helsinki's World Peace statue, with the intention of selling the image. The majority of EU countries allow this (Germany, Great Britain, Poland, Austria, Spain among others). Current Finnish copyright law restricts freedom of scenery. The current law allows taking pictures of public buildings, but not public artwork, and I therefore suggest that taking pictures of public artwork with intent of making profit would be allowed.

In the end, this idea, operating on the level of legal principles, also presents a rather technical improvement. The young people's ideas show that changing something familiar and concrete appears as possible and imaginable. A bad traffic arrangement, such as an intersection, can easily be seen as something that can be improved. In addition, it makes sense to think that such an e-democracy service could affect such issues.

The civic imagination emphasizing community and solidarity is quite literally absent from the young people's ideas. Few of the ideas demand better possibilities for influencing school lunches, which comes closer to communal power and the civic imagination that emphasizes solidarity. However, it should be noted that the nature of the data we have used affects these results. It is no surprise that when studying local social movements – as Baiocchi et al (2014) did – the community gets emphasized more, compared to a setting of mostly individually submitted ideas. Even though it is quite natural that people do not attempt to change, for example, Finland's tax system via a service such as Youthideas.fi, nevertheless it could just as well be used to demand more power for students or put more emphasis on local communities. The fact that there were only a few of these kinds of ideas is illustrative of an individualistic political culture.

Even though most of the ideas and comments were based on private interests or advocated technical improvements, there were also ideas that could be thought of as a conflictual form of politics, directed towards power and structures (see Figure 4.2). The majority of these 20 ideas related to immigration, multiculturalism and refugees. All but one of them shared a tone situated between a 'critical stance' and open racism.

The amount of racist, anti-immigration and anti-refugee ideas was not surprising as such, as support for parties promoting these themes has been high among the Finnish youth for quite some time (YLE 2019). In addition, many of the most active places for political discussion in the Finnish (language) internet have revolved strongly around these themes (Ylä-Anttila et al 2020; see also Chapter 6).

At the same time, some of the important issues for young people such as the accessibility of public transportation (see Figure 4.1) are often debated with a quite heavy emphasis on moral argumentation in the sphere of 'grown-up politics'. Even the young candidates in Chapter 3 present these issues in moral terms. This was for the most part absent on Youthideas.fi. The most frequently used register had more in common with customer requests for more grocery stores and cafés in the neighbourhood – something which would be nice and would make life easier.

This in no way makes these ideas worthless or less valuable. But if these ideas are situated in the context of democracy education and, more widely, as taking part in public discussion, the difference is striking. Racist opinions demanding that borders should be closed usually explicate their moral groundings which are supported by resorting to a form of common good. Those demanding better bus connections, on the other hand, state that it would be more convenient or more economical for the city if the bus line to the school would be better. Even though there would be a conception of fairness lingering in the background, it is not commonly expressed. As a contrast, one of the ideas explicitly demanded equal grading for Finns and immigrants, based on an urban legend claiming that different grading scales were used. These arguments appeal to definitions of common good and use public justifications.

When the sample size is approximately 400 ideas, one active user can skew it all by themselves. The person using the nickname 'TheRightCause' submitted 15 ideas to the service, all of which opposed multiculturalism, feminism and reading books in schools, and promoted loosening copyright laws in various ways. These ideas formed a significant part of that portion of the data that can be termed 'generally political' – that is, those that dealt with more general themes than the immediate surroundings of young people. Therefore, the conclusions that can be made on the general politicization in the materials are limited: had there been even a single active leftist user, the political bias in the materials could have skewed significantly more 'woke'.

As the ideas show, the majority of ideas submitted are requests for sport facilities, local events and various improvements to schools. These ideas are justified by referring to private interests or by appealing to the common goods of efficiency and technical rationality – overall, the civic imagination is that or technical problem solving. Despite the loftier goals, young people use Youthideas.fi as a feedback channel and a tool for asking things from the officials, and less as a possibility for public deliberation.

As a channel for influencing matters, Youthideas.fi clearly shows how little influence young people actually have over significant matters in their lives. In one of the most concise and pointed ideas submitted to the service, students demand the permission to stay indoors during recess. The actual text in its entirety is as follows: 'Let us in it's f***ing freezing'.

Conclusions: formal participation and technical problem solving

Based on the content of the Youthideas.fi service, the culture of doing society among young people can be characterized as follows: the most important thing is to influence everyday issues in life, be they sports facilities or practices in local schools. This influencing is structured according to a conception of politics based on (liberal) private interests: improvements should be made not so much because they are elaborately argued and defended, but because 'that's what people want' and because executing them would not be technically too hard or too costly. When arguments based on the common good are expressed, this common good is quite often efficiency, based on industrial justification. The overall civic imagination sees the world as problems to be solved. This is *doing society through individualist technical problem solving.*

Technical problem solving, industrial justification, individual interest and the underlying engagement in a plan would seem to also share theoretical underpinnings, which makes them a natural fit together. Seeing the world as something that can be acted upon and improved through single acts instead of continuous involvement is both a defining feature in engaging in plan, industrial justifications and a particular kind of civic imagination. Whereas Boltanski and Thévenot's conception about different common goods and Thévenot's conception of a political grammar based on private interests provide a tool for identifying ideas based on technical solutions and equality, as well as differentiating between the common good and private interests, Baiocchi et al's civic imagination situates technical justifications and private interests into a wider context. One could assume that a civic imagination favouring problem solving includes more technical justifications based on the common good of efficiency. However, justifications based on private interests also go more easily with this form of civic imagination, as they do not include themes connecting with power and societal structures, nor are they based on communities and solidarity. Instead, private interests are promoted specifically through smaller, more narrowly defined issues and problems. Forms of common good based on, for example, equality can be considered suitable argumentative tools for a civic imagination focused on inequality and power.

If we compare individualist technical problem solving to the cultures of doing society presented in the two previous chapters, we can see obvious similarities. The participatory-industrial path to political influence goes through similar individualistic and problem-oriented landscapes, whether we are talking about participatory budgeting, youth councils, e-democracy – or the people who through these become actual politicians.

This sort of techno-rationalist and problem-based conception of democracy does not differ significantly from the one identified among Finnish adult citizens. Technical justification, measurability and presenting things first and foremost as easily achievable and rational are very effective means of arguing in the Finnish political culture (Luhtakallio 2012). In this comparison, it seems that young people have accessed mainstream political culture quite well. From this viewpoint, the service succeeds in producing a similar kind of participation as participatory practices 'directed to grown-ups', which are not commonly seen to hold an educational function (cf., for example, Eranti 2014 and 2017: individualist technical-rational problem solving would describe quite well all Finnish participation in urban planning).

Demands for improved mobility and better moped and microcar infrastructure communicate a desire among young people to expand their capacities and freedom of agency. Ideas like this, advocating for the rights of individuals is typical among the ideas submitted to the service, while only a small fraction of the ideas related to communities or collective action.

There were hardly any actual conflicts between political opinions or justifications in the ideas analysed. This might not be surprising because, as discussed, technical improvements fit better with the nature of the service. The channel directs how democracy is actualized: opinions are submitted primarily by individuals, and anything actually happening based on them is dependent on a civil servant being able to act on a specified level (city, school, youth house). In this kind of service, it makes more sense to raise minor technical details than to dream of a better world. In some sense, Youthideas. fi gave a more realistic framing for the whole process than what we saw with youth councils or participatory budgeting in Chapter 2: instead of vague promises of power and influence, or misleading marketing about realizing one's wildest dreams, the pitch was a channel for submitting ideas. Maybe they would be acted upon, or maybe not. As can be seen in Chapter 2, this also turned out to be the case with participatory budgeting.

Approximately half of the young people's ideas presented in the service are justified by not referring to any form of common good. One can assume – and it would be worthy of further research – that ideas structured according to the common good were more successful in constructing the legitimacy needed to bring about actual changes. If this is the case, the service sets requirements for young people's literary expression in a deliberate influencing channel. A well-formulated idea and justification more easily gains the necessary support than a vaguely defined initiative based on private interests.

If democracy education communicates one specific way of doing society that is characterized by individualism, technical problemsolving, and an emphasis on personal interest, it is not surprising that these young people's culture of doing society aligns with these attributes. More deliberative participation would both bring out different viewpoints, arguments and justifications, so that participants could understand other people's viewpoints better and find common solutions.

But even if the ideas presented here were sometimes posted in jest or did not hinge on complicated societal argumentation, they all represented a kind of participation that was done according to what the system wanted from these young people. In the next chapter we leave the well-oiled machine of formal participation and enter the world of marginalized and stigmatized youth, where this kind of participation is far from people's minds.

5

Imagining Alone: The Necessity of the Atomized Self among Stigmatized Youth

Taina Meriluoto and Lotta Junnilainen

Let us start with an interview extract where Utu, a young transgender person with experiences of homelessness, mental ill-health and substance abuse, describes society:

> 'If I start from how I've experienced it in my reality, then it's very much something that I am outside of. And that has defined society for me. That I'm outside it. Society is something that is made up of its accepted members. Specific accepted professions for example. Ever since I was a child, I was ashamed of my parents, their professions, their status, everything. Ever since I was a kid, I have strongly felt that we are the ones who do not belong. Anywhere.'

In this chapter, we discuss how young people in stigmatized positions do society. Based on ethnographic research among Finnish young people living in stigmatized low-income neighbourhoods or with stigmatizing experiences (see the Appendix), we examine how these young people imagined society and its problems, their position in (or out of) it and, in particular, their actions towards a better future from these circumstances.

Many of the young people we studied share Utu's experience of an outsider. Indeed, this is also the lens through which their societal participation – or lack thereof – is often studied; their passivity and 'inaction' are diagnosed, and different cures are proposed. In this chapter, we argue for a shift of perspective. If we understand doing society more broadly than simply as the usual acts of citizenship, we will see how the 'disengaged' youth are doing society in various ways. This chapter is about their imaginations of – and acts for – a better future.

The young people who are the focus of this chapter inhabit different stigmatized positions in Finnish society. All of them come from socioeconomically underprivileged positions and have suffered from different stigmatizing experiences throughout their lives. Some of them live in stigmatized, low-income neighbourhoods, some have suffered from homelessness, and others still suffer from substance abuse or mental ill-health. Some are transgender, while others have an ethnic minority background. While we recognize that the youth's varied experiences cannot be reduced to a single category, by interpreting their descriptions of the cultural norms and their positions, we can conclude that they all share experiences of stigmatization and marginalization in Finnish society (see Tiidenberg and Allaste 2020: 315–316). Despite Finland ranking high in terms of economic and social equality by international comparison, experiences of marginalization are as powerful there as in countries with higher degrees of income and social inequality, such as the UK or the US. As Barnes and Hall (2013: 22) argue, this is due to the country's egalitarian culture and tradition of a welfare society, which shapes people's expectations and deepens experiences of injustice in a situation where the upper classes take off economically, culturally and socially.

As we started discussing our findings from different field sites, we were surprised by the strong similarities between the experiences the youth shared and the strategies they employed, despite their different backgrounds and contexts. We use the term 'stigmatization' in this chapter as the youth's shared experience of how they are ignored, overlooked and underestimated by others in society (Lamont 2014).

Like Utu at the beginning of this chapter, most of the young people we studied viewed society as a separate entity from them and their lives, and as a community of people who disregard them. They frequently described experiences of unrecognition and loss of dignity as examples of 'what is wrong' with the current state of things, and longed for a society where everyone would be seen as worthy. This observation is our point of departure in this chapter: the main characteristic of our society, and simultaneously its main problem that the stigmatized young spoke about, was the *lack of recognition* (see also Fraser, 2000; Lamont, 2018, 2023; Lamont et al, 2016).

To understand their opinions about (the lack of) recognition, and the different ensuing ways of engagement, we use Gianpaolo Baiocchi et al's concept of civic imagination (2014). In contrast to the politically engaged and active citizens studied by Baiocchi et al (2014), most youth in our data could not, by any means, be defined as politically active. While some of them had, at the time of the fieldwork, started to engage in party politics or activist efforts, making them 'on the verge' of becoming active, many of them did not engage in any explicitly political activities. Subsequently, our following analysis is an extension of Baiocchi et al's work (2014; see also Bennett et al 2013), exploring how the youths' shared understanding of their lack of recognition translates into certain kinds of acts for a better future. For the young people in our data, these acts were primarily rooted in individualistic tools of public action rather than collective mobilizations and conventional political tactics for a better society. However, as we take seriously the youth's descriptions of lack of recognition as the main characteristic of society, we highlight that all their acts of seeking recognition are societal by nature; it is through these acts that the youth do society.

We first illustrate how the youth imagine society primarily through the main problem – lack of recognition – with which they identify. We then describe their engagement with the more formal and institutional ways of doing society – namely voting and institutional politics. However, our focus is on how the youth sought to tackle the dilemma of recognition – that is, what sort of engagements and action arose from their recognition-oriented civic imagination. Our primary interest is not with *what* the future aspirations of the stigmatized young in our study look like, but rather *how* they seek to get there. We identified three acts for a better future the young employed: (1) self-transformation – changing oneself into 'a respectable citizen'; (2) opting out – flipping the finger to 'the system'; and (3) subversion – critiquing the valuation schemes of society.

We conclude that the major problems young people identify within society today, alongside their responses to the situation, are highly individualized. The significant problem for them was their lack of recognition and value as individuals. Instead of focusing on and mobilizing for common concerns, such as economic redistribution, most stigmatized young people engage in envisioning and acting for a future in which they and their individual lives are valued. In addition, most of their responses relied on individualized tools. Instead of organizing collective mobilizations, most of them focused on individual solutions: changing themselves into 'respectable citizens' or distancing themselves from the 'broken system' altogether.

However, we also found a small minority of stigmatized young people who engaged in more collective efforts of political action. These young people sought to affect the valuation schemes of society so that people 'like them' would also be recognized as worthy. Intriguingly, the prominence of individualized cultural tools is also visible in these cases, as mobilization for recognition often takes place through the sharing of personal stories and experiences.

The society we don't belong to

At the beginning of this chapter, Utu described society as a composite of 'accepted members'. This was a common approach for young people to perceive society. They recurrently described society as a community of 'valued people', in which they and their families were not included. This became particularly evident in their descriptions of shame and condescension; they felt that 'the society', in the form of its 'accepted members', only cast a judgmental eye on them and perceived them as the wrong kind, as people that could and should legitimately be left out.

As many previous studies have also revealed, young people develop civic identities as reactions to the daily life experiences of their surroundings and their experienced place in the world (for example, Rubin 2007; Roberts and Evans 2012; Breeze et al 2017; Lannegrand-Willems et al 2018). In particular, the youth in stigmatized positions compose an image of society and of their place in it through an interwoven process of self-making, valuation and comparison. As they seek to understand their societal context and 'social location' (Irwin 2015), they scan and interpret the people and processes that seem to compose society. Particularly important are the boundaries the youth perceive: who is part of the society, who is left out and on what basis? Within this process of boundary making, processes of valuation and comparison become crucial tools with which the youth form a sense of society, but also of the underlying valuation structure that sustains it (Lamont 2012, 2023). As they compare themselves to the 'commonly accepted values' of their society, the young develop a sense of their own position and value.

Suvi powerfully described the feeling of being disregarded and a profound sense of being excluded in her interview. She grew up in an underprivileged neighbourhood with her mother. Her father died of overdose when she was a small child, and she has been suffering from hard-to-diagnose mental ill-health since her early teens. She is now 26 years old and has been on a partial disability pension for five years. When we asked her what the most important facts about herself were in order to truly understand her, her immediate response was that she is "someone who is not ashamed of the fact that she does not fit into society's moulds". With her hair dyed green and yellow and the multiple piercings on her face, she has become accustomed to getting comments about her looks. However, the feeling of not belonging has in-depth roots:

Taina: What does society mean for you?
(Suvi thinks for a long time)
Suvi: Maybe it's something from which I've always been at the fence on. You know, whether I'm in or out.
Taina: What makes you feel that you're at the fence?
Suvi: Okay, there's an article that was written about me that will give you an idea. The journalist who wrote it described me as 'exemplary stigmatized' – I actually took it up as a sort of stage name! It was a piece on youth marginalization, and

I had this outrageous struggle with the journalist because they tried to twist my words. They went like 'Do you feel stigmatized?', and I was like 'No!', and then they insisted and tried to put words into my mouth, like 'Well, but aren't you, anyway?' According to the article, I was an example of a young, stigmatized drop-out. So OK, I have been on disability pension for years, and before that, I've been living with public income support. So, I am in no way included. And to top it off, I am stigmatized, as they say. I've never been a good citizen.

Taina: What is a good citizen?
Suvi: Someone who is not me.
Taina: Who, then, is part of society?
Suvi: People who work, who are successful, and who have a family. Who have a golden retriever and 1.5 children.

Both Utu and Suvi described an outside gaze that made them feel unwanted, unaccepted and excluded, and created a strong rupture between them and 'people who belong'. This is how Michèle Lamont and her colleagues describe recognition. From a cultural sociological viewpoint, recognition is the result of culturally patterned (e)valuative practices that induce some voices being highlighted and valued while leaving some silenced or disregarded (Lamont 2018; Lamont et al 2016). Lamont and her team, for example, identified how 'neoliberal scripts' affect how poor people are regarded as lazy and undeserving (Lamont 2018) or how race affects people's everyday experiences of stigmatization (Lamont et al 2016).

Although people might not use class as an identity category (Savage et al 2001), they often organize their experiences of society based on the key characteristics of class, such as the distribution of economic resources, occupation and material wealth (Irwin 2015). Indeed, the young people made the distinction between the groups primarily based on material and economic basis: people are recognized as worthy if they have decent professions and the outside markers of a middle-class lifestyle (see also Irwin 2015). However, people who are 'not successful' – who struggle to make ends meet, suffer from different social or health problems, or quite simply live in underprivileged neighbourhoods – can be sure to know how they fail to meet society's demands. As Suvi described earlier, a key part of feeling excluded is the labels that are being attached to underprivileged people, assigning them a clear position as 'problematic' or 'the wrong kind'. However, the problems they identified had little to do with economic redistribution or injustice; rather, they highlighted how "not everyone is valued equally" describing the injustice experienced primarily as a matter of recognition.

This profound experience of being 'of the wrong kind' also manifested in several encounters the young had with public officials who tried to change them into 'something better'. The young people of stigmatized neighbourhoods repeatedly described how teachers, or other adults present in their lives, treated them as deviants. They felt that these adults thought that people who stayed in the neighbourhood could not make anything of their lives. They also understood why the officials told them to leave the neighbourhood when they grew older (Junnilainen, 2019). Leaving behind the influence of the people of the wrong kind and becoming exposed to the lifestyle of the 'normal' society was a strategy that was supposed to save the youth of stigmatized neighbourhoods from deviant trajectories.

Here, Afaf describes how a youth worker gives her advice on how to change herself for 'the better'. She is a 15-year-old second-generation immigrant who has suffered from school bullying, and she feels that, despite their efforts, adults have never been able to help her; rather, they have left her to solve all her problems on her own. Instead of valuing and seeing her as a whole person, public officials have treated her as a misbehaving problem, implying that the solution to these problems lies in her own hands – in better controlling herself:

> 'I used to end up in fights repeatedly at the time, so I had to go to a children's organization – or something – with my curator. Anyway, there was this woman who told me that I should put more effort into calming down. She said that if I'm in a difficult situation I should just sit down and squeeze the armrests. Which wasn't really helpful. I could tell she was trying, but usually when people try to help me, things just get worse.'

Similarly, in the following interview extract, Karo, a transgender man with experiences of homelessness and substance abuse, describes their experience of how society – as an active being – refused to recognize them for who they were:

> 'When I did not yet have the diagnosis [of being transgender], and therefore had not been able to change my name or my social security number, I felt like I did not have an identity at all. Like, if I went anywhere to run any official errands where you need your personal ID, they just slap you with some details, like: here, use these, be this person. I mean, I could not do anything or be included in anything with my own name and my own identity. And I felt like society tried really hard that I use certain kinds of clothes, for example, or that one particular name that others used of me. That I go and study to be a

seamstress, start a family, and marry a man. Those sorts of things that are not me at all.'

These institutional efforts to change young people into 'better' citizens had profound consequences for the youth's sense of self. In particular, the young people described a merging of shame and loneliness, as they felt that they were the problem and needed to change. These experiences of exclusion and stigmatization, coupled with the effervescent institutional efforts to change the youth into something 'better', caused the youth to identify a lack of recognition as the key problem in society today. Subsequently, their efforts to do society were strongly oriented towards questions of recognition and respect. Thereby, society was defined as an entity that does not recognize them, their experiences and struggles. For these young people, the main problem with society became its main characteristic.

Loviisa, a 26-year-old woman with experiences of mental ill-health, who had recently assumed a role as 'a mental health activist', phrased this problem explicitly into a political objective when asked what she would want to change in our society:

> 'Well generally, be it related to mental ill-health or anything else, really, I would like to change and widen the representations. To find the people and themes that are not seen right now … Now, it's about broadening the imagery related to mental ill-health. And through that, challenging what kind of work is important and what kind of activities are important. In general, what is seen as valuable in this society. I want to broaden that.'

Next, we turn to the youth's engagements and strategies of action – how they sought to change the problem of a lack of recognition. We start by examining the youth's approach towards traditional means of political influence, meaning their attitudes and engagements with institutional politics.

"I don't do the voting stuff"

Laura was a 15-year-old girl for whom school had always been fairly easy. At the time of the interview, she was not living at home with her mother, but she slept on her older sister's couch, giving her company and protecting her from her abusive boyfriend. Her teacher had encouraged Laura to take part in a youth participation programme aimed at 'giving a voice' to the local youth and providing them with channels to improve their living environment. However, Laura said that "none of that stuff" is for her. She was not "that kind of person", and neither was her family:

Lotta:	Do you think that it's important to have an influence on societal matters in general? Like voting for example?
Laura:	Well, no. At least, I am not the kind of person who would be doing much of the voting stuff.
Lotta:	Do you ever talk about voting at home?
Laura:	Well, they are all like they don't vote. No one has ever really voted.
Lotta:	Do they talk about not voting?
Laura:	Yeah. Whenever there's an election.
Lotta:	Have they ever said why [they don't vote]?
Laura:	They don't say why. I guess they just think it's useless.

Laura's approach towards institutional politics, and voting in particular, was extremely widely shared among our informants. Many expressed a mix of distrust and indifference towards institutional politics and described, with a somewhat bored tone, how they could not see the point in such activities. It was "useless", "a waste of time", and "led nowhere" – it "did not change anything anyway".

As Baiocchi et al (2014) describe, the 'skeptical engagements' of the people in their study reveal how the statement 'I am not political' carries more meaning and significance than simple withdrawal from civic life (also Bennett et al 2013). According to Baiocchi et al (2014), people make these statements to express their identity as citizens. In the cases they describe, when people said they 'are not political', they conveyed a conception of a good citizen who does not 'do politics', but is instead invested in 'fixing it' – meaning the present problems of society – themselves. As Bennett et al (2013) note, we should look beyond these statements to investigate what the imaginary behind them is like: if politics is bad and unbecoming for these people, they also hold an ideal about what politics and society ought to be like. Subsequently, instead of assigning the label of 'politically passive young' to our informants, we need to push further and investigate what these statements of indifference and disengagement reveal. As Bennett et al (2013: 521), following Eliasoph (1997, 1998) and Norgaard (2006), put it, 'displays of apathy actually take significant work to produce – in this way, apathy is a mechanism that people have developed to preserve faith in democratic ideals in the face of feeling powerless'.

The first thing we noticed when looking beyond these sceptical statements is that they are indeed composed against an ideal: voting, now, would be useless and a waste of time, alluding to the notion that, ideally, voting should be a way for people to have their voices heard.

More concretely, politics should be a route to 'change things' and, furthermore, an environment where everyone's viewpoint would come across. This latter point is made poignantly clear by a conversation with

Kaarlo and Jere, two young men with homelessness and substance abuse backgrounds now living in a rehabilitation institute. As we sat to eat kebab after having browsed some secondhand stores for clothes, Taina asked them whether they vote. They replied with a slight grin on their faces:

Kaarlo: Well, I can't say that I have done much of that voting thing. There really is no one who would get how it is for the least well off. I mean, yes, there are the housewives from Kauniainen [a particularly well-off city in the Helsinki capital area] who *say* that they get it, but they haven't' experienced it themselves.

Jere: Yeah, I haven't done much voting. I've had bigger concerns in my life so far.

In a good society, then, the decision makers would also include those with difficult life experiences. Their voices and viewpoints would be heard, and their experiences would influence the decisions made. However, this is often just a distant dream in the eyes of our informants and, subsequently, they distance themselves from politics that does nothing to ease their struggles. This disappointment is also reflected in the youth's choice of words when describing voting. Instead of talking about voting, many of them use diminutive terms, such as "the voting stuff" or "a little bit of voting", to highlight their disregard towards the whole business.

The youth's disengagement also reflects their experienced social location, and the disjuncture between this experience and their notion of a better society. As Aleksi, a young man living in a stigmatized urban neighbourhood, describes in the following, it would be better for everyone if 'those people in there would decide among themselves', clearly indicating that for him, society and its institutions function completely detached from him and his life:

Lotta: Have you thought about whether you're going to vote when you turn 18?
Aleksi: I won't.
Lotta: Have you thought about why not?
Aleksi: I think it is completely pointless, or a waste of time, that voting stuff.
Lotta: In what way is it a waste of time?
Aleksi: They could just decide among themselves who sit there. It would be easier that way.
Lotta: Do you think then that it does not impact your life, who is there and who isn't?
Aleksi: No. I really don't think it does.

Aleksi's description of disengagement not only reflects his indifference towards the political system but also a profound feeling of detachment from society; not only does he feel that voting would be useless because nothing would change, but also it is useless because it has nothing to do with his life. In contrast to a system that would have a meaningful impact on Aleksi's life and in which he could also have an impact, he feels absolutely no connection to society and its decision-making processes.

With a similar feel of detachment, Pihla, a young woman with experiences of homelessness and substance abuse, describes her reasons for not voting as "potentially harmful for the whole system":

> 'When I went to live in the rehabilitation centre, I did not even want to vote – I think it was the parliamentary elections or whatnot when I got there – because I felt that I am too stupid, and that it's a really bad thing if I vote because I have no idea who I should vote for and then it's detrimental for the whole system if people who have no clue go out and vote. (Laughs) I mean, I just had this really profound experience that I am not a part of this society. Even if I concretely knew that I had the right to vote, I still somehow felt that participating is not something that is intended for me. I felt that it's a thing that's detached from me and revolves on its own.'

Pihla and Aleksi both described a profound detachment from society as their undergirding reason for not participating; society is something that functions with or without them, and whether they take part in it has very little, if any, meaning. Moreover, for Pihla, her participation appeared to be a potential threat to democracy, should 'a person with as little knowledge as her' go out and participate. While, through their experiences of exclusion and detachment, they envision a society in which everyone would feel included, Pihla also imagines democracy as a system in which people would make considered decisions. Hence, their disavowal of politics has a slightly different character. While Aleksi seems to express disinterest, even disdain, towards the political system, Pihla seems to hold it to a rather high regard – so much so that "a person like her" has no business taking part in it. However, for both, the experienced result is the same: that institutional politics and "the voting stuff" is not for people like them.

Regarding the young people studied here, not voting and often vocally proclaiming not voting was not (just) a declaration of distrust or a uniform expression of disappointment towards the system, and of feeling detachment from society as a whole. It also indicated the failed ideals that these young people measured their present conditions and evaluated the meaningfulness of their participation against.

By looking at their expressions of disappointment, we can picture the ideals against which these disappointments emerge. Why is politics in its current form such a big source of disappointment for the stigmatized youth and how should things be instead? We argue that the democratic ideals our informants seek to preserve, but that they experience being constantly violated, are about inclusiveness, respect and recognition. The young are disappointed with politics, as they see no one taking note of their views or even their existence. They are not seen or heard in the system, and neither is anyone who shares their experiences. Even if they are seen, they are disregarded, regarded as problems and 'targets' of varying policy actions. The system and politics, then, are 'not for them', although they feel that it should be. In a good society, everyone would be seen and heard, but as this is decidedly not the case, it makes perfect sense not to partake in the useless circus of politics in the first place.

Acting for a better future

As it was not institutional politics to which many of our young informants turned, we further discuss the ways they acted for a better future, and by so doing 'did society'. We identify three acts for a better future that the young people assumed as their response to a society characterized by unrecognition: (1) changing oneself into a 'respectable citizen'; (2) flipping the finger to the system; and (3) challenging the valuation system that now disregards them.

Self-transformation: changing oneself into a 'respectable citizen'

Rather than politicizing the unfairness of not being seen and heard, and voicing claims for recognition and respect, most young people we interviewed focused on *changing themselves*. For some, this meant making a radical break with their past self, which was often accompanied by an implicit assertion that their past self had indeed been part of what is wrong with society today.

Here, Anna and Klasu provide examples of such radical breaks. Anna, who grew up in a stigmatized neighbourhood, now studied law at the university and had recently joined the National Coalition Party, which drives a neoliberal political agenda and boasts a reputation for promoting the interests of the most well-off in Finnish politics. Anna had come a long way since she had lived with her low-income grandparents, who had helped her mother to raise her. Her accounts of changing society went profoundly in parallel with changing oneself to meet the current demands for a respectable citizen. In the following interview extract, Anna explains her motivation for joining the party:

> 'Of course, I've always had all sorts of opinions, mostly critical, everything sucks you know. But then I thought that okay, all we Finns

ever do is complain. I think it's our original sin that we only complain about everything. Like, OK, maybe there's something I can do about these matters. That it's better to join people who do something rather than complain in some corner.'

Throughout her interview, Anna highlights her hard work in leaving stigmatized neighbourhoods and the grades and positions she has achieved, despite her underprivileged past. In her view, this is the strategy everyone should assume in order for a better society to take shape. The most significant societal change needed, in her view, is that people would start assuming more responsibility for themselves and change themselves for the better:

Anna: Personally, I have worked so hard, and I have seen my grandparents work so hard. So, I just can't comprehend it. Sure, if you have some physical injuries or something that prevents you from working, but in the end, you have so many people who just choose to stay at home. I think we should support them only if they contribute something in return. That's the thing that has always bothered me the most: that we throw out money for people who decide to do nothing.

Lotta: Have you seen many people like this?

Anna: A lot. I mean, ridiculously many. And then you have alcohol and drugs that you add to the mix. There was a guy that burned down his flat because he had left a cigarette burning in his mouth. The apartment was completely ruined. He got a new flat from the city just like that, and there are people waiting in line for an apartment. And then this junkie gets a flat just like that, and a voucher for a thousand euros to buy new clothes. And this person has not worked a day in his life for this society! He has gotten everything free ever since he was a kid, and he has never done anything.

For Anna, the problem and the solution lie within the individuals: it is the undeserving and lazy freeloaders who need to change themselves, just as she has done.

Klasu, a recovering addict with a homelessness background, provides a similar account of how change for a better society starts with yourself. In the following fieldnote excerpt, Klasu recounts his life story as we get to know one another in the living room of the rehabilitation centre. Klasu is one of the rehabilitation community's 'eldest'. He has lived in the centre for about a year and has recently started a work experiment outside the centre.

Klasu describes his work experiment with a huge smile on his face. He says that he feels pride that he "can pay taxes now":

'I make my own money. I smile at people. I say hello to the cashier at the grocery store. Now, I am fit for this society and a respectable man. And that's what I want to be. [Being fit for society] means that I am no longer filth in this society, or problem material, but that I do what's right. Before I used to laugh at people who were on their way to work, like "you fucking idiots, there you go running around while I'm just chilling". Now I love to watch people running about in a hurry. I'm like, hey, why didn't you leave 15 minutes earlier to go to work? Now I work, too, and I've been thinking that helping others might be my thing. I love that grandmas now sit next to me on buses and start chatting with me.'

Klasu, like Anna, believes that changing himself is the key towards a better society. Instead of questioning society's demands, he sees his past self as the problem and is happy and proud to report how he now meets the demands of an active, contributing citizen who no longer imposes fear on grandmas. When mirrored against the problem of recognition, Anna and Klasu have chosen a strategy where they start seeking recognition by transforming themselves to meet the criteria they have witnessed as hegemonic in our society today. To put it bluntly, they saw it only fair that people need to make an effort to be seen as worthy and, furthermore, to make an effort that complies with society's demands. Their strategy is that of self-transformation and not collective or political mobilization.

In her study of young working-class adults, Jennifer M. Silva (2013) made a forceful observation of the cultural background of these individualistic strategies. She argued how their life experiences

> teach young working-class men and women that they are completely alone, responsible for their own fates and dependent on outside help only at their peril. They learn to approach others with suspicion and distrust. Many make a virtue out of necessity, equating self-reliance and *atomic individualism* with self-worth and dignity: if they had to survive on their own, then everyone else should too. (Silva 2013: 83–84, emphasis added)

We acknowledge the notion of atomic individualism in our data as statements of self-reliance, independency and desolation. Afaf, whom we got to know earlier as she was taught how to control her feelings, had – if not necessarily anger management – adopted a script of the self that is resilient, undaunted and lonely:

'I take a deep breath and tell myself that I'm a strong person and can do this. I'm proud of myself. Despite all the shitty things I've experienced,

I've made it this far. I've had no one to talk to. There is nobody in this world I could really trust. There is no one to count on but myself. Only me. If I have a problem, I try to solve it by myself. I believe that if you believe in yourself and try hard, you can make it.'

We argue that the strategies of self-transformation among stigmatized youth reflect a similar accustomising to and acceptance of highly individualistic, if not necessarily neoliberal, strategy in doing society. Throughout their childhood and across their harsh experiences, their surroundings have taught the young people that they must make it on their own and that the key to a better life lies within them to transform themselves. Instead of growing up to demand something from society or rising up to challenge the criteria based on which they are being judged as problematic, they accept these criteria for an active, self-sustaining and independent citizen, and start working on themselves to meet this vision of a better world.

Opting out: flipping the finger to 'the system'

While transforming oneself – and demanding it from others – was a common strategy of action among our youth, we also found regular accounts of strategies that were decidedly not focused on transforming oneself according to society's norms. We call these the strategy of 'flipping the finger to the system'. Here, society's current criteria for worthy individuals are acknowledged but not obeyed.

To illustrate this strategy, let us return to the kebab joint with the two young rehabilitation centre inhabitants, Kaarlo and Jere. As our conversation about voting continued, Taina asked the guys whether they would now consider voting. Probably yes, they responded, and Kaarlo proceeded to share a story concerning last year's parliamentary elections:

Kaarlo: I was informed by the staff regarding voting. I had gotten the voting paper in mail, you know, what is it called anyway. And I had just glanced at it, gone like 'OK, right' and thrown it in the trash. The staff had found it in my trash bin, and I got a punishment for anti-societal behaviour and isolation. They then forced me to vote. But out of revenge, I voted for this most ridiculous bloke.
Taina: A revenge to whom?
 (Kaarlo laughs)
Jere: As a revenge to the staff that they made Kaarlo vote.

Later during the conversation, Kaarlo envisions the possible way in which he could see himself participating politically: "I could become a political influencer with an agenda of an 'anti-societal person'. I could bring out stuff that no one wants to see and say the things that no one else says out loud."

Kaarlo, who by 20 had moved from one foster care institution to another and had been imprisoned once, was now making a break from his "criminal past", as he put it. However, for him, this break did not mean a self-transformation to meet the current norms of an acceptable citizen. Instead, he continued to pride himself over not knowing what an aubergine is and not eating greens with any of his meals. While he toyed with the idea of assuming an active, political role as someone who would say all the things that are currently left unsaid, in practice, he was quite content with his position in society's grey area, where he could see society's demands, but could also choose to ignore them. Although he did notice that currently not everyone who should be seen and heard is given adequate attention, he did not engage in any collective mobilization to this end. Instead, he sought his recognition elsewhere. Kaarlo was a sauna enthusiast, who went to public saunas several times a week to unofficially compete with his sauna club over who manages to sit in the heat the longest. This recognition, it seems, was enough for him.

In contrast to what Anna and Klasu chose to do, Kaarlo and Jere did not strive to right any societal wrongs by transforming themselves. While they acknowledged similar demands of a good citizen as they describe themselves as 'anti-societal', their strategy is the linear opposite of the self-transformation strategy of Anna and Klasu. Instead of starting to 'play by the rules', they opted out. By proudly proclaiming their 'anti-societal' stance, Kaarlo and Jere figuratively flip the finger to the system and make their detachment from society a crucial component of their selves. As they paint a vivid picture of how they deliberately act against the expectation's society has for them, they also proclaim how little they care about how society perceives them. Whether or not they are seen as worthy and valuable by society's majority seems irrelevant to them. For this, they turn to their smaller group of peers in various subcultures.

A similar wish to position oneself in society's grey area is painted by Karo in the following quote. As we discuss how Karo sees society, they use the metaphor of a castle. As we ask whether Karo sees themself inside the castle, they hesitate:

Karo:	Well, yeah, I guess I am there. Even if it feels like a somewhat uncomfortable thought.
Taina:	Why does it feel uncomfortable?
Karo:	Well, I mean, somehow, I feel that there are these walls or norms. And when you are inside you need to fit inside them. That is somehow a scary thought.

Taina: Is it possible to *not* be inside them?
Karo: Yeah. Or at least I have imagined and hoped to be outside them.

The finger-flipping strategy also relies on individualistic tools of action. While it does not rely on the individual's willingness and ability to transform themself to meet the norms of recognition, it is rooted in their choice to construct themself as atomized individuals, detached from society. As Karo forcefully describes, they are painfully aware of not meeting the norms of a worthy individual in today's society. Instead of fighting the norms or transforming themself, they choose to ignore them.

This strategy is the mirror image of the devaluing experiences many of our young informants recounted having: as they strongly felt they could not meet society's demands and thus did not fit what seemed to be the hegemonic vision of a good society, they showed equal disregard and indifference towards society. If they felt unworthy and devalued in the eyes of society, they would deem society as unworthy and irrelevant for them.

Subversion: critiquing the valuation schemes of society

Finally, some young people engaged in various forms of societal and political action to explicitly challenge the valuation structures that they currently felt unjust and unrecognizing of their worth. These actions take the form of experience-based activism, where the objective of the activists is to counter the current valuation schemes of society that allow the stigmatization and devaluation of people with difficult life experiences. This strategy, then, stands in contrast to the two other ways of acting for a better future identified previously: it does not focus on the individual as the root of the problem, but places the problem at the structural level of society. However, as we will notice, this more explicitly political strategy is also rooted in quite individualistic tools of political action.

To illustrate this strategy, we describe a situation in which Taina is planning a talk with Lilja, a young activist with a background of homelessness and substance abuse. Taina and Lilja have been invited to speak at a seminar intended for public officials working around homelessness services, and they meet at the university cafeteria to plan for their talk. We ask Lilja what she would ultimately want the audience to understand and what she would like to have an effect on:

> 'That I am not just a recovering addict, I am a human being! You know, the drawing of boundaries between us and the normal people. I mean, what normal people?! When you go listen to someone with some rough life experiences and then you have the people who are a little bit more normal there in the audience. Then you only

see that side of the person that isn't normal. Fucking stereotypes! They drive people to a role where they are diminished to their mere experiences ... There's the scale of valuation that I want to be disassembling. That no one's past is that person.'

Lilja's account was a widely shared attitude among societally active young people. These strategies were targeted at changing people's perceptions and attitudes or improving public services so that people would be treated with respect. Lilja strongly feels the unrecognition, dismissive labels and judgmental gaze that society associates with people in her positions and situations. Unlike the first strategy identified earlier, she does not feel that it is her who needs to change. Neither does she choose to walk away from society, but instead expresses a strong investment to do something about the system that is unrecognizing of her worth.

Similarly, Loviisa, the mental health activist we met earlier, described how her participation is based on the conviction that 'It's not me, it's them':

'We need to see that it's the society that's faulty here, and not the individuals who happen to have problems. The clearest example is that it's not the problem of the person in a wheelchair that they can't access a building, it's the building's fault for not having a ramp.'

Nancy Fraser has suggested the term 'transformative strategy' to describe efforts to claim recognition that seek to destabilize the patterns of cultural value that enable making hierarchical distinctions and valuations between groups (1997: 27). This was the strategy adopted by an active minority, who placed the problem of unrecognition in the wider society instead of themselves and who engaged in efforts to do something about it. They sought to change the unjust valuative criteria by, first, exposing them. Quite concretely, they wanted people to notice how, and based on what, they currently judge people in stigmatized positions.

Interestingly, this political mobilization is also strongly rooted in individualistic repertoires of action. To change society into a place where everyone would be valued, the young people engaged in creative activist practices, most of which relied on them sharing their personal stories and experiences in public. These practices, as the mental health activist Suvi explains in the following, were explicitly meant to dispel the shame that is currently being placed on people in stigmatized positions. They entailed boldly sharing highly stigmatizing experiences and personal stories both at activist events, in everyday encounters and, increasingly, on social media (Meriluoto 2023). The young activists put their own lives and experiences on the line to show how they were currently being disregarded and to make a point that this should not be the case.

From her early teens, Suvi has boasted a keen interest in "all forms of political participation". She has been active and vocal in highlighting her bad experiences with mental health and child supportive services, and now defines herself as a mental health activist because she wants to "dispel the shame associated with mental ill-health". She shares her experiences and emotions openly on her social media account, and makes a point of not only posting smiling selfies but also images of herself crying, her make-up all messed up, or in the middle of a panic attack. Contrary to the strategy of self-transformation, she has no interest in transforming herself into anything. However, it is society that should change to make room for her:

Suvi: It has always been very important for me that I am faithful to who I am, and I don't want to be fitting into anyone else's moulds. Be it talking about mental health issues or whatever ... I have always wanted to be vocal about my experiences with my own face and my own name. Because if no one speaks about these issues with their own name and their own face, nothing ever changes! The openness is key. And by talking about these things in public, I also want to encourage others to share their experiences. To show that there is nothing to be ashamed about here.

Taina: You said that if no one does this, then nothing changes. What needs to change, then?

Suvi: Attitudes.

Taina: Why do they need to change?

Suvi: Because people still think mental ill-health is something to be ashamed about ... People have this need to appear perfect, which leads them to hide everything that's not. And that's really harmful for everyone.

While Suvi, Loviisa and Lilja share the diagnosis of the lack of recognition as society's biggest problem, their strategy is to mobilize politically in order to change society instead of changing themselves or retreating from society altogether. In traditional terms, their way of doing society is the most civic of the three, but intriguingly is not much more collective than the first two highly individualistic strategies. Although all of them were part of activist groups whose objective was to fight the stigma and tackle the prejudice associated with their experiences, the actual practices they adopted relied on them sharing their individual experiences alone, either offline or online. They shared images of themselves at their worst, coupled with short stories and descriptions of how life with mental ill-health, homelessness, substance abuse problems or other stigmatizing experiences felt like. This kind of sharing of testimonies has long been a central strategy of grassroots mental health activism, but as researchers have stated, focusing on 'stigma shattering' (Tyler and Slater 2018) by sharing personal 'mad stories' also risks bypassing more fundamental cultural, political and economic questions regarding the distribution of distress in our society (Costa et al 2012; Davies 2016).

Loviisa explained her position as 'an independent activist' concretely, as she described what her activist group meant to her:

> '[The group] provides me with background support and boost to act as an independent activist. But it also means that I don't have to tie myself to any one political agenda. In a way, it's more my own, and it allows me to be unique while also having the group's support ... As an individual, I get to speak about my experiences any way I want and not have to link my experiences to a specific movement or a cause.'

What the active youth seem to describe is an intertwined objective of being recognized for who they were, and claiming this recognition as themselves, free from any collective agendas or frameworks. They also want to be recognized and valued as themselves in their activist practices, making their societal participation rely on individualistic tools while striving for collective goals (see Chapter 8). In the final section of this chapter, we discuss the possible roots of these individualistic tools and, in particular, their meaning for the political action of youth in stigmatized positions.

Imagining alone together?

Here, we have first shown how underprivileged youth perceive society as an entity to which they have no access. In their view, society is for 'successful people who belong', and this does not include the youth or their immediate surroundings. In contrast, they constantly and repeatedly feel looked down upon, labelled as problems and made to feel unwanted and unwelcome. This led us to observe that the joint problem identified by most youth in our data was the lack of recognition in society.

Furthermore, we investigated how youth navigated the problem of unrecognition. We started by showing how institutional politics and other conventional means of influence was not the go-to strategy for most of our informants. Instead, we identified three ways to act for a better future the youth employed: self-transformation, opting out, and subversion. We pinpointed how all of these operate with individualistic tools of public action, and instead of collective mobilization for policy changes or economic redistribution, for example, the politically active youth adopted individualistic means of activism to achieve their goals for being recognized as valuable.

Instead of this being a mere symbol of the increasingly 'individualized culture' in Western societies, we argue that this individualistic style of action is an adaptation to the youth's experiences of how society perceives and treats them and, subsequently, a necessary survival strategy for the stigmatized youth. As the only group attachments on offer for them are highly stigmatizing, with 'those who belong' assigning collectively stigmatizing labels upon them, the youth markedly construct themselves as unique individuals and seek to distance themselves from the stigmatizing group memberships. Peculiarly, however, most formal and organized possibilities of participation, including the myriad of 'inclusion projects', treat the youth as precisely parts of 'a problematic collective'. Assuming an active role through these routes means first accepting an outsider label of being part of 'the less well-off', 'the weak', 'immigrant youth', NEET youth or 'housing estate youth' as the basis of one's active role. The youth are invited to participate as 'an exemplary stigmatized young', as Suvi forcefully described. They are assumed to be interested in topics that deal with these hardships that determine them, and are offered a role to take part as a representative of this stigmatized group.

While a few young people accept this role and then use it to change common preconceptions about people with such experiences, many find it compelling to make a clear-cut distinction between them as individuals and the problematic group in which they are commonly placed. This, we argue, hinders disadvantaged youth's societal participation in a political system where the promotion of collective interests and group identification form the basis of political participation. Identifying shared sources of injustice and mobilizing behind shared political claims become significantly harder when the recognition of your self-worth is highly dependent upon you making a point of being an individual unlike anyone around you.

However, the youth's striving for recognition as unique individuals has some characteristics that, we argue, cannot and should not be reduced to mere signs of increasing individualism. Notably, the youth's imaginary of a society in which everyone would be recognized often translates to pleas for *everyone's* right to be recognized as unique individuals without preassigned labels and identifiers (see also Lamont 2023). Some youth, as we have shown, sought to turn this ideal into reality by living their own lives as detached from the collective identifiers described earlier as possible. Meanwhile, many of the more societally active young engaged in explicit actions that fought for everyone's right to recognition and self-determination. Perhaps the right to carve out your own way of being and dreaming is the vision of a good society behind which today's youth mobilize collectively as individuals.

In the next chapter, we continue with different ways of dealing with tensions of individualism and collectivism: online imageboards.

6

Online Transgressions: Imageboards and Cultural Practices of Anonymous Citizenship

Tuukka Ylä-Anttila and Veikko Eranti

In this chapter we continue with somewhat marginalized young people with problematic connection to broader society – but with quite different focus and methods. If the previous chapter was based on ethnographic encounters with marginalized people, here we take a look at imageboards: anonymous online discussion forums that have spawned peculiar subcultures, resulting in memes and discourses which often cross over to the mainstream public sphere. They are popular particularly among young men with interests often considered 'geeky/nerdy', such as games, computers and comics. Imageboards are also interesting because they have recently been associated with right-wing, antisemitic and misogynist politics, even though their roots are in more benign discussions about popular culture such as anime. Looking at online spaces such as these is crucial for understanding how society is done, not only by the traditionally politically active citizens or the upright civic heroes that keep the machinery of civil society humming. We must also see how these right-leaning nominally rule-free online environments contribute to creating the culture, and the cultural tools, shaping our political reality.

We focus on Ylilauta ('Überboard'), the most prominent Finnish language imageboard, basing this chapter on a previous article about the politicization of Ylilauta (Ylä-Anttila et al 2020) as well as on continued participant observation and qualitative analysis. In our survey of youth aged 15–25 in the Finnish capital region, presented in Chapter 1, around 25 per cent of the respondents had visited Ylilauta, so it is a somewhat mainstream experience. Imageboards are discussion forums divided into tens of thematic 'sub-boards', in this case including the likes of 'Anime', 'Vehicles', 'Relationships',

'Bodybuilding and Fitness', 'Politics' and so on. A discussion thread on these sub-boards always starts by a user posting an image or video, and each reply may or may not also include one.[1]

To browse Ylilauta as an outsider is a curious experience, to say the least. After large online casino ads, one browses most active topics on different sub-boards. There are several threads about female social media microcelebrities, where borderline harassment and hate-following mixes with genuine affection that comes from investing one's time into something. All these threads have hundreds of comments. There is a thread where a poster shows off his antique Roman coin collection and a thread asking for job-market advice. Another thread starts with a long post about the Finnish tax code and how after joining the European Union, Finland is no longer a sovereign state. In the 'Random' sub-board, the first post is an antisemitic tirade about how the Jews are to be blamed 'for immigration and cultural policy that are destroying Europe'. One thread starts a detailed rewriting of the Finnish Constitution from a populist right-wing viewpoint. All the threads are laden with profanities and all imaginable types of slurs.

To understand how society is done on Ylilauta, we first look at the general history of imageboards to understand where their culture comes from. We then look at how technological features – such as anonymity – affect their political culture. Lastly, we zoom out and look at how the bigger picture of politics on Ylilauta has evolved in recent years.

Culture on Ylilauta

Imageboards have their origins in Japanese internet culture and have undergone numerous literal and metaphorical translations. Ylilauta, founded in 2011, may be considered a Finnish localization of 4chan, which in turn was founded in 2003 as an English-language localization of the Japanese imageboard 2chan. Imageboards, or *chans*, were originally focused on discussion about Japanese popular culture, which is now a minority topic on both Ylilauta and 4chan. Many of Ylilauta's structural features – such as including a 'Random' board, the most popular one – are directly translated from 4chan.

Online subcultures thriving on imageboards are characterized by carnivalesque irony, trolling, specialized vocabularies, inside jokes and myriad cultural references (Phillips 2016). Despite the increasing cultural significance of imageboards and the increasing social acceptance of related subcultures (such as gaming), imageboard users still often see themselves as belonging to a 'scene' that is alternative, niche or even marginalized (Marwick and Caplan 2018: 5). Many imageboards, including Ylilauta, have been used to coordinate harassment campaigns, primarily against feminist activists (Typpö and Pullinen 2016; Marwick and Caplan 2018).

The cultural tools, practices, repertoires and styles through which young people understand politics (Swidler 1986; Eliasoph and Lichterman 2003) are collaboratively created, shared and learned in places such as Ylilauta. Since styles of interaction in general are culturally patterned, they have effects on interaction beyond the immediate context in which they are observed (Eliasoph and Lichterman 2003: 738), especially in the case of influential subcultural communities such as Ylilauta. Moreover, the cultural patterns and styles of political interaction young people now create online and offline will be the tools by which citizenship is acted out in the future. It has been argued that concepts such as 'the public sphere', 'communicative action' or even 'politics', as typically understood, may not grasp what actually happens with politics in the unconventional setting of imageboards, and that we may need new concepts instead (Watts 2019). This chapter suggests some such concepts for understanding citizenship in action on online platforms, based on pragmatist theories of politics and citizenship (see also the introduction of this book).

Ylilauta has been previously understood as a peer support community for those withdrawn from society, rather than a political platform: 'conversations do not become politicized in the conventional party-political or activist sense because the critique is stuck at the personal level' (Vainikka 2018: 12). But several studies have found that 4chan, the most well-known imageboard, experienced a far-right politicization in the latter half of the 2010s (Hine et al 2017; Nagle 2017; Phillips 2019), and we have argued that a similar development happened on Ylilauta (Ylä-Anttila et al 2020). Moreover, the line between personal-level critique and political articulations is thin. Some of the most interesting facets of political culture may in fact be found in areas of life not considered 'political' *a priori* (see Chapter 5; see also Eliasoph and Lichterman 2003).

On the other hand, anti-immigrant, anti-feminist far-right politics enjoyed a sustained rise in popularity in Finland in the 2010s, a development in which networked communication and its associated cultural logics were central (Hatakka 2017; Ylä-Anttila et al 2019; Ylä-Anttila 2020). Far-right movements that challenge the mainstream on identity-political terms often shape politics through culture; that is, influencing the public's worldviews, not just through elections and government (Eatwell and Goodwin 2018: 283–292). Media accounts have claimed that Ylilauta has become a seedbed for the right-wing radicalization of young men (Typpö and Pullinen 2016; Ikola 2018), like its anglophone predecessor 4chan (Hine et al 2017; Nagle 2017; Marwick and Caplan 2018; Phillips 2019). Identity-focused youth subcultures grow in grassroots spaces online and offline, and ideologues of contemporary politics, particularly on the identity-focused 'alt'-right, see subcultural communities such as imageboards as battlegrounds in waging their 'culture war' (Hine et al 2017; Nagle 2017; Lewis 2020).

Technological affordances and cultural tools

One central feature of Ylilauta is that threads with no recent replies automatically disappear as new threads take their place, making the nature of discussions on them fleeting and ephemeral. On the most popular sub-boards, such as Random, only around 24 hours of most recent messages can be viewed, and users tend to browse the front page, consisting of the most recently active threads. But the feature that defines the whole arena as a place for doing society is anonymity, which is strongly encouraged both technologically and culturally. Anyone can post without creating a user account or even choosing a nickname: the platform has traditionally identified each poster only as 'Anonymous' by default. The poster can of course include their name or handle in the post, but revealing one's identity is considered a faux pas in imageboard culture, and identities would rarely be verifiable. Anonymity may be considered a radical democratization of the public sphere, in that only the content of each message matters, rather than the status of the speaker – but it has also made possible some rather more unsavoury features of conversation culture on anonymous boards.

Here, we come concretely to the intersection of technology and culture, in which the concept of affordance, coined by Gibson (1979: 115), is useful: 'The *affordances* of the environment are what it *offers* the animal, what it *provides* or *furnishes*'. Affordances can be used as a conceptual tool to observe similarities and differences between online and face-to-face interaction, and different online platforms, in terms of the effects they have on sociality. What kind of (political) culture is made possible and/or salient by the affordances of the platform? This has become a crucial question for research on citizenship and politics, as more and more of our daily lives, including our political lives, are lived online. A large part of the research literature on imageboards, social media and other online platforms focuses on this, specifically: which technical features of online platforms result in what kinds of social action? For instance, what kind of sociality does the Facebook like button create and support (for example, Eranti and Lonkila 2015)? Do algorithmic 'filter bubbles' inherent in social media create political polarization (for example, Bail et al 2018)? What about enforced anonymity, as in the Ylilauta case?

Technical features of online platforms directly influence action, since users typically cannot change the platforms. However, what they can do is to use the affordances offered by the platforms for creative action, resulting eventually in habitual practices of action, which through repetition are sedimented as culture, which in turn shapes action through providing established practices ('toolkits' and 'repertoires'), which actors use to act. As such, practices are the social and cultural analogue to technical affordances, such as recommendation algorithms or enforced anonymity, in that they define the kinds of action that are possible. However, they differ from most technical features in the sense that they are always in flux, constantly created and recreated in social action, while being based on the more rigid determinants of action formed by the technological features of the platform.

Transgression and shock value as group style

Let us now look at examples of how Ylilauta users create local cultural practices based on platform affordances. Despite the anonymity and ephemerality of communications on imageboards – which are affordances dictated by the platform – certain practices and norms of interaction are upheld by users and their collective memory. Accumulating shared culture is one of the functions of *memes*, probably the most well-known example of imageboard culture. Users create, collect, creatively modify and use memes on and beyond imageboards – an example of a cultural practice which has spread from chan culture to social media and popular culture more broadly (Shifman 2013). 'Memetic' expressions such as images and catchphrases are repeated by participants one after the other, so that the meme 'travels' from one person to the next, often changing somewhat on the way as each user creates their own variations, while still remaining identifiable (Nissenbaum and Shifman 2017: 484).

English-language memetic expressions are often translated literally into Finnish by Ylilauta users – with deliberate comic effect – and a memetic lingo including such translations is used to signal familiarity with English-language chan culture, which is a form of cultural capital on Ylilauta (cf. Trammell 2014; Nissenbaum and Shifman 2017). Deriding new users by calling them *uusihomo* ('newfag') does not make much sense unless you know it is a literal translation of an obscure homophobic/homosocial meme: calling new users 'newfags', experienced old users 'oldfags', social justice oriented users 'moralfags' and so on. Of course, 'newfag' as a concept does not make much sense either – to an outsider – but on the boards, it is a repeated signifier of belonging, discursively constructing the in-group, while excluding uninitiated newcomers who do not know the group's deliberately offensive *speech norms* (Eliasoph and Lichterman 2003).

To give an example, consider this exchange between a few users in a thread about investing in cryptocurrencies. This discussion starts when two users disagree as to whether a particular crypto coin is a worthy investment, and one of them tells off the other one – but there is an empty line in their post before the actual message. This etiquette faux pas leads to the following reply:

> Empty line ruthlessly exposes you as a newfag, coming back at you as an ad hominem

to which another user replies:

> Post your oldfag tag if you yourself are so old. Don't have one? Epic, owned : D Greetings, differentfag

A third user, who may or may not be the same one as previously:

> Only wannabe oldfags are using any fucking tags. Tags are a fucking sign of being a newfag.

Such practices bond together those 'in the know' and exclude those who do not understand. This hierarchy building between 'us' and 'the normies', as well as between more and less esteemed members of the community, is central to chan culture. Membership and status in the community must be earned by proving familiarity with the community's norms. In the case of 4chan, it has been argued that rather than a rule-less space where 'anything goes', as the rather loose organization of the technological platform would suggest, users are in fact 'highly invested in delimiting and policing the borders of what counts as "acceptable" posting behaviour within the community' (Trammell 2014: 1) – that is, cultural practices. What is acceptable on imageboards might be unacceptable elsewhere, but this does not mean that there are no social rules – they are just different from those of the mainstream public.[2] This comes close to a cultural level institutionalization of the opting-out strategy explained in the previous chapter of this book: mere belonging to Ylilauta culture requires certain pushing away of conventional norms.

Imageboard culture in fact reminds us of Nina Eliasoph and Paul Lichterman's (2003) seminal work on culturally patterned *group styles* of interaction and how they tie in with politics. By 'group style', Eliasoph and Lichterman refer to the local culture of interaction of a group: shared assumptions about the *boundaries* of the group, the *bonds* between group members and the *speech norms* guiding interaction between group members. These are implicitly reaffirmed and learned from others in social action. Eliasoph and Lichterman's ethnography exemplifies their theory by observing 'The Buffalo Club', a group that regularly meets in a bar in a West Coast suburb of the United States for country and western dancing and beers (Eliasoph and Lichterman 2003: 764), which may seem like quite a departure from the online subculture that is our example here. But while the Buffalos' material affordances for social action were indeed quite different – they met face to face, knew each other's names, danced and drank together – the cultural practices of their interaction, as described by Eliasoph and Lichterman, were surprisingly similar to those of Ylilauta. The norms called for not revealing too much about one's life outside this particular social setting and for telling offensive jokes about outsiders, especially politicians and activists, as does chan culture.

Like the Buffalo Club, Ylilauta has never had any consistent political ideology or goals; how could it, with thousands or of users contributing without much organization or stated purpose? Imageboard culture has in fact explicitly shunned politics and morality, denouncing those who care about justice as 'moralfags' (Deseriis 2015: 170) and mocking those who care about social justice (Phillips 2019). Such a style of mutually affirmed disavowal of politics is in fact political in itself. Eliasoph and Lichterman (2003: 760) describe the Buffalo Club's 'rude and crude' group style of 'constant raucous, racist, sexist, and scatological joking'. The function of this style, they argue, is to seem authentic, to 'debunk the pieties and con games that they saw everywhere' (2003: 761) in society. Thus, the most important speech norm was 'Do not talk seriously in the group context, and try to appear to be breaking rules' (2003: 761) – transgression, that is (see Nagle 2017). Eliasoph and Lichterman claim that the 'distant, ironic relationship to the wider world' is 'a kind of political position' (2003: 764). The point of the Buffalo Club's casual, joking racism was not in fact to 'say that blacks, Asians and Latinos are bad' (2003: 770), but rather to show that the group was 'inclusive of anyone who had a reasonable, open sense of humor' (2003: 770). Still, the club's racism had exclusionary consequences, as when a member's Black son-in-law would not attend Club meetings because of it (2003: 767).

A similar dynamic is at work in the case of Ylilauta, where racist and misogynist imagery and rhetoric is frequent. Such a style likely also has other functions and meanings for the participants than the racist and misogynist content itself, such as its 'edgy' shock value, which is particularly important to its core demography: young men. And in the case of Ylilauta, the technological affordance of anonymity is likely at least a part explanation for such content: it allows such behaviour and in fact creates an outlet for it. This, of course, in turn affects who turns out to frequent the boards, thus partly explaining the core demography of often disaffected young men.

To exemplify the everyday cultural transgressions, here are a few comments taken from a discussion collecting videos and photos from Kabul Airport in August 2021, depicting a chaotic scene with people running and dying while trying to climb on planes to escape the Taliban:

> These people are even more retarded than gypsies!
> They look like ants: D Makes me wanna step on them
> Where's the minigun when you need one [helicopter-mounted machine gun used by US troops in the Vietnam War]
> What the fuck! Mind your social distancing! Everybody's gonna fucking get covid and die!
> How about social distancing? Face masks? HELLOOOOOOO

Next, we analyse Ylilauta's culture in more depth in terms of their group style: boundaries, bonds and speech norms (Eliasoph and Lichterman 2003) created within the constraints and affordances of the platform. Ylilauta's group style, we argue, is defined by boundary work towards a constitutive outside of 'normies', and boundary work between 'elites' of the board and unwelcome newcomers. Lacking personal connections between participants, as the space is anonymous, these in-/out-group boundaries in fact constitute most of the *bonds* of the community that is Ylilauta. Deeply intertwined with this way of self-defining the community are the speech norms of self-reflexive irony and cynicism, which also act to separate the group from outsiders.

Anonymous group style

The category of 'normies' (people outside imageboard culture) is a central group boundary on Ylilauta – one of the most common memetic expressions on Ylilauta is 'huutista normoille' ('lulz at the normies'). The few bonds between users who do not know each other as individuals, only as an anonymous mass, and who are technically and culturally bound to not reveal too much of their own lives, arise from boundaries: shared ideas of who they are not. The constitutive outside of 'normies' makes politicization of group identity easy, since the out-group category can easily be given a political meaning: those who, because they do not understand and accept our worldview, enable politics we do not want, whether actively or passively. This definition of a common enemy gives birth to a political identity for the in-group:

> In many issues I agree with the green-left, however due to the feminazism and failed multiculturalism of the left I sympathize more with conservative forces at the moment. >>True Finns

Explicitly political enemy categories on Ylilauta include the 'green-left', the 'feminazis', the 'Social Justice Warriors' (SJWs) and the 'toletards' (a portmanteau of 'tolerant retard', the 'useful idiots' who make multiculturalism possible by their excessive 'tolerance' of difference) – all of which are quite familiar from Finnish right-wing activist discussion forums, showing clear cross-pollination between them and Ylilauta (Ylä-Anttila 2018; Ylä-Anttila et al 2019). In discussions critical of SJWs, political Ylilauta users explicitly and implicitly define an enemy category of people who have taken social justice ideology 'too far', obsessing over 'identity politics'. They are typically described as 'coddling' self-victimized minorities and ruining the moderate left. These are, of course, quite typical contemporary criticisms of parts of the left by right-wingers globally, echoed by some on the left as well (Nagle 2017). The following quote illustrates how many users identify broadly with the right and expect other users to share this identification, together with a common perception of 'our opponents':

> Yeah, the board is obviously biased towards the 'right wing', although even this 'right wing' isn't any kind of uniform bloc and it's also criticized from several different viewpoints. There are True Finn supporters here, reactionary conservatives, national socialists, Fennoman fascists, ecofascists, right-wing liberals etc. The whole bunch. And there's no consensus. And yeah, with this bias, people aren't that interested in criticizing let's say the violence perpetrated by the American extreme right. Why would they be? I don't give a shit even though I don't particularly support violence as a strategy. I'm more interested in the mistakes of our opponents.

In contrast to political articulations arising out of a personal register of grievances (such as 'incel' politics), which do exist on Ylilauta (Vainikka 2018), surprisingly many political discussions on Ylilauta deal with mainstream party politics, grand ideological narratives and political theory, often in a self-reflexive and rather deliberative fashion, discussions one might find at first-year political philosophy seminars. Consider the following quotation in which direct democracy is argued for:

> Referenda are best-suited for issues in which there is no right or wrong answer: the functioning of society is not significantly endangered whether gay marriage, marijuana or abortion is forbidden or allowed. Everyone understands moral issues and knows their opinion on them, but they're impossible to justify with objective argumentation. Thus, making collective opinion the law is as good a solution as any.

There is some debate (Phillips 2016) about whether anything said in a culture in which ironic trolling is central can or should be taken seriously. We have argued (Ylä-Anttila et al 2020) that rather than a dichotomy between 'serious' and 'insincere' political expressions, the situation is much more complex. This can be seen, for example, in discussions where users self-reflect on their irony:

> hitler and right-wing forcing is also a meme fucking newfag. It's a protest against the cancer spread by the mainstream media. Not everyone is a nazi fan. I might post just to fuck with people and to piss off the hippies.[3]

Apparently stepping out from behind the veil of irony to speak directly, this user confesses to another user (whom they also accuse of being a 'newfag' who does not understand the irony permeating the board) that far-right and Hitler posting is 'a meme' rather than an expression of being 'a nazi fan'. The purpose is simply 'to fuck with people' (on trolling, see Phillips [2016] on what she calls 'fuckery') and 'to piss off the hippies'. Perhaps on the surface this can be taken as a dismissal of politics, but it is 'hippies', a politically determined out-group, an enemy, that the user is 'fucking with'. And this 'fuckery' is 'a protest against the decay of the mainstream media', a grievance of the contemporary far right (the mainstream media as a puppet of the 'multiculturalist elite'). Here, 'Hitler posting' can be 'ironic' in the sense that it is not an endorsement of Nazism per se, maybe even considered nonpolitical by the authors, *while at the same time containing a right-wing political agenda.*

The political right used to always resent accusations of (proto-)fascism, but these online trolls revel in the accusations and make fun of them. 'Over the top' political posting (Nazi symbolism), in this spreading subculture, are often used to convey a political position that is somewhat similar to the surface-level interpretation (right-wing or at least against the left). Rather than ironic – the underlying interpretation being opposite of what is said on the surface – these expressions are hyperbolic: the difference of the literal meaning and the contextual intended meaning is of degree, not of kind. What matters is common enemies (see, for example, Lewis 2020). What decidedly does *not* matter is whether 'normies' accept your style of doing politics. If you can 'fuck with the normies' while making your point, all the better. After all, 'normies' and 'SJWs' are most hated by most Ylilauta users for their moralism, for example, being concerned about hate speech online and sometimes supporting limitations on free speech, which is directly oppositional to the beliefs of many Ylilauta users. This makes transgressive, cynical, irreverent mockery an effective political retort. This style may, of course, be adopted for nonpolitical reasons (to belong to the group, or just for 'the lulz'), but one cannot escape its political implications.

Conflicting politics

In our previous work on Ylilauta (Ylä-Anttila et al 2020), we conducted a mixed-methods analysis of hundreds of thousands of messages posted between 2012 and 2019 to look at general macrolevel trends in politics on Ylilauta. We noted that political talk on the board is often perhaps surprisingly analytical, abstract and philosophical in style, as in the following example:

> Perhaps I should have spoken with more care about the middle part of the 19th century, and instead of national freedom I should have said national uprising, which happened quite some time before they gained independence as a state. In any case, the brainless circus that today's

trogdolytes are calling 'ethnocentrism' has nothing to with neither 19th century nationalism nor 20th century regressive nationalism – it is just pure farce.

We estimated that around one tenth of all content on Ylilauta was political in nature and that political talk was interspersed within discussions of other topics (see Highfield 2016). By using computational techniques (see the Appendix and Ylä-Anttila et al 2020), we found that the most prominent topics of political discussions were party politics, capitalism, ideologies in general, race, political philosophy, human rights, immigration, the economy and sexual assault (in effect politicized as part of the discourse on immigration). Many of the far-right identity issues such as race, immigration and crime increased in popularity between 2014 and 2018 at the expense of discussions on the economy and political philosophy. Right-wing and even far-right ways of politicizing and doing society clearly gained saliency during this time.

However, this is not the whole story. The community is far from unanimous on anything, or simply an 'echo chamber' of like-minded people enforcing each other's beliefs. Many discussants were in fact highly critical of what they see as the recent far-right politicization. Such comments included: 'This / pol/ bullshit of the last few years has nothing to do with real chan culture', 'Being edgy has always been part of chan culture but this obvious alt-right infowar bullshit is new' and:

> This meme conservatism is only a few years old. Ylilauta just always wants to be edgy and countercultural, at this very moment Nazi roleplay is the thing you can use to separate yourself from the normies.

Thus, Ylilauta highlights an interesting paradox of online political communities, and especially ones that place value on openness and anonymity: at the same time, the culture, the ways of talking about politics, and the constructed enemies seem to create a cohesive radical right whole, and yet Ylilauta also contains poignant critiques against this way of doing society online. It remains to be seen whether the current politicization is a permanent change in online arenas or only a phase. The administrators, for their part, have become quite active in 'cleaning up' the most popular board, Random, of political discussions, to avoid the board becoming all about politics and preserve what they apparently feel is the true nonpolitical nature of the board – or perhaps to avoid accusations of hate speech, together with police attention, often resulting from anti-feminist or anti-immigration threads. Or even more cynically, to secure their continued ad revenue by making sure the board is not too controversial for companies to advertise on. In October 2020, there was a permanent, untypically sincere and official banner text at the top of the Random board: 'Let's keep political and societal discussions in the "Politics and society" board. Thank you!' At the same time, the administrators' commitment to what Colley and Moore (2020) have termed 'free-extremist' thinking (free-speech fundamentalism) seems to remain, at least considering by the board's main motto: 'Ylilauta – the spokesman for free speech.'

Conclusions

The most striking feature of Ylilauta culture, we argue, is the hierarchies that users construct between themselves and the 'normies', outsiders who do not understand their worldview, as well as between 'elite' users and 'newfags', 'moralfags' and other subgroups of users whom the 'higher-ups' consider unworthy. This boundary work, while sometimes 'merely' social (who are we and who are we not), also sometimes gives birth to at least a temporary, discursive 'community' of the like-minded, a political identity, a people with common enemies (Laclau 2007), we who understand certain inalienable truths about the world, and are 'enlightened', against a 'them' – hegemonic society at large.

This is a somewhat similar way of building a political subject than what is evident in conspiracy theorist communities, also fostered by online anonymous communication (Ylä-Anttila 2018; Ylä-Anttila et al 2019). Participants of political discussions on Ylilauta often share an opposition to feminism, multiculturalism and related 'social justice' advocacy – a position deeply interconnected with Ylilauta's transgressive, ironic, hyperbolic and cynical style of interaction: those who are easily offended should stay out. Whether the style comes first and the political positions second or the other way around likely differs from person to person: some users probably become politicized through this group style, while some who already have such political views join Ylilauta because it allows them to say things they could not elsewhere.

Whether this ends up being the 'final form' of doing politics on Ylilauta or not, such an extreme-right-leaning way of doing society now forms part of the political imaginary and repertoire of Finnish young people.

We have argued previously (Ylä-Anttila et al 2020), in line with Phillips (2013), that a possible interpretation of the 'take nothing seriously' group style of imageboards is that the participants, being mostly White straight men, occupy a societally privileged position, from which most forms of political mobilization are in fact status threats. A political belief that 'any challenges to the societal status quo are unnecessary, immoral or laughable' may follow quite naturally if the status quo is that you hold power. However, we also note that such an interpretation hinges on the understanding of Ylilauta users as 'privileged', which may also be questioned, considering that many of them in fact consider themselves marginalized (Vainikka 2018; Ylä-Anttila et al 2020).

Intentional cultural work by the 'alt-right' has harnessed the compatibility between 'internet culture' and the cultural right, as well as the self-perceived marginalization of some online subculture members (Hine et al 2017; Nagle 2017; Marwick and Caplan 2018; Lewis 2020; Phillips 2019) and, as such, the right-wing politicization of Ylilauta must be seen in its national and international context. Ylilauta has a segment of users who are active on global imageboards and translate the cultural conventions and ways of doing society for Finnish audiences. It also has a segment of users active on online right-wing activist sites, bringing that discourse in. And Ylilauta of course reflects broader trends in Finnish politics: the overall saliency of far-right themes, as well as a broader popularity of meme-based ways of doing society and presenting critique, a development in which Ylilauta has played its part.

Even more so than parties or movements, Ylilauta, as an imageboard, is composed of a diverse and constantly changing group of people (different every day), acting in diverse ways. One could argue that it is more of a platform than a group, although it has elements of both. We do not know who reads and posts on the anonymous platform that is Ylilauta at any one time, and anyone could join the discussions at any time. At the same time, if one would do so, one might find it hard to fit in without deep-seated cultural knowledge of how to act in the group that is Ylilauta. An anonymous online space may be, at the same time, a seedbed for harassment, a recruitment place for radicalism, an outlet of hate speech, a safe space of playful humour and camaraderie, a peer support and therapy group for marginalized people, and a democratic forum, all functions which may be participated in by the same or different users. And they are fertile ground for the creation of memes, speech norms and political strategies – cultural tools used to do politics both within the confines of online spaces, and increasingly also in the world at large.

The next chapter moves from the creation of an online community to a physical community, but continues to examine the question of what kind of culture is needed to create a community out of fleeting individuals.

7

Street Party: Urban Individualism and the Culture of Commitment

Maija Jokela

Introduction

What does collective civic action look like in the age of individualism? How does individualism change belonging to a collective, the common good it pursues and the kind of politics in which it engages? This chapter will explore these questions through a case study of an urban neighbourhood movement – the Kallio movement – that takes place in a gentrifying neighbourhood in Helsinki. The chapter is based on online and offline ethnography, interviews with ten Kallio movement participants, and a survey conducted during the Kallio Block Party (KBP), an annual street party organized by the movement, in 2019 (n = 327).

Since 2011, the first Saturday in August each year in the Helsinki district of Kallio has witnessed tens of thousands of (mainly) young people enjoying the last summer days by walking and dancing on streets usually occupied by cars, listening to music or sitting on the pavement or standing on top of a tram stop, perhaps having a drink or two (or more) at the KBP. The party is a free, one-day festival that is mostly focused on music with several different stages, ranging from techno to indie rock to punk. For a day, all traffic is closed, in good understanding and cooperation with the City of Helsinki, while people take over the streets to enjoy the drinks and food that is sold in food trucks and a programme that, in addition to music, has included for instance a children's area, a roller derby disco, a photo exhibition, skateboard ramps, spoken word stories about Kallio, poetry, short films, walls to paint graffiti on and so on. The event is organized by the Kallio movement: a loosely structured neighbourhood movement that, especially in contrast to the Finnish tradition of registered associations, wanted to emphasize the freedom of the movement's members and the movement itself. But how does a collective endeavour, such as organizing a block party, work out in practice with these individualistic tendencies?

Individualism is changing the cultural structures of doing society, as was already detailed in Chapter 1. In Finland, it is especially the tradition of (registered) associations that is being challenged by individualism. The crumbling of this associational form has raised concerns that ultimately boil down to loss of the common good-based public action and, in some accounts, 'the political' altogether. Increasing individualism in collective action is feared to turn that action into 'egoprojects' (Siisiäinen and Kankainen 2009: 101) and 'retreat into lifeworlds' with no connection to institutionalized politics (Blühdorn and Deflorian 2021: 260).

However, individualism and collectivism are not necessarily a dichotomy. Negotiating them within organizations creates different types of commitment cultures (Lichterman 1996). In addition, 'individualism' can mean several things, such as personalism that emphasizes the expression of a unique self (Lichterman 1996: 5–6), and some forms of individualism, as I claim in this chapter, are also new ways of keeping a collective effort together, such as by assigning responsibility to individuals. I also demonstrate that an idea of a common good may still be present despite the lack of connections to institutional politics or clear political goals. In the case of the Kallio movement, this common good was prefigurative and built through concrete doing and organizing events.

Therefore, this chapter shows, on the one hand, that individualism, in its many forms, can work as a basis for commonality, but on the other hand, it also illustrates that individualism does change and often also complicates matters. Individualism makes *belonging* to a collective less important and places emphasis on *doing* things. Individualized responsibility can be used as a tool to keep a collective effort up and running, but, as I demonstrate, with limitations. However, perhaps most importantly, individualism makes it difficult to formulate common values or a collective political stand.

The rearticulation of individualism and collectivism

While there is an individualizing tendency in the current Western societies, with collectivism and individualism pitched in opposition to one another (Craddock 2019: 83), collective action is still taking place. However, individualization is changing the way in which people come together to practise their citizenship: not only the issues that movements politicize, but also the ways in which people attach themselves to the movements and the forms that the movements take (for example, Johnston et al 1994; Melucci 1994; Lichterman 1996; Bennett and Segerberg 2013). The articulation between individuals and collectives are being remade and 'collectivistic collective action' is being replaced by 'individual collective action' (McFarland and Micheletti 2003).

How individualism is replacing or changing collective organizing has been discussed at least since 'new social movements' were coined at the turn of the 1980s (for example, Johnston et al 1994; Melucci 1994). Collective identities were no longer forged by class or locality, but instead the formation of a collective identity became one of the goals of new movements. This individualizing tendency has accelerated with social media and the 'digitally networked action' it affords (Bennett and Segerberg 2013). The logic of such action has been coined by Bennett and Segerberg (2012, 2013) as *connective action*, in distinction to collective action. Togetherness is no longer necessarily based on locality, similar structural position or strong ties like in old social movements and contrary to collective action in new social movements, in connective action people engage in movements *as individuals*, through personal and not collective interpretations and meaning making of values and symbols, such as memes, that are shared on social media platforms (Bennett and Segerberg 2013). Digitally networked activists only share 'minimum common denominators' (Milan 2019). This means that there is not necessarily an ideological unity and even if there are some shared values, they can carry very different meanings. Social media enables a flexible and inclusive form of togetherness, and the form of organizing resembles networks rather than organizations (Bennett and Segerberg 2013; Milan 2019: 122). For instance, membership and boundaries of the movements, who belongs and who does not is fuzzy, and there are often tensions between online and offline participation.

However, what is not sufficiently considered in the theorization of connective action is the understanding that as soon as there is a common goal among different people, there is a need to coordinate action (for example, Eliasoph and Lichterman 2003; Gerbaudo 2012; Baiocchi et al 2013; Kavada 2015). Also, any kind of collective organization always requires the building of some kind of understanding of who we are as a collective in order to function (for example, Eliasoph and Lichterman 2003; Thévenot 2007). In order to understand how it is people create togetherness, we need to look beyond technological affordances and investigate the actual practices in which people engage in these networks (Gerbaudo 2013; Kavada 2015; Uldam and Kaun 2019) that often blur online and offline realities.

Also, exactly what kind of collective cultural structures individualism (such as connective action) is changing varies from one political culture to another. In Finland, it is the cultural form of a registered association that is being challenged. Finland has been characterized as an 'association society' where the establishment of an associational sector went hand in hand with the building of the state and the nation. In an international perspective, the field of associations in Finland is 'exceptionally broad and diverse', and the political and societal role of associations has been greater than anywhere else (Siisiäinen and Kankainen 2009: 91, 122), associations carrying the representative task of portraying the will of the people (Alapuro 2005). Finland has a tradition of a national register of associations to which most associations apply once established. Even new social movements in the 1990s and the house-squatting movement in the 2000s had mostly, no matter how reluctantly, formed registered associations (for example, Siisiäinen 1998; Jokela 2017), but, as this chapter illustrates, this is no longer self-evident.[1]

Several meanings of individualism

Changes in the Finnish (and Nordic) field of civic action from registered associations to less formal movements, groups and projects has led to questions about the common good and the political in these formations. Their political and societal impact has been questioned as they lack the connection to formal politics that national associations used to have, and due to their operation in seemingly nonpolitical fields, they can be seen as 'ego projects' instead of 'places of the production of the collective good' (Siisiäinen and Kankainen 2009: 101) because they lack a 'deeper ideological foundation and change orientation' (Sivesind and Selle 2010: 98). As Dag Wollebæk, Bjarne Ibsen and Martti Siisiäinen (2010: 146) put it, 'the mainstream of associational development seems to follow the lines of bourgeois, seemingly non-political, non-commitment'. They continue: 'the new form of associations catering to individual interests and neighbourhood concerns are clearly compatible with increasing individualism' (Wollebæk et al 2010: 147).

These concerns are of course not limited to Finnish discussions, but they are also what the newest forms of civic action such as 'DIY urbanism' have been criticized for, since they are feared of being pierced by individualism and neoliberalism, leading to the 'erosion of the public' and a 'retreat into everyday practices and personal lifeworlds' (Finn 2014: 391; Blühdorn and Deflorian 2021: 260). As Alteri et al (2016: 719) put it: 'Is participation suffering a "neoliberal" transformation, merely becoming an individual tool to express individual concerns and to pursue individual interest? Or does networked individualism, challenging old structures and interaction modalities, allow people's uniqueness to converge in building a collective long-term project of political and social change?'

When discussing individualism, it is crucial to note, as Lichterman (1996) has pointed out and as Alteri (2016: 719) hints at, that individualism does not always mean the pursuit of individual interests, but can appear in the form of 'personalism' that emphasizes the *expression of a unique self*: 'It is the individualism women and men practice when they seek self-fulfilment and individualized expression, growth in personal development rather than growth in purely material well-being' (Lichterman 1996: 6). Personalism does not render collective organizing redundant, but it rearticulates the bonds between the groups' members by accentuating 'an individualized relationship to any such communities' (Lichterman 1996: 5–6). When individuals practising this civic style of personalism unite to form a collective, they are likely to engage in 'personalized politics', or 'personalized commitments', which Lichterman (1996) identifies prevalent in (US White, middle-class) grassroots activism since the 1960s and 1970s. '[P]ersonalized commitments ... both create and are sustained by a form of political community that emphasizes individual voice *without sacrificing the common good for private needs*' (Lichterman 1996: 4). In other words, within the civic style of personalized politics, individualism is compatible with the common good. This style relies on inspired individuals, who carry their 'portable political commitments' from one movement to another, thus fitting well with digitally networked activism that enables multiple belongings and that relies on 'flexible individual commitment'. 'Networking young citizens are ... are more likely to participate in horizontal or non-hierarchical networks; they are more project orientated; they reflexively engage in lifestyle politics; they are not dutiful but self-actualizing' (Loader et al 2014: 145).

This chapter takes the concepts of personalism and personalized politics as points of departure since at first sight, these strongly resonated with the culture of doing society in the Kallio movement. However, the chapter takes a step further in dissecting individualism in the movement with the help of pragmatist theorizing. Pragmatist theory takes no normative standpoint as to what a collective can or should be based on, and in the extreme, commonality can also be embedded in regime of engaging in a plan that is based on individual interests instead of a common good (Thévenot 2007, 2014; Luhtakallio and Tavory 2018). However, as I argue in this chapter, in practice this works in a collective only to a limited degree.

This chapter unfolds as follows. I will first present the Kallio movement and its form as a non-association and ideology of no ideologies. Then, I will look at how individualism, in the form of personalized commitment, was visible in the movement in its emphasis on doing instead of belonging. This is followed by an examination of personalism in action that shows how easy it is to slip from personalism that is motivated by common good to the pursuit of individual interests only. Lastly, I will illustrate how difficult it is to communicate a political message from these grounds.

The ideologically non-ideological Kallio movement
The Kallio Initiative

> A politically nonaligned community of people living, working and hanging out in and around the district of Kallio, Helsinki. The Initiative endeavours to influence the City's decision-making and policy-building, and to organize block parties.
>
> Kallio is the throbbing urban heart of Helsinki, a romanticized old working-class district not only known for its population of students, bohemians and beer-fond denizens, but also increasingly identified as an abode of families with young children at home and middle-class IT workers. There's room for everyone in Kallio!
>
> A vocal number of Nimbys also call Kallio home. These are individuals who have trouble abiding anything even slightly controversial in their immediate vicinity. A Nimby audibly complains about bread lines, noisy terraces, refugee reception centres, bar culture, boarding houses for the homeless, street festivals, graffiti and other so-called 'disruptions' in Kallio …
>
> Helsinki's official decision-making concerning Kallio is influenced by Kallio-seura (i.e. the Kallio Society), which has opposed such initiatives as the Hursti bread line and the reception centre on Kaarlenkatu …
>
> The city's bread lines have to be abolished not by relocating them out of sight and mind, but through improving social welfare.
>
> How about we form a kind of Kallio Initiative? It would be a loosely structured, politically nonaligned community of people living, working and hanging out in Kallio, and it would endeavour to influence the City's decision-making – and crucially, to arouse public discourse on matters concerning this neighbourhood. The Initiative could also put together some Kallio block parties, build on an already strong bedrock of solidarity and above all avoid congealing into a district society per se.
>
> Join this group, and let's get all sorts of things done together! (Kallio movement's Facebook page; original language is English)

Kallio is a former working-class district next to the city centre. Despite its gentrifying trajectory, Kallio has been and still is treasuring its romanticized working-class history and is considered to have a distinct character, where certain amount of restlessness – meaning usually drunkards – is a part of the district (Mäenpää 1991: 59, 78–79). Especially in relation to the racist and/or populist right that has risen in the 2010s, Kallio has become a symbol of the green-left 'tolerants' (see also Junnilainen 2019) as well as hipsters.

'Kallio Initiative' was launched on Facebook in 2011 as a response to plans by the City of Helsinki not to renew a rental contract with an organization 'Hursti's Help' (Hurstin apu) that distributes free food to people in need in Kallio, and was soon after renamed as the 'Kallio movement'. The pressure inserted by the Kallio movement online initiative led the City to rent another space for the organization and, after this success, the initiative also became a face-to-face movement. It was established in the beginning that the movement would not be a registered association with hierarchies or representatives and that the movement would remain independent of religion and party politics. The participants of the Kallio movement, and the organizers of the KBP, were nearly all-White, aged roughly 20–40, many of whom worked in the field of culture or in nongovernmental organizations (NGOs), marketing and communications.

The initiation of the Kallio movement was a part of a larger boom of new urban activism that took place in Helsinki at the beginning of the 2010s, including, for instance, Restaurant Day, which enabled everyone to set up a restaurant free from bureaucratic control (see Weijo et al 2018), urban and guerrilla gardening, and the temporary use of sites that were to be built in the near future. Instead of a broader political change, new urban activism pushed for the creation of an urban feel and a 'breaking free' from unnecessary bureaucratic regulations that restrict the creativity of individuals as well as a 'new we-spirit' and a sense of community based on individuals and voluntary belonging, with openness, surprise, enthusiasm and intrigue as the affectual register (Hernberg 2013). Therefore, in relation to their civic imagination, the Kallio movement falls into the category of building solidarity and community, instead of redistributing power and privilege or advancing problem solving and technical solutions.[2] As summed up in Chapter 1 of this book, 'civic imagination valuing solidarity and community see communities themselves as vehicles of change the world for the better, and therefore the task is to enhance the possibilities of these communities which then leads to positive outcomes'. This new wave of urban activism was in stark contrast to the previous wave of urban activism in Helsinki, such as the house squatting movement, that was clearly framed as anticapitalist and that centred around the anarchist/autonomous left (Jokela 2017).

From the very first meetings in 2011, it was clear to the participants that they wanted to avoid the cultural forms of both registered associations and radical activism: "Kallio movement is a mixed bunch of people that arranges things but is not an association but a community of people." This quote is from a KBP meeting where a more experienced participant in the Kallio movement explained to newcomers what the movement is. The distinction from traditional Finnish associations was a crucial pillar in the movement's self-understanding and the decision to not form a registered association was made in their first meeting. Instead, they aimed to build a community of free individuals[3]: "This is supposed to be *free civic action* and not this kind of association thing", as one of the participants, Katri, explained to me. Associations were interpreted in the Kallio movement as bureaucratic and hierarchical entities that suffocate individual freedom and where power and responsibilities fall on those with official positions. To Lilli, another activist, not being an association meant that "everyone is equal and everyone has the same freedom of speech". In addition, as can be seen in the originating statement given earlier, neighbourhood associations were considered to be powered by NIMBY (Not In My Back Yard) thinking – in other words, by being concerned over one's own interests. The Kallio movement wanted instead to oppose NIMBY-ism and create open and accessible urban space through its actions. Therefore, in contrast to the Finnish political tradition, *not* forming or joining the already-existing Kallio neighbourhood association was seen as a better way to reach a common good that extended beyond local apartment owners' interests.

Radical activism, on the other hand, was also off the table. This can be explained in a few ways. First, a more radical form of activism would have required a common political goal or an ideology, both of which the movement had opposed (in an ideological manner) since the beginning. Second, it was important to the movement from the beginning to do things by the book, since the participants strive to increase citizens' right to use city space without constraints of bureaucratic guidelines by showing that they could arrange events responsibly. This was why the main target of the Kallio movement was City bureaucrats instead of politicians. Therefore, in contrast to the previous wave of urban activism, activism was now perceived as a practice of 'active citizenship' and 'positive civil disobedience' (Hernberg 2013) instead of something disruptive to the structures of the society. Kallio movement resembles 'small-p politics' of Canadian eat-local initiatives that Kennedy et al (2018) researched. They discovered that the participants in these initiatives opted for unconventional small-p politics, such as organic farming, because unlike emotionally straining traditional activism, which has to deal with conflicts, it was comfortable, convivial and pragmatic: it made sense in the local setting of food markets. The avoidance of conflicts is also typical of community-oriented groups that aim for community solidarity rather than structural changes (Baiocchi et al 2013).

The avoidance of both of these cultural forms, associations and radical activism also have to do with how politics was understood in the movement, as party politics, which, like associations, were interpreted as pushing one's own interests instead of pursuing common good more broadly.[4] During my fieldwork, there was a Facebook discussion as to whether the Kallio movement should include associations as exhibitors in the festival area. Most discussants opted for not accepting their participation, for two reasons: first, because they perceived that the Kallio movement was already sending out a message through the KBP, one that communicated the movement's values; and, second, since organizing an event would be enough to promote their values. However, it was also because institutional politics should be kept out. As one of the discussants said: "It would be great if even for one day a year there would be one area free of politics and agendas in this country."

This comment is revealing as it conflates institutional politics with 'agendas'. It resembles the idea of 'dirty politics' (see, for example, Baiocchi et al 2013: 1–3), where politics is not about the common good, but about particular 'agendas' and interests, which in the Finnish context have traditionally been represented by associations. According to this logic, serving the (universal) common good is better accomplished by staying clear of institutional political organizations.

However, another important reason why politics and ideologies were avoided in the Kallio movement was because of the high value placed on individualism. As was noted earlier, this was already visible in the movement's difficulty in forming a collective opinion and taking a representative stand.

Organizing the KBP has almost since the beginning been the Kallio movement's most visible way of organizing. The Block Party closes off streets in one part of Kallio for one day, in cooperation with the City of Helsinki and with all the required permits, to hold a free, noncommercial culture festival. The movement has also, for instance, rented out urban gardening crates and arranged occasional soup kitchens. It is an example of prefigurative politics, hands-on action where means become as important as goals and where activists live the alternative, desired future in the here and now (see Yates 2015).

Even though it reads in the statement given earlier that 'the Initiative endeavours to influence the City's decision-making and policy-building', this was never the movement's main form of action. The movement was often contacted by the City officials, as part of the official participatory process, about issues concerning Kallio, such as a construction of an electric structure, but at least during my fieldwork, these requests were often not responded to. Partly this was because it was difficult for the movement to formulate a collective statement – they lacked the tools and perhaps even a civic imagination for that. The participants' civic imagination was pierced by individualism, and this was also visible in their ideas of representation:

> 'I mean if we take a stand on some [City of Helsinki planning matter], then it's pretty much like "Kallio movement says", like "us in Kallio movement", can one say this?' (Julia)

It was clear that individualism was valued highly in the Kallio movement and ideas about individualism pierced the movement's practices throughout. In what follows, I will delve deeper in the different forms of individualism, beginning from the movement participant's ideas of belonging – or not belonging – in the Kallio movement.

Personalized commitments: doing and not belonging

One aspect where individualism became visible in the Kallio movement was how it emphasized doing over belonging. In the Finnish civil society, that has historically relied on registered associations, passive *belonging* to an association, either formally or informally, has been as important as *doing* (Stenius 2010: 46–47) and associations have provided identities for their members. In contrast, and in the spirit of personalized politics, Kallio movement participants did not want "associational activities for associational activities' sake." They didn't want to sit in meetings and keep the movement alive just for its own sake, but prioritized doing. As the founder of the Kallio movement stated in an interview magazine interview for the Green Party magazine (*Vihreä lanka*, 27 April 2012): 'Younger generations no longer want to commit themselves to parties or organizations but want to do concrete things.'

This is of course logical: if the purpose of civic action is to organize events, only belonging and not doing becomes almost impossible. In the Kallio movement, doing was emphasized together with the freedom to decide whether they want to do anything at all. Susanna noted: "We can actually agree that right now no one wants to arrange anything, and we'll call it quits. That people aren't committed to absolutely anything."

This freedom was also considered an asset in recruiting new participants. During the second year of my fieldwork, there was a fear of there not being enough people organizing the festival and those involved were afraid that the entire festival was at risk as a result. Participants in a general meeting in June discussed how to get more people involved and someone said they should emphasize the freedom involved in the organizing: 'Don't be afraid, you don't have to tie yourself up. You're not gonna have to sell your granny!'

With busy people and a buffet of grassroots projects to choose from, it was an asset to keep participation light and the binding ties loose (Lichterman 1996, 2005: 68). This motivating was considered important, especially since the Kallio movement was not clearly a political movement that participants would be passionate about, as one of the original members, Janne, told me:

> 'The doing of this kind of light action is not such a strong motivation, this kind of nonpolitical action is rarely a thing like "I'm going to do this at any cost". In some cases, a political revolution might be a thing people are ready to sacrifice their entire lives for, but street parties, not so often.'

In the civic style of personalized politics, individuals are the 'locus of political efficacy', and they carry their 'portable' political commitments within themselves, to be practised in everyday life as well as in different organizations. A prime example from the portable political (or civic) commitment is the plug-in volunteers that come to organize the KBP, without taking part in the overall Kallio movement. The following quote is from an interview with Markku, who was an active organizer of the KBP during my fieldwork but was not interested in Kallio movement: "If we're in a movement it doesn't mean anything to me, what matters is what it does. And Block Party is doing, Kallio movement is not doing."

Markku had previously been involved in the Finnish Occupy movement and an economic reform movement, yet he assigned no meaning to belonging to a movement; he simply carried his political commitments within himself from one movement to another, looking for opportunities to do things. This plug-in type of activism does not require or necessarily build durable ties between activists (Lichterman 2005).

Separating the wheat from the chaff: individual responsibility and the culture of commitment

But how does a collective that emphasizes individual freedom function in practice, or at least well enough to be able to organize a festival with tens of thousands of attendees? As Lichterman (1996: 35) notes, 'people acting as citizens or community members would assign each other different sorts of responsibilities, and create different bonds of obligation, than those that are available when people assume political agency resides in a personal self without strong institutional grounding'. For instance, the form of registered associations ensures that key responsibilities are named, as usually there is at least a chair, a secretary and a treasurer. Therefore, if there are no commitment *structures*, groups need to build a *culture of commitment*. In the Kallio movement, one of the means to ensure commitment was to emphasize the participants' individual responsibilities for the organizing process. This is in line with personalized commitment, since this civic style emphasizes individual responsibility instead of or in addition to collective responsibility (Lichterman 1996).

Paradoxically, the binding ties of responsibility were stronger when taking part in organizing the KBP than in the Kallio movement. In the movement, one was free, for instance, to take a year off from arranging the block party and come back the next year, but once one got involved in the organizing of the festival, which always meant one had at least some individual responsibility for a given task, it was considered a faux pas to drop the ball. More specifically, taking part in organizing the festival meant taking up individual responsibility. Although often I would hear the phrase 'doing together' that was at the core of the KBP 'way of doing', in practice it was often individuals who did the doing as 'solo gigs' (see Lichterman

1996: 55, 2005: 82): they contacted sponsors, recruited volunteers from their networks, and worked on the KBP website.

In a general meeting in early June, two months prior to the festival, Alex, who had taken the lead in the overall organizing of the KBP in the spring of 2018, asked the meeting attendees to raise their hands if they were going to be in town in July – the most popular month to go on holiday, often away from the city, and also the month when the organizing of the KBP was most intense as it was only a month or less away from the festival. About half of the people present raised their hands, some of them hesitantly, to which Alex commented: "Some of the hands are halfway up." He said: "Take a good look at this bunch, the party is done in July when there will be half the amount of people [from the meeting] around. Everyone has to take care of their slot. That's when you separate the wheat from the chaff."

During the meeting, Alex had emphasized several times that this was a chance to do a big event and the most important thing was to take responsibility and carry it. In a hierarchical association, responsibilities are visible as each position is appointed and the tasks and responsibilities of each position are listed and known to all. In a seemingly nonhierarchical organization, responsibility does not disappear, it is just hazier and less visible – although it is at times made visible in occasions such as the one given previously, where those who had their hands up proved themselves to be the responsible and committed ones.

In the next general meeting ten days later, Alex repeated that the people who wanted to take part in organizing the festival must "catch the ball" and that responsibilities were now being carried by too few shoulders: "The party isn't done just by going to meetings." Belonging to the movement was not enough, not even by going to meetings: one had to be ready to take on practical tasks. Tuuli told me how she was annoyed when there were new people coming to organize the festival who did not know the organizing principles of the event – that there was (in principle) no money involved and that nothing came for free:[5] "I was annoyed by those who asked, 'what's the budget for our stage' … And I was just like, well come to the group and make that money … and if you're not up to doing the work, then you don't need to come at all."

This emphasis on individual doing and individual responsibilities that the preceding quotes from Alex and Tuuli illustrate portrays as a rather draconian requirement for participation. A passive belonging to an association (Stenius 2010: 46–47) has, at least in part, been replaced by the requirement to take individual responsibility and do one's part. This was true at least in Kallio movement whose explicit purpose was to arrange events and not to sit in meetings and, for instance, discuss topical issues in the Kallio area. However, what Alex's and Tuuli's comments also reveal is that individual responsibilities were used as a tool to advance a collective effort. In other words, individualism in this case did not equal 'ego projects' (Siisiäinen and Kankainen 2009: 101), nor were individual tools used to express individual concerns or to pursue individual interest (Alteri et al 2016: 719), contrary to what some writers have feared.

However, assigning responsibility to individuals had its limits. Since the movement was not a registered association and thus not a legal person, each year someone had to sign the necessary event application to the City of Helsinki under their own name, ultimately taking the responsibility of the entire event. Unsurprisingly, it was difficult to find a person willing to take on that risk, even if the volunteer was jokingly offered a bottle of good whisky and the experienced organizers ensured that the entire group of organizers would share the responsibility if something unexpected occurred. Another problem each year was the lack of a collective bank account. This meant that the money involved in the organizing process would have to be circulated, for instance, through one of the participants' companies or a personal bank account. The KBP became bigger and more popular each year, which meant growing responsibilities and greater monetary and safety risks. For these reasons, during my fieldwork, the Kallio movement eventually opted for the pragmatic solution of forming a registered association – the Block Party Association – in order to become a legal entity. A lot of discursive work (see Kuukkanen 2018: 110) had to be done within the movement about this being just a practical solution and not a game changer in any way. This goes to prove, first, the strength of the cultural form of registered associations and, second, the practical limitations of individual collective action.

Thus far, we have been safely within the civic styles of personalism and personalized commitments as described by Lichterman (1996). Next, however, we will take a look at how easy it is to slip from this style to the pursuit of individual interests – something that is not looked upon kindly in the style of personalized commitment.

Slipping from individualized expression to the pursuit of individual interests

In the spirit of personalized commitment, the Kallio movement wanted to promote itself as a platform for realizing individual aspirations. The arranging of the KBP in particular needed aspiring individuals, 'self-starters' (Lichterman 1996: 50) to come up with new ideas for the programme, since there was no producer and the programme was not curated by the movement. The following excerpt is from the meeting where the Block Party Association was founded. The meeting attendees are discussing how the association should be introduced to the KBP organizing team, leading to discussions about what the KBP is about:

Alex: There should be three questions over a [local bar's] pint of beer and people would think them through in small groups: why is KBP organized? Why are you organizing it? Attaching it to your biggest dream, what is it?

Leena: 'Which dream would you like to realize through KBP?' We should raise the spirit that you can aim for big things.

The organizing of the growing KBP meant that there was a need for a lot of volunteers and, as was noted earlier, the core members were not sure how to motivate them. Therefore, in addition to "not having to tie oneself up", another motivator was the possibility for the volunteers to pursue their individual dreams through the KBP. As the festival had grown in size and become a well-known event, it had attracted a lot of people outside the movement who were interested in advancing their careers in culture and music. The movement members were aware of this and instead of categorically denying this self-interested motivation, they clearly thought to make the most of it, since it meant having enough volunteers, who in addition were skilful and motivated. In the meeting, the participants even talked about providing volunteers with a certificate. However, as I will shortly explain, this kind of flirting with individual interests came at a price.

It is also crucial to note here that being motivated by individual interests was acceptable only as long as it was possible to harness and attach these interests to the overall framework and values of the KBP and the Kallio movement. In general, this combining was seamless, as in Tuuli's reply to what motivates her to take part in organizing the KBP: "Obviously to take over the streets. And I mean, from the point of view from organizing, I'm interested in getting to know likeminded people. And then the fact that one can learn things and affect the kind of spirit of this area." In her reply, individual motivations such as getting to know likeminded people and learning things, is intermingled with more common good-type motivations, such as taking over the streets (from cars to pedestrians) and affecting the spirit of the Kallio area. However, at times the tension between individual interests and the common good became visible, especially when collective responsibility and common values were threatened and had to be discussed in the meetings. This tension was also brought up in the interviews, as I will explain next.

One of the continuous struggles in organizing the KBP was to get enough people to do the more tedious tasks. The more obvious target and source of passion, and an outlet for the required dreams, was to organize a stage or some other programme for the festival, such as 'spoken word', 'stories from Kallio' or perhaps a karaoke of famous movie citations (all of these were part of the KBP programme in 2019). It was never a problem to get enough people to organize the stages and programme content, but there was a constant worry about getting enough people to take care of the less visible and glamorous infrastructure such as communications, arranging portable toilets and trash cans for the festival area, contacting sponsors, arranging the necessary permits from the City, contacting the City public transportation office and so on. Especially in interviews conducted with the participants, many brought up how some – especially semi-professional and aspiring producers or musicians – only came to "strum the guitar" or produce a stage without attending the general meetings or taking collective responsibility for common tasks such as cleaning the site after the party:

> '[The people who produce a stage] have to understand – the processes behind the event that take up more work. And it does cause irritation that there is supposed to be someone present from each stage in the general meeting [and there aren't]. It does annoy the people [who go to the meetings] that [some people say that] "I want to set up a stage" and then you don't attend the meetings. Because everything is tied up to everything, then if you're not involved and don't know anything that's going on, you can't just come and build the stage.'

As this quote succinctly illustrates, selfish interests – the regime of engaging in a plan – were used when there was a need to denounce others (see Moody and Thévenot 2000: 285). Individual pursuit of self-interest was juxtaposed, first, with collective responsibility, as in the preceding quote: setting up a stage of one's own without taking part in the larger collective effort.

Individual interests were also contrasted with the values of the Kallio movement. Elina told me why she had been involved in the Kallio movement and organizing the KBP for such a long time – six years at the time of the interview:

> 'Somehow it becomes such a close and important thing, and you also want to maintain the original values and principles, to see that they're still there. No matter how much pressure there is because Kallio Block Party attracts a lot of commercial actors and the kind of people who want to prove themselves, then, somehow it's OK, it's fine, but it's still a part of the Kallio movement and it ... you can't ... I mean there's sometimes the need to really have a conversation but, I'm not alone in defending it, it really is an important value.'

In summary, it was 'somehow OK' to have plug-in volunteers who 'want to prove themselves' and commercial actors, whose main logic of action is to make profit, but not at the cost of losing sight of the fact that the KBP was a part of the Kallio movement that had certain values and principles. In other words, individual interests were tolerated because there was a need for creatives and doers, but there was a constant worry over the preservation of the common good. However, what common good the KBP pursued or what the values of the Kallio movement were was not clear to everyone, especially the newcomers. This is a question to which I will turn next.

Challenging prefigurative politics

> 'It's not just "hey, let's have a party!" even though parties are also nice. But it's also about transforming the urban space into something kind of magical or at least into something else. It becomes seen as something a little bit different and there's this kind of sense of community and openness. It's everyone's celebration and not a gated event one has to pay to get into.' (Maria)

Thus far, we have explored the different forms of individualism within Kallio movement and established that individualism does not always equal selfishness. The pursuit of a common good is possible for groups that practise personalized commitment. However, there are limitations to the individual responsibility and how easy it is for these civic groups to slip into selfish motivations. Therefore, while the different forms of individualism are clearly changing the way in which collective action is structured, collective action and pursuing, and serving the common good is still possible in the age of individualism. But what exactly was the common good in the Kallio movement? As noted earlier, the movement displayed a civic imagination of building communities, in which conflicts are avoided. Is it possible to maintain and communicate a certain common good if ideologies are ideologically opposed, and an open discussion on values is not an option, especially since conflict and disagreements are a prerequisite for understanding politics (Mouffe 2005; Eranti and Meriluoto 2023)?

The participants of the Kallio movement had a dual understanding of politics. 'Politics' was generally understood as party politics, and displaying any symbols of institutional politics such as political parties as well as associations were explicitly opposed within the movement, even though many of the participants voted and were members of an association or even a political youth organization, and a few participants had even taken part in an electoral campaign. However, on a few occasions I would hear someone say that the Kallio movement was not political and then quickly add "well, not party political". While the Kallio movement denounced institutional politics, many with whom I talked thought that the movement was still political or at least had political elements. In particular, the original or long-time members (and the committed new ones) of the movement assigned political meanings to the movement and the KBP. This confusing double standard of being politically and ideologically nonaligned while at the same time claiming that the Kallio movement had always been political was rooted in different understandings of 'political'. In addition, these political meanings were hardly ever explicitly communicated, but were left to individual interpretations.

The main idea in the Kallio movement was to organize events in Kallio instead of advocating or protesting. These events were meant to follow and communicate the values of the movement, such as making urban space accessible for everyone. Therefore, even though the Kallio movement had declared itself to be politically and ideologically nonaligned, it *prefigured* values that were part of the left-green movement family, or practised nondiscursive, 'hands-on' social critique (Pyyhtinen and Lehtonen 2023). The following excerpt, from the Kallio movement's soup kitchen (called the 'block kitchen') that was a part of Night of the Homeless in October 2017, exemplifies Kallio movement's prefiguration. The block kitchen served apple pie and coffee for free (or with a voluntary donation to the block kitchen) in one of the several tents set up by civic organizations:

Customer:	So, what exactly is this block kitchen?
Sauli:	Well, we cook food together and then distribute it.
Customer:	So there's no ideology behind it?
Sauli:	Well, the ideology is kind of precisely it …
Matias (under his breath, from the back of the tent):	Well, it's Left Green.

This excerpt illustrates two things: first, it confirms that many of the movement participants perceived the movement to be part of a left-green alliance; but, second, it shows that this ideology was practical in nature. There were certain values that guided the movement's actions, but these values ought not be vocalized but practised, and the KBP was the movement's main tool for this. The following citation further clarifies this point: "We're doing a good, free urban festival for people according to the values of the Kallio movement and I don't think we need to do any greater deeds than that. The *values are visible in our action* and … are that way communicated also to the city residents."

Nobody ever really explained to me why the values should not be explicitly and verbally communicated, but it was a part of the movement's civic imagination of avoiding politics and ideologies, and therefore also avoiding conflicts, and of reluctance of forming political coalitions since, as Julia said, "one should remember that one speaks on one's own behalf … since everyone has their own opinion".[6] This kind of reasoning is typical to connective action where participants engage as individuals, through personal and not collective interpretations of values (Bennett and Segerberg 2013;

Milan 2019: 122). As this section shows, communicating the values of the Kallio movement both internally and externally was difficult, since they could not be vocalized, making the attempt of prefigurative politics unsuccessful.

The idea of the KBP was to celebrate the Kallio area and further build a sense of community that was open to all, but also to close off streets from cars for one day to show an alternative reality, or to "transform the urban space into something kind of magical", as Maria stated previously. As already noted, there were a lot of new volunteers each year organizing the festival. Some of these volunteers knew the festival, but not the movement or its values directing the event, or that there were any values to begin with – that KBP was not just a cool, free festival. It didn't help that here was no manual for organizing the Block Party, and hardly any induction to newcomers. This was, again, a way to preserve the absolute creative freedom of individuals and the movement, like Susanna said: "there should be no code of conduct, like 'this is how you organize Kallio Block Party'. It should be left really open and free, so that this can be anything".

Thus, on the one hand, in a thoroughly individualistic spirit, the organizing of the KBP should be 'really open and free', but on the other hand, the festival should still prefigure certain meanings and values of the Kallio movement, which were not explained to the newcomers. Unsurprisingly, these contradictory guidelines led to confusion. For instance, the principle of occupying urban space was not clear to all first-timers. In a meeting in 2018, a newcomer, Eija, asked: "Do we need to block a road? 'Block party' as in block a road?" Someone replied: "Otherwise it's just a festival, a concert. The idea is that we want to do this one thing, have people partying on the street." Another principle that was not known to all the participants was that of noncommerciality, which became evident during my fieldwork.[7] In KBP 2019, there was a stage for a national breakdance competition that was part of a global competition, sponsored by the energy drink Red Bull. The organizers of the stage were clearly unaware of the noncommerciality principle since the morning of the KBP revealed a terrifying sight: the Red Bull logo was painted on the dance stage, as big as the stage itself. The other block party organizers were horrified at the sight, but it was too late to do anything about it. Since Red Bull was the sponsor, it was apparently part of the competition concept to have the logo in sight, and it was too late to cancel the entire competition, which was a part of the festival programme (or rather, no one wanted to take such drastic action).

It was this mishap in particular that led to the clarification of the KBP values. However, this clarification was not an open discussion, but a practical Facebook vote. The Block Party Association, consisting mainly of experienced Kallio movement members and block party organizers, made a preliminary list of values, or the "quiet ethos" of the Kallio movement, as the original member posting the poll phrased it, and posted them on Kallio movement's private Facebook page. Members of the movement could then vote for the five most important ones out of the suggested options.⁸ The fact that the values of the movement were chosen through a Facebook vote instead of discussion in a face-to-face meeting is illustrative of: first, a social media era where the affordances of platforms such as Facebook guide civic groups' actions; and, second, the Kallio movement's ethos, which respected each individual's opinions and avoided conflicts that may have resulted from an open discussion. Voting is in fact the prototypical way to solve issues within the regime of engaging in a plan (Eranti 2018: 15), since while there may (or may not) be an open discussion before a referendum, the act of voting itself is an individualistic act (Adut 2018: 72). The purpose of the voting of the values itself also had a practical tone to it, as it was mainly supposed to make the organizing of the KBP smoother and more consistent, and to minimize 'slippings' from, for instance, the principle of noncommerciality (such as the infamous Red Bull stage).

If the values behind the event were not clear to even all the organizers, were they 'read' by the visitors to the KBP? In order to find out, I conducted, with the help of Tampere University sociology students, a survey of attendees (n= 327). A vast majority (73 per cent) were aware that the KBP was arranged by the Kallio movement as a volunteer effort (80 per cent) and also the majority (65 per cent) of respondents said they knew the movement's values. However, only less than a quarter (22 per cent) of respondents wanted to name these values in the survey's open-ended question about them.⁹ Most respondents said they had come to the KBP that day to have a good time and only few of them mentioned more ideological reasons such as "I'm interested in taking over urban spaces in a non-commercial way". But on the other hand, the more ideological motivations to attend the KBP were not absent either: they could be read off the event if one wanted to. As one of the respondents said outright, there was an *implicit* assumption that the KBP was for "liberal and open-minded people" if one wanted to see it. This is perhaps the key to unlocking the message in the KBP. The event caters to those wanting a good, free party as well as those who have more ideological or political motivations.

Civic imagination of building communities, which avoids conflicts, is suitable when driving for cultural change (Kennedy et al 2019), whereas structural and political changes require dealing with conflicts – both within the group as political goals are deliberated and outside the group in communicating the values or goals of the group. The Kallio movement's prefigurative politics were vague and ultimately individualistic: if an organizer or attendee of the KBP wanted to perceive the event as political, it was possible – but so was a completely opposite interpretation.

Conclusions

This chapter has established that individualism can take several, different forms and that it does not necessarily mean a threat to collective organizing – in fact, individualism, in the form of individual responsibility, can add another (even if rather draconian) tool to the toolkit of collective action. (However, I also presented that coordinating a collective effort had its limits: when it proved too difficult to get one individual to sign bureaucratic papers in their own names and to manage monetary flow through someone's personal bank account, it became reasonable to form the registered Block Party Association.) By utilizing the concept of personalism, this chapter has demonstrated that the kind of individualism that the Kallio movement cherished was one that emphasizes the creativity and freedom of individuals. Therefore, on the one hand, increasing individualism does not automatically mean 'ego projects' (Siisiäinen and Kankainen 2009: 101), as has been the concern in the literature on the newest forms of civic action both in Finland and beyond. This is one reply to Alteri's (2016: 719) question whether participation is becoming merely 'an individual tool to express individual concerns and to pursue individual interest'.

On the other hand, it is clear that individualism is changing collective action in several ways. As Lichterman notes, 'organizational stability' based on personalism *is* more fragile and a 'tenuous accomplishment' compared to established organizations (Lichterman 1996: 35). One of the most evident manifestations of this fragility is the emphasis of doing instead of belonging to a movement, which meant that long-time commitment to the movement was not something that was expected of the members. Instead, the movement did expect that one would commit, in the short term, to the action. However, perhaps more importantly, I have presented this fragility of togetherness in the Kallio movement as a slipping from personalism towards the pursuit of individual interests, and as losing sight of the common good, which in the Kallio movement was to prefigure the movement's values through their action. Since there were a lot of newcomers and plug-in volunteers, and no open discussion on the common values of the movement, what exactly this common goal was was not clear to everyone, leading to a mixed bag of messages, such as a huge Red Bull logo in an event that was meant to look like a noncommercial event. Hence, unsurprisingly, the Kallio movement's prefiguration, in terms of communicating its values to the partygoers, was not very successful. Therefore, concerns over 'the erosion of the public' and of the political in collective action penetrated by individualism (Finn 2014: 391; Siisiäinen and Kankainen 2009: 101; Sivesind and Selle 2010: 98; Wollebæk et al 2010: 146) are, perhaps, reasonable after all. The fragility of commonality in the Kallio movement makes it rational to ask whether it is possible to maintain a political coalition (whether this political is prefigurative or more institutional in nature) in a group that values individualism as much as the Kallio movement does.

8

Reluctant Rebels: The New Climate Movement and the Individual Activists

Maija Jokela, Jenni Kettunen and Eeva Luhtakallio

Introduction

Any research aiming at covering the current political concerns of young people is eventually bound to land on the climate movement. The current climate movements, global and internationally connected through social media and personal contacts between activists, are an unavoidable object in the quest of understanding youth political engagements. While also studied in abundance from various angles, young people taking part in the climate movement deepen our understanding of the final key piece to the puzzle of doing society presented in the previous chapter: what do the dynamics of individualism and collectivism look like at the heart of today's social movement activism? How does engagement in the context of the climate movement unfold and what kinds of civic imagination tools are in use in the biggest political mobilizer of young people today?

In this chapter, the climate movement is represented by one of its most well-known current branches: the Extinction Rebellion (XR). XR is an international movement established in 2018 in the UK and is nowadays active in 45 countries. It describes itself as 'an international movement that uses non-violent civil disobedience in an attempt to halt mass extinction and minimize the risk of social collapse' (Extinction Rebellion 2020). In Finland, XR[1] organized its first actions in November 2018. Today, the movement has local groups in more than ten cities, and countless groups organized around specific themes or participant profiles, such as professions (Scientist Rebellion and Doctors for Extinction Rebellion), some focused on engaging people on different topics such as 'artivism' (combining art and activism), anti-discrimination or social media outreach. XR's goal is to 'create a mass movement able to disrupt the daily life so that it's impossible for anyone to ignore the climate and environmental crisis' (XR 2022). In a relatively short period of time, XR has been able to mobilize hundreds of people onto the streets of Helsinki. With its often-spectacular civil disobedient approach, including sit-ins on busy and central streets, the movement has gained significant attention in the news media, as well as both loud criticism and strong support on social media, especially on Twitter and Instagram (Luhtakallio and Meriluoto 2020; Nykänen et al 2023).

The analysis in this chapter is based on 17 interviews of young climate activists, aged between 14 and 30, supported by ethnographic data on XR (see also Malafaia et al 2024).[2] The interviewees have been engaged in the Finnish chapter of XR and/or in climate strikes. In the interviews, we have asked the climate activists about their actions in the movements and motivations to take part, but also their perception of the place of activism in their lives and in the society, as well as their future expectations.

XR has been criticized for its 'politically 'neutral' framing of climate change' (de Moor et al 2020: 619), as well as for using scientific argumentation as its primary style of claims making. As our analysis also shows, climate activism operates on a short timespan where changes in climate politics are expected urgently, within the next few years. This affects both how the activists commit to action and what they expect from activism, from the others and from themselves. It may be that climate activism therefore differs from many other forms and causes of activism, such as feminist or LGBTQ+ activism, in terms of its temporality that should be considered when analysing the movement(s). Moreover, as our analysis will further elaborate, this general temporal aspect has deep consequences to the coordination of the movement, as well as the activists' individual reasoning thereon. Namely, this feature plays a key role in making the movements emphasize *project* as their primary mode of action, coordinated much with an engagement in a plan (Thévenot 2007), and driven by a dominant understanding of the movement context as a community of *interest* in which individuals come together to claim a preferable direction for politics, as opposed to a community of identity in which the internal logic is centred around a common affinity (Lichterman 2020; see also Eranti 2018). Surely, the movements make claims about climate justice and carry other clear markers of the repertoire of public justification (Luhtakallio and Ylä-Anttila 2023), but the unfolding activist practices and activists' sense making thereof are more varied. The climate movement, hence, can be portrayed rather as a frictioned set of scenes than a unified entity (see Lichterman 2020).

Furthermore, talking with the XR participants, we met a band of *reluctant* activists. The interviewees' accounts often suggest that the urgency of climate change had *forced* them to take action even if they would have much rather spent their time doing something else. The somewhat uneasy picture that unfolds is one where the movement, in its mission statements, places great emphasis and value on the collective – by way, for instance, of its (standardized) practices of group debriefing, to which we will return later on – but where, simultaneously, the activists were ultimately individuals engaging in personalized politics (see Lichterman 1996).

Living an activist life seemed to be a source of hardships for many. The activists found it difficult to combine climate activism to what they considered to be 'normal everyday life', such as having a job or kids or doing travels, because of both ideological and practical reasons. In the XR activists' talk, climate activism appeared as a demanding, even overwhelming form of political action, considered impossible to combine with having a family or a regular job.

Up against these recurrent accounts, the uneasiness of the combination of elements at play in the action of participating in the climate movement shows itself in full. Indeed, doing society by engaging in the climate movement is full of contradictions: it is lonely while extremely, even intimately collective at times, it patterns into ultimately individualistic – and often accordingly burdensome – responsibilities and choices, while creating a culture of nearly compulsory sharing of personal emotions and accounts of one's experiences. We argue that the culture of doing society unfolding among the climate activists portrays a difficult hybrid between a strong engagement in a plan, and coordination anchored in familiarity that is subordinate to the plan and project at hand – not a community of identity with a long line of history together or a strong shared affinity of sorts (see Chapter 1; Thévenot 2007; Lichterman 2020).

In the previous chapter, the concept of prefiguration was shown to be one of the (unsuccessful) coordination devices of the Kallio movement. Prefiguration refers to 'attempted construction of alternative or utopian social relations in the present' (Yates 2014: 1), where the means of action are as valuable as the goals. In the literature on recent climate activism, prefiguration (or prefigurative politics) has been identified as the most characteristic feature of XR in particular, including its dramatic performances such as the Blood brigade, die-ins and roadblocks, but also for its practices of self-care and the heavy emphasis on the wellbeing of the members by way of debriefing sessions after protest acts, as well as mindfulness practices (Westwell and Bunting 2020; Sauerborn 2022). These practices, and the seemingly important role of the community, are well in line with what has been written about the new climate activism and new social movements in general (Yates 2014; Blühdorn and Deflorian 2021). However, as Sauerborn (2022) has also suggested, we argue that while the emphasis on the wellbeing of the members and the community-building practices of the movement can quickly be interpreted as prefiguration, this is a misrecognition, since these practices, as we will show, do not have intrinsic value, but are instead means of efficiently reaching the political goal. Asking how are the climate activists doing society, what kind of civic imagination guides their meaning making and what are the dominant repertoires for coordinating engagements in the movement settings, we show that both the spectacular performances and practices of care – and, ultimately, the community – have little value in themselves, but are rather means to an end, which is to ensure efficient activism with a clear and urgent political goal of changing climate politics.

Reluctant activists

> '*It's kind of like, I wouldn't want to be an activist, but I guess I just have to be* ... *But if it looks like I can no longer change it to a direction that is more worthwhile, then I'm off doing something else.*' (Solja)

> 'Because most of us probably wouldn't want to do this for real, I mean sure the friends and new acquaintances mean a lot, but I'm pretty sure that quite many would rather spend that time to something else, be it your work or hobbies or family or anything, even travelling. *I hope that XR will not exist in five years, that we're not needed, we can do whatever we want on our free time, and I don't have to spend another second to this.*' (Carita)

The first thing that struck us in the interviews was how reluctantly the activists described their activism, expressing in various ways that it was something they didn't really want to do, but had to. They described activism as taking up the responsibility that adults and politicians were not taking. They did not do activism because it was fun, exciting or cool – on the contrary, they told us they would much rather spend their free time doing something completely different. This rhetoric was also repeated in the wider public when one of the most well-known public figures of young climate activists in Finland, 16-year-old Atte Ahokas, said in a Finnish public broadcasting YLE interview in 2019: "We young people shouldn't be here [in a demonstration]. It is not our job to tell how this crisis will be solved. We are here to demand that adults begin to do their jobs."

One can think of different interpretations of this recurring pattern of talk. Perhaps it was a way for the activists to emphasize the urgency of climate change and remind us all that not enough is done to prevent it, and that it would not be the task of young people to prevent the disaster (see Huttunen 2021). This is what the activists, such as Atte, cited earlier, as well as many of our interviewees, were also literally saying. However, there also emerges a strong emphasis on individual responsibility and a portrait of activism as a functional tool to solve a concrete problem – in other words, not activism that is valuable as such, but a means to an end. This departs from how leftist critique and activism is usually seen: as action and aspirations of change aimed at the structures of the society (Zivi 2012: 74; Hansen 2019: 300). This finding is in line with the critique to which XR has been subjected of being apolitical and 'not critical enough' (for example, de Moor et al 2020). For instance, only one of the informants described XR as a leftist movement and hoped that the movement could also take a stand on other issues in addition to climate change.

What do these accounts disclose about the civic imagination that is prevalent among the activists? Perhaps surprisingly, climate activists mainly shared a civic imagination of problem solving (Baiocchi et al 2014; Chapter 3). Solja, who was quoted earlier, said that if XR seemed like it was no longer worthwhile, they would leave the movement. Similarly, Carita even said they hoped XR no longer existed in five years. This would mean that XR was no longer needed since climate politics would have taken a leap forward, and that they could use their spare time to do something else. Their activism, even though collective in appearance, was not centred around the collective as it is described to be, for instance, in the case of civic imagination that promotes community solidarity. But it was not an imagination focusing on dismantling societal structures of inequality either. For these activists, XR was meant, simply, to be a short-term medium to reach a specific target, and once that target was met, they would be off doing something 'completely different'. Ultimately, as Sauerborn (2022: 461) notes about XR, '[t]he individual constitutes the rebellion's foundation'.

The interview theme that, nonetheless, brought up a prefigurative dimension was connected to the activists' plans and hopes for future life, which was imagined as one on which climate change had had a profound effect. None of the activists appeared to see themselves able *or* willing to lead a normal life with a regular job. This was partly because of XR taking up so much time and energy in the present, but partly also because the activists did not want to be 'cogs in a wheel'. In a sense, prefiguration among the XR activists was negative: not taking part in the current system and disillusioned about the future one. There seemed to be no collective utopias in XR and, ultimately, each individual was left to their own devices to cope with the (current and future) 'toxic system'.

Next, we look at how the XR activists approached activism individualistically. Even though the collective was important in motivating the activists and helping them cope with emotions related to activism and climate change, we argue that belonging to the activist community had no intrinsic value in a prefigurative sense, but a mere instrumental value instead.

Collective as a tool

The activists had a strongly individualistic repertoire of talk. Rose's following description of their activism (also quoted in the preface of this book) is especially illustrative of this. When we asked how they ended up in XR, they said they did not see themself as really part of the movement, despite being very active in it:

> 'I'm just not really involved with XR. That's part of it, but I'm mostly affiliated with Withdraw the CAP, which is the common agricultural policy, and looking to withdraw it … I've also been protesting every week by myself outside my library … And then being involved in many different campaigns. But I don't know, I wouldn't say that I'm particularly affiliated with any group. *I'm more like a personal entity for climate justice* is how I've always described it.'

When we asked if they see themself as being part of XR after five years, Rose replied: "I'm not, I'm part of all movements and I'm part of none of them." Strikingly, it was not that they felt unable to fit into the movements or communities, but this was not even something they wanted: "I just could never see myself being so attached to one particular group. That's not something I ever want for myself."

Rose's descriptions of their activism as "a personal entity for climate justice" and not wanting to belong to any particular activist group resonate strongly with the cultural repertoire of belonging Lichterman (1996) has coined as *personalized politics*, whereby commitment to civic action is sporadic and short term. Members of groups that practise personalized politics commit to certain causes instead of groups and carry their 'portable political commitments' from one group to another. As in the Kallio movement (see Chapter 7), this patterned civic style of personalism also emerged in our XR interview data. Personalism was an elemental part of the culture of doing society in both these movements.

This repertoire of personalized politics became evident especially when we asked the informants whether they would be part of XR in five years or not. Nearly all the interviewees replied that they didn't know or that probably they would not be. Most obviously, they all hoped that there would be a leap for the better in climate politics and therefore XR would no longer be needed, at least not in its current form. Five years seemed like a long time within the urgent timeframe of climate change, but also in the temporality of the activists' personal belonging, as Maria explained:

> 'I don't know if in five years XR will be a thing where I will be involved anymore, or where my growth and road will take me, and is

it the same place where XR is going, because it keeps changing and growing all the time and I'm also changing all the time. It could be that we change in different directions.'

Personalized politics is based on individualized expression and the pursuit of personal development (Lichterman 1996) – very much the kind of individualism reflected in the preceding quote. It was impossible for Maria to know whether they would still be in XR in the future since they didn't know where their personal development would take them.

However, there was also another kind of meaning to individualism that the informants displayed in the interviews, one that assigned a heavy responsibility to the individuals. As with the block party in Chapter 7, our data reveal an emphasis on individual *doing*, not merely taking part, or, like Rose said: "I'm a big believer in doing and *not just advocating*" and continued "you know you can only change something if you go out there and do it". This emphasis on individual doing is, indeed, equally point of similarity to Kallio movement.

Also, Solja, when they talked about what made acting in XR meaningful for them, said they thought that as an individual they "could always do more" – *themself*, not XR as a collective. This idea of individualistic doing put a lot of pressure on the activists. They were battling to change the course of a looming eco-disaster – as individuals. As Maria said, "if I don't do this, then I won't have a chance to impact in anything else either, because our civilization will be destroyed". The activists were carrying the weight of the world on their shoulders. They felt they were supposed to give to activism everything they could "squeeze" out of themselves, as Solja put it, and continued, "maybe it's about using all of one's potential". Giving 100 per cent to activism while still blaming oneself for not doing enough was the harsh equation many interviewees used to describe their engagement to the movement. Solja reflected about the moment the declaration of climate emergency XR demanded was turned down:

'It's been a concrete cause of bewilderment, confusion, frustration, but somehow, to me it's like OK, *I wasn't doing enough*, as if it was about me not mobilizing all my near and dear ones and so the climate emergency was not declared. I mean, I give myself too much credit, it's not about that, but somehow, *it's easier to blame oneself than a collective movement.*'

In other words, even though there was a collective structure, a motivating community one could (and partly even had to) share one's emotions with, ultimately the activists felt alone in fighting climate change. This is the flipside of the importance personalized politics places on individuals, those (brave, anxious and often burned-out) "personal entities for climate justice", in Rose's words.

Despite both the Kallio movement and XR emphasizing individual doing, XR as a movement made more effort to coordinate action collectively. In contrast to the Kallio movement, in XR there was an explicit political goal and new members were trained in how to take part in the movement's actions. However, as we showed earlier, despite these efforts, a sense of individual responsibility dominated the activists' thinking. The XR activists display the power of the individualistic tools perhaps the most illustratively because of this controversy: they are involved in a collective movement, yet there is no escaping the context in which the liberal grammar is considered normal action (Thévenot 2007), and personalized politics has for a long time been the dominant civic style in progressive movements (Lichterman 1996).

Nonetheless, and as another contradiction of sorts, the interviewees also emphasized making new, like-minded friends, networking and being a part of a community through joining XR. Nearly all the informants mentioned that the community had become very important and motivating to them, especially the movement's affinity groups that Carita, for instance, described as 'safe havens'. The affinity groups comprise 8–12 people and 'are autonomous to do the actions they want to in the name of XR'.[3] These groups are part of the 'regenerative culture' of the model structure set by the international XR that emphasizes caring and sharing feelings, and has institutionalized in the movement practices such as mindfulness (see Westwell and Bunting 2020; Sauerborn 2022). Regenerative culture and a caring community were repeatedly brought up in our material, as well as a kind of longing for a community, now found in XR. This community was emotional and felt close, as Maria explains:

> 'After an action, we debrief our experiences with the affinity group or some other group, for instance Summer Rebellion that was an intense and heavy experience, and we debriefed with our affinity group and we all just cried for being so tired and because it had been so emotional. We were all somehow really happy and then I felt really close to my entire affinity group, because we were able to share really personal things even though we only knew each other through XR … We were all really sensitive and open together and it's really safe and comforting … it's moments like these that are really important in XR.'

The intense experience of taking part in civil disobedience and the following practice of debriefing those experiences in one's affinity group created an emotional community that felt "safe and comforting", as Maria said. This description resonates with the regime of familiar attachments (Thévenot 2007, 2020; see also the regime of 'the presence' in Brahy et al 2023) and it seems to be in a stark contrast to how the same activists describe their nonbelonging to the collective and the burden of acting as an individual. However, this paradox becomes understandable if the community is seen, as Sauerborn (2022) has suggested, as an instrumental resource for efficient political activism. In other words, the regime of familiar attachments and the emphasis on presence were subordinate to the regime of engaging in a plan. The emotional support that the community provided, with practices such as debriefing and mediation, enabled a particularly demanding and time- and energy-consuming form of activism – one that included civil disobedience, an intense and emotional form of protest that in XR was carefully organized beforehand and, as shown earlier, was treated with designated debriefing practices afterwards (Nykänen et al 2023: 300). In addition, the felt urgency and importance of climate action increased the activists' stress.

Sauerborn (2022) claims in a rather cynical approach that XR's regenerative culture with its institutionalized 'emotion programmes' can be seen as instruments that establish order in a decentralized movement: 'Caring for the feelings of others becomes an instrument of activism. However, this is not merely an act of charity, but rather a functionalist, self-preserving, and order-maintaining moment for the movement and ultimately of the political issue behind it' (Sauerborn 2022: 465). This means-to-an-end thinking potentially also plays a part in why none of the activists saw themselves as part of the movement after five years. Carita stated: "The purpose is not to build up XR as an association or a movement, instead we want to have this rebellion, we want the rebellion to succeed, and then we can start doing something else."

Next, related to individual doing, we discuss how the activists valued efficiency in their activism.

Optimizing political protest

A key word to describe the XR activists' views on activism could be 'optimizing'. In the previous section, we established that, for the activists, the community was a functional tool to deal emotional stress with. Similarly, Sauerborn (2022: 464) notes how the XR practices to reduce stress and burnout were a means to an end: '[A political] subject is supposed to submit to the imperative of emotional self-care, not only for improved well-being, but also to increase and *optimize the political effectiveness of their protest.*' Efficiency was the yardstick against which action in XR or other collectives was measured, and the value of efficiency did not require further explanation. Therefore, paradoxically, while XR is critical of the 'toxic system' responsible for climate change, the activists of the movement are not free from the demand of efficient individuals. For instance, when we asked why they decided to take part in XR, Joel said "action in XR feels like the most efficient means". Again, contrary to prefigurative politics, activism was not considered to have intrinsic value, but its value was measured in terms of what it achieves. Rose, who declared themself a "believer in doing", further talked about how activism is useless unless it is able to achieve something:

> '[A]ctivism is a bit useless. I don't want to use really crass words here, but sometimes … the activism scene is a bit circle jerky … I mean, it's a very tight knit circle. Activism is just a bit performative for other climate activists. It's no good protesting every week, if the only people that's going to see it are your four followers, who were also your friends and also in the same group. Like, who are you influencing? *You have to actually achieve something with your activism*, if you want to get somewhere.'

In Rose's opinion, it was no use preaching to other activists who were already on one's side; instead, one should reach people outside the activist clique. While reaching new and especially powerful audiences is a crucial goal for most activism, a prefigurative approach would also ascribe value to the group of activists of which one is part. *Belonging* to an activist community (or *building* that community) had no prefigurative value in XR; the only value of activism was in efficient and individual doing.

Joel, like others we interviewed, compared XR to traditional associations like Greenpeace and deemed XR to be "more efficient" because of its nonhierarchical structure. However, another interviewee, Matias, would have wanted more hierarchical structures to increase the movement's efficiency. For them, especially the meetings felt often long and heavy because there were always newcomers who had to be briefed. Maria, too, described the meetings as frustrating and inefficient:

> 'Meetings are often frustrating and slow and decision-making is really slow because there are so many people, and the discussion is so thorough. Sometimes I feel like nothing goes anywhere in the meetings and you can't get into the direct action, you just have to sit somewhere and discuss the same things all over again, sometimes it feels like I'm not up to this. It's unmotivating and it's heavy … It's somehow numbing but luckily meetings usually lead to action, so that finally all the frustration is unleashed, when you have the euphoric action experience.'

The emphasis on efficiency, and on doing, in XR surfaced in how Maria disliked the slow and frustrating meetings, but tolerated them since they usually led to actions that they described as "euphoric". Many of the informants mentioned acts of civil disobedience as the spice of XR action; as Maria put it, "maybe civil disobedience has, for myself, always been an empowering and even rewarding part of this action". It is noteworthy that despite Maria describing action as "euphoric", in general, acts of civil disobedience were justified by their efficiency, measured in terms of media visibility:

> 'I no longer think protesting is enough, there has to be civil disobedience for something like XR to be more impactful. I mean there are plenty of other ways of influencing than civil disobedience, but in this environmental thing the necessity of civil disobedience has only gotten stronger ... I mean it seems like there's been so many times that you get more attention when you're being civil disobedient.' (Liisi)

However, Maria's description of the "euphoric action experience" also fits well with XR's regenerative culture and its emphasis of emotions. The focus of this regenerative culture is on the *feelings* of individuals, used as a resource, 'fuel' (Sauerborn 2022: 460–461) for such demanding form of activism that, ultimately, strives for efficiency:

> 'Actions are these kinds of moments, you get such a strong feeling and adrenaline and everything and somehow it's such an impressive experience to be in an action ... It's perhaps difficult to describe, but it's a really strong experience that creates a strong feeling in your body.' (Maria)

In other words, feelings and efficiency were not juxtaposed, but instead, feelings were harnessed to serve a political purpose, in this case to get more attention by engaging in direct, disobedient action.

In addition to efficiency, a closely related, and almost consequential, topic that emerged from the data was talk about exhaustion. It is noteworthy that practically every activist we met with mentioned, without us asking, health-related issues, mental health, having enough energy, coping or exhaustion. Good physical and mental health and having enough (time and) energy were listed as resources for activism, either on an abstract level or through the activists' own experiences, some of which included experiences of burnout. The activists' talk about health is illustrative of XR as a movement, with its emphasis on the wellbeing of its members, as well as of the current society and its exhaustion epidemic (see also Chapters 3 and 5). On the one hand, talk about health and energy as something that needs to be taken into consideration when taking part in activism is a 'natural' element of an 'exhaustion culture' in which talk about exhaustion is constant and normalized. This culture is clearly visible in XR through its 'recurring narrative' of how 'the ongoing and strenuous battle against climate change involves the great danger of burnout' that must be avoided 'through deliberate and strategic stress reduction' such as debriefing, yoga and mindfulness practices (Sauerborn 2022: 466). Our interviewees also mentioned that XR perceives exhaustion as part of the toxic culture that has produced the environmental crisis. Thus, if exhaustion, and the prevention thereof, is regularly discussed in the movement, it is no coincidence the activists bring up the topic in the interviews.

However, an exhaustion culture is obviously not only talk but also embodied experiences, as Esko demonstrates: "If I was at home and had nothing to do, I would just lay in bed and take a nap because I was just so exhausted, all the schoolwork and the climate things, there was just no energy left after that."

Solja describes the time they joined XR: "I was somehow really busy at that time, as always." Activism was often yet another factor that may lead to exhaustion, as Esko's quote illustrates. If activists feel they have individual responsibility for the fate of the planet, and that they are trying to steer away from a disaster by optimizing their activism into as efficient as possible, is it any wonder they wear out? As Solja noted earlier, XR activism was about "using all of one's potential". Maria echoed Solja's approach to activism, saying they had an "all or nothing attitude", which had led them to experience burnout:

> 'If I get excited about something ... I get into it intensively and I have this all or nothing attitude. That's why, when I joined XR, after a few months my calendars were already completely filled with XR things ... and I was like this is great and meaningful, I get so much out of this, this is what I want to do all the time. Then, in the summer I had a wake-up call when I realized that I'm completely burnt out ...
>
> I've also heard from others that [XR] has swept them away pretty intensively and that quite many get a really bad 'fomo' [fear of missing out] if they think that they should rest but there's that action. If you don't go there, you get a ... a feeling that *nothing* [*else*] *I do could be more valuable than this*. When you think about the climate crisis, that is such as huge thing and it took me, I actually had to be in a point where my body and mind wouldn't function to realize that I can't go on like this, I have to do other things, too and I have to rest and I can't give so much of myself to this as I would like.'

This section has demonstrated how demanding a form of participation XR was considered to be. Next, we show how at least partly because of this, the activists considered it impossible to combine activism with living a 'normal life'.

Giving up 'normal life'

> '[M]aybe acting in XR has somehow opened my eyes, like I'm not sure if I'll apply for studies, I've left it kind of in the background ...

or I've given them up, *giving up is the right word, for instance dreams of travelling … You give up your own time and dreams about, like, career and stuff.* Like a decent income and things like that, because there's simply no time for that.' (Solja)

Several informants pondered their past, present and future life course in the interviews, and what these recollections, plans and hopes revealed was that they considered it impossible to lead a life that could be called 'normal'. The activists compared their current or imagined future lives with what they considered as nonactivists' lives, including travelling, a family and a steady job, and distanced themselves from this image. There seemed to be an insolvable contradiction between being an XR activist and (leading a) 'normal' life. In particular, giving up travelling and working full-time or building a career were recurrent themes upon which the activists reflected. While it was not a timely matter to any of the activists, they also doubted the feasibility of leading a family life *and* being an XR activist. Both time and energy scarcity and ideological choices portrayed as reasons. In this section, we look more closely into these reasonings that made the activists' future lives seem challenging and bleak.

First, as the previous section illustrated, acting in XR was considered so demanding and time- and energy-consuming that it seemed impossible to combine activism with building one's career or working full-time, or at least this combination would not be wise considering one's health and coping with one's life. Carita noted: "[XR] has taken a lot of time so I haven't been able to concentrate, like develop my career, even now I'm working part-time and the big plus side is the fact that I can do XR and not be completely dead every day, because I can do it as a kind of a second job."

The exhaustion talk of the previous section was also present when the activists talked about their current life situations and future plans. Like Carita (quoted earlier), many XR activists weighed up their physical and emotional resources when they estimated what else they could do besides activism. Matias talked about a medical doctor who was very active in XR. They wondered how it was possible for them to be so active in the movement despite having such a challenging job. Matias, who worked in a nongovernmental organization (NGO), said that they was able to scroll XR social media discussions during their workday, but doubted this would be possible for a doctor: "I mean they clearly are coping on top of a job like that … You must have a situation in your life, like not have a family, I mean children of your own … It must take a lot of coping."

Matias mentions 'coping' twice: clearly in their view, combining a demanding job with activism was only possible for those (rare) people who have enough energy for both – and who do not have children.

In the climate activists' thinking, activism came first, then the rest. Here, however, the age of the participants played a role, so that activists from the higher end of the age spectrum like Matias, who was 30 years old, were mildly concerned about how being a visible part of XR would affect their reputation and future employment. Matias also reflected on this prioritization more than the teenagers:

'At some point in the meeting I … caught myself thinking, hey, I'm a 30 year-old adult, I should be thinking my own personal life's next big steps at 8 o'clock in the evening, but here I am exercising with people ten years younger than myself, how we, you know, this is the kind of personal pondering and a kind of frustration.'

Elisabeth, aged 22, who worked as an artist, also said they questioned their choice of using their time:

'I do think about it all the time that darn, all my other colleagues are for instance developing their practices and going forward with their work and … I myself am using so much time for [XR], so occasionally I'm like what do I get out of this?'

These personal struggles expressed in the interviews bring to light how it was *not always self-evident* for the activists to prioritize the greater collective good over their own life plans and career moves, but that this choice was something they had to justify to themselves (and probably to others too). Self-sacrificing activism is not easy in a world that expects and rewards life plans based on individual interests (see Thévenot 2007). This is also in stark contrast to the block party activists discussed in Chapter 7, who were openly motivated by self-actualization and whose recruitment as volunteers had to be done by connecting the action to the individual dreams of the participants.

What made the activists choose activism over their career then? After reflecting on what they "got out of" activism, Elisabeth continued by saying: "But it's not about what I get out of this and it's good to remember that *this is just such an urgent thing*, that if nothing is done to [climate change], then it will get too bad."

Simply, climate change was too urgent and threatening to be sidelined. This brings us to the second reason the informants gave to the impossibility of combining their activism with normal life – namely, their values. Climate activists did not want to be part of the toxic system by working for it, and obviously travelling was off-limits for them. As Rose stated straight out when we asked them what they thought was the best way to take part in society: "I don't really want to be a member of society, so that's a bit of an odd question." Solja echoed this in their own way:

> 'It's about values and what kind of person one wants to be and what kind of world one wants to build ... So, if you don't want to, like, produce destruction and live as some weird cog in the wheel, then it's pretty challenging to tread this kind of non-conventional path.'

For these young people, work was not the primary medium for self-expression or fulfilment of dreams. Instead, what working life offered was exhaustion and burnout, and being part of a system advancing climate change. In the previous section, we described how the things that could be expected to have intrinsic value, such as the activist community and self-care practices, were instead functional means to ends, contrary to prefigurative politics. However, this unwillingness to be a "a cog in a wheel" was very much prefigurative in nature. This made the activists' future life, "treading a nonconventional path" seem challenging. In the opening quote of this section, Solja said they would have to give up dreams of a decent income – quite a drastic vision for the future which in some sense puts these activists in a similar position to the marginalized young people in Chapter 5 (this comparison continues in Chapter 9).

Some of the informants had difficulties in thinking about the future in general, especially when we asked where they saw themselves in five years.[4] There emerged no clear dreams or utopias, whether individual or collective. Liisi was struggling with their mental health and said: "When I don't know how my life will be even in a month, it's difficult to say anything about five years." Maria had great difficulty in responding the question of where they saw XR in five years and whether they saw themself as part of the movement then: "Five years, wait a second. [A 24-second pause] This is a really difficult question."

Thus far, we have looked at the place of activism in the participants' lives and established that doing society as a climate activist was a heavy-duty form of civic engagement patterned around fastidious temporalities, merciless demands of individual action and responsibility, and coping practices that seemed to emphasize community, but did not manage to build one in a lasting sense.

Next, we look at how the activists perceived the place and role of activism in society and their perceptions of institutionalized politics.

'Slow and stuffy' political structures in need of repair

XR, both internationally and in Finland, has become known for its performative acts of civil disobedience. However, the movement has at the same time been criticized for being apolitical, since its political goals are based on science, not political vocabulary (de Moor et al 2020). XR is moderate in terms of 'ideology', focusing *only* on climate issues instead of challenging the political or capitalist regime (de Moor et al 2020; Erpyleva and Luhtakallio 2023) and a 'no blame' policy that holds the 'toxic system' responsible for climate change and not individuals, politicians or companies (in contrast to, for example, Greenpeace's policy of explicitly blaming companies for polluting). These insights from previous research resonate with our data where XR activists appear more like reformists than revolutionaries, and where even the acts of civil disobedience are justified with efficiency.

Reformist characteristics unfolded, for instance, in that while the XR activists we interviewed said to have hardly any belief left in institutionalized politics, most of them participated in it nevertheless by voting (if they were of age) and by membership of registered associations (which they, like the Kallio movement activists in Chapter 7, considered to be a part of institutionalized politics). Some even belonged to political youth organizations. These young people were not the ones to shatter the foundations of the society, and even civil disobedience was justified with 'reasonable' arguments and efficiency. Efficiency was understood as media visibility and changing people's attitudes, as well as directly influencing a political change.

The XR activists, when asked how they understood 'the society' and 'societal participation', gave replies illustrative of the reformative rather than revolutionary character of the movement. For instance, Maria said that society is "a construction that is broken". Seventeen-year-old Eero described the society as "maybe even subconsciously accepted structures that being inside a society consists of" and continued: "I don't really even see a reason to question, or I wouldn't think to question something like the schooling system, because it just is. I mean it's not like a law of nature, but still people just think that it just is."

Quite logically then, societal participation for Eero was "accepting these structures and wanting to mould them from within". This viewpoint aligns with the critique XR has received of its lack of profound analysis and rejection of capitalist structures.

Solja echoed the reformative approach when they described XR's actions and compared them to how much more radical the movement could be: "XR just sits on the road, I mean it's not very radical when the alternative would be to start smashing places and destroying infrastructure, or do cyberattacks and things like that."

The question of where XR would be in five years, from a societal perspective, provided responses in which many saw two optional futures. If XR still existed in five years, without having achieved changes in climate politics, the movement would have become either more legitimate with more participants or, alternatively, it or some other new movement would have become more radical. This kind of turn was not necessarily what the activists hoped for, but, rather, it was seen as an unfortunate necessity in the event that climate politics were lagging. For instance, Eero said they was "even a bit worried that XR will be replaced by some significantly more radical movement".

It is interesting to note that despite this moderate, almost legalistic approach to society, many activists named civil disobedience as the best way to change things, at least in relation to climate change, since it was considered the best way to gain media visibility. "I mean it seems like there's been so many times that you get more attention when you're being civil disobedient", said Liisi. Even Eero, who had very modest viewpoints about changing society, said that in order to best get their voice heard in a societal matter, they would opt for nonviolent civil disobedience. Such a combination of radical means of action and not-so-radical goals differs from how progressive, relatively radical leftist movements are usually thought of: as wanting to change the society throughout, often in a prefigurative manner (for example, Yates 2014). From another viewpoint, it also differs from what was going on in Kallio movement (see Chapter 7), where the prefigurative idea of a community following its values was an important, albeit often a failing part of the organizing process of the street party.

However, the previous sections of this chapter help us to make sense of this paradox. The strict demands of efficiency resulted in the choice of civil disobedience as the method, which was portrayed almost as a calculated, means-to-an-end device. Maria said that they thought XR was a good way to make an impact and that their "opinion is based strongly on research and history of what kind of civil movements have been able to make a change". This justification echoes XR's widely used scientific – or, in pragmatic terms, industrial – argumentation (see Chapter 3; de Moor et al 2020; Luhtakallio and Ylä-Anttila 2023). In addition, civil disobedience in XR was not spontaneous or about smashing windows; rather, it was an almost stoic practice, in relation to which everyone taking part should undergo training.

For the activists in XR, activism was as much about visibility in the media, generating reactions on social media and changing people's attitudes than it was about advocating. Matias noted that: "I take part in [XR's] actions because I want to be involved in arousing people's reactions, questioning established ways of thinking and acting and maybe even challenge them, or challenge this current democratic decision-making system."

Perhaps raising reactions in and through media and social media felt a more approachable and efficient way to drive change than institutional channels. Institutionalized politics was, for these activists, a far-away sphere, an old remnant of something that perhaps used to work in the past, but one that is no longer able to deal with current life-threatening crises such as the eco-disaster:

'What speaks to me in XR is that this kind of an extraparliamentary actor can pose the question whether representative democracy is efficient enough medium to solve threats like climate crisis or should there be solutions like citizens' assemblies. I think broadening democracy is a really interesting theme and something I genuinely believe in … *Securing one's position as a member of parliament* shouldn't affect what kind of decisions are made.' (Matias)

Matias thus believed in democracy, but not in representative democracy. Other interviewees also talked about how they had lost their belief in institutionalized politics. One reason to be doubtful of representative democracy is the idea of 'dirty politics' (Baiocchi et al 2014; see also Chapter 7), where politicians are thought to only advance their own interests. Another reason for the disbelief was the *inefficiency* of the democratic system. Solja, for instance, said how voting and the democratic system "[f]eels like it's slow and stuffy and somehow incapable, toothless in many things. Somehow I hope the political structures could be renewed".

Activism, then, felt like a more active and efficient approach to solving climate change than taking part in institutionalized politics. Solja said that a part of why they wanted to participate in XR was the feeling that they could really affect things, both inside and outside the movement: "Even though they teach at school that political participation is primarily voting and consuming, I find it really disactivating."

However, it is noteworthy that despite this loss of belief, the activists did not opt out of politics altogether or become more radical. Instead, like Solja said: "Yeah, I myself definitely vote even though it feels like it makes no difference".

With the kind of culture of doing society the XR activists were forging through their actions, they stood, in many ways, in the middle ground between other actors we have encountered in the chapters of this book. They were reluctant and disillusioned, much like the marginalized youth of Chapter 5, and yet echoed the trust in their own capabilities of influencing and having a voice of the young electoral candidates of Chapter 3. They were disappointed in the toxic system, but did not think themselves to be completely excluded from it, and were not imagining actions that would foundationally disrupt the society. They did not want to be cogs in the wheel, but did not feel like the system pushed them out – it was their own choice, and not being part had its limits. In the end, many of them were bending towards 'the system' rather than further away from it.

These activists were superparticipants who were ready to use all legitimate channels to drive political change (even if the legitimacy of XR is debatable and debated). For instance, 17-year-old Eero said that in particular, acting in XR gave them an "equal chance to make an impact" since they was still too young to vote. In addition to XR, they said they also took part in "a more party political, more traditional associational activities". Climate change was at the time the only reason many of the activists wanted to participate societally, but practically everyone said they hoped to continue participating in some form or other in the future. Twenty-three-year old Maria noted: "XR is the first step in finding my own pathway of making an impact ... I'm excited that my journey in civic engagement is really only beginning and I still have a lot of new things ahead of me, so many opportunities which direction to go to."

In this respect, the activists stood in the middle ground between their colleagues in the Kallio movement and the young aspiring politicians. The former were also fueled by dreams and excitement of what they themselves could do via the movement and the Block Party, while many of the latter saw politics similarly as a vehicle to expand their own opportunities. However, two important differences emerge. The Kallio movement activists, although they were individual dreamers, never hoped for their movement to make itself dispensable. They were happily part of a relatively stable and lasting project, even if not everybody kept volunteering year after year. In addition, their quest for individual fulfilment was clearly different – they wanted to do fun and cool things and develop their skills, while the XR activists were in it for a livable planet (also for themselves to live on). The electoral candidates, for their part, calculated their opportunities with varying degrees of cynicism, but nonetheless gratefully accepted the collective support of the party machinery.

Finally, what distinguished the climate activists' form of engaging most clearly from the forms fostered by most other actors in this book was the essential urgency of the climate issue. As the direct opposite to, say, the sardonic deriders on Ylilauta in Chapter 6, these activists were dead serious. Their plans and dreams about the future were conditioned by the climate crisis. Should they not succeed in their efforts, there would be nothing left, no future to build. Climate activism presents a unique case since the future engagements of the activists, as well as the future of the planet and humankind in general, were described as directly dependent on the success or failure of climate politics. The activists were doing society in an emergency.

In the concluding section, we elaborate on this argument by returning in a more in-depth manner to the comparison of the actors in the climate and Kallio movements already touched upon previously.

Conclusion

Civic imagination 'comes alive' in civic groups that are the manifestations of different kinds of civic imaginations (Baiocchi et al 2014: 23). What does collective civic action look like in the age of individualism? What do civic groups' civic imaginations look like in terms of collectivism and individualism, and what kinds of cultures of doing society thus emerge?

Despite their very different goals, the Kallio movement and XR share many similarities. The participants in these groups display a longing for a community, but they join these communities in individualistic terms, along the lines of personalized politics, with individuals carrying their 'portable political commitments' from an engagement to another (Lichterman 1996: 35).

From the point of view of Finnish civil society, one of the most significant similarities between the two movements is the fact that both perceive traditional associations as part of institutionalized politics, and therefore something to be avoided. In both movements, this avoidance had to do with their emphasis on *individual doing*, in which the collective was only a supporting structure. "This is not about associational activities for associational activities' sake", said a member of the Kallio movement. Compare this comment to a quote from XR's presentation: "The purpose is not to prop Extinction Rebellion as an association or a movement, instead we want to have this rebellion, then the rebellion succeeds, and we can start doing something else."

Similarly, in both movements, institutionalized politics was not seen as a sphere where the common good is forged, but where politicians pursue their individual interests. However, despite their lack of trust and belief in politics and associations, the activists of both movements – those over 18 – voted, some belonged to political parties, and many were members of different associations. Activists in either of these groups were not challengers of the status quo, not even the XR activists with their civil disobedience practices, and both groups were careful to do everything by the book.

XR had clear and urgent political goals, and 'activism' to achieve them was supposed to be efficient. Here the two movements part ways. The Kallio movement can be characterized as prefigurative politics, where the action – taking over the streets of Kallio for a celebration of the spirit of the area – was a goal in itself, considered to mediate the values of the movement to the partygoers. In XR, acts of civil disobedience were only means for changing climate politics. Therefore, the Kallio movement strove to practise prefigurative politics, whereas XR did not. However, it is worth noting that because of the emphasis on individuality, the Kallio movement did not succeed very well in terms of being prefigurative: common values were not explicit even to the organizers of the Kallio Block Party, at least not until the values were voted for (see Chapter 7).

In both Chapters 7 and 8, the inherent frailty of political coalitions is tangible and visible. Kallio movement members, on the one hand, were hesitant in speaking on behalf of the movement in any situation, since 'everyone has their own opinions'. XR is, on the other hand, a showcase of a *possible* political coalition in an extremely individualistic setting, while being a political coalition only in a very minimalist sense.

The cultures of doing society patterning in the cases of the Kallio movement and XR, respectively, are marked by perhaps the strongest tensions between individualism and collectivism of this book. Albeit in different ways, in both cases the participants were torn between the demands on the individual and perplexity on what to do with the community, and how to position it and oneself in relation to it. In the Kallio movement, prefiguration was the answer – common values and visions of the future were to guide the individuals. However, this turned out to be like herding cats, since it was impossible to come to an agreement on the visions, or even on whether such agreement was necessary. In XR, the community had many outspoken missions and tasks, but one by one, these all revealed to be means-to-an-end tools to ensure the maximum efficiency of the individual activists' actions to influence climate politics. In both, engagements emphasized 'doing' over 'belonging', fairly often with the effect of leaving individuals quite alone with their to-do lists or planetary responsibilities.

Acknowledgements

Jenni Kettunen contributed to the data collection and early drafting of this chapter.

9

Conclusions: Cultures of Doing Society

Eeva Luhtakallio and Veikko Eranti

This book has explored the cultures of doing society among Finnish young people. The aim of this methodologically and empirically manifold approach, as well as the conceptual suggestion of *doing society* in place of more specific terminologies of political and civic participation, has been to provide a holistic view of cultural patterns of reaching towards the common, irrespective of the group or type of political action the different actors could be categorized in. The necessity for such a conceptual turn, we argue, lies in two observations: first, actors – not just the young, and not just in our contexts, but all over where social researchers go to them – tend to dismiss the definitions of politics applied to them, often refusing the label 'political' to begin with; and, second, the range of included activities in sociological definitions usually reserved for societal participation – from politics to activism to civic and civil actions or spheres – leaves out the experiences of societal life of probably the great majority of people in an abundance of situations. For some, this is because they are not 'civic' – they do not adhere to normative ideals of common good and deliberation-based collective action – while for many, it is because they fail, willingly or unwillingly, to express themselves in ways recognized as civic participation. Yet such people, such situations and such engagements are also part of the common world, and they leave their mark in terms of how the common is forged. Leaving them out because of conceptual limitations leads to blindspots that social sciences cannot afford to have in our current world of complex, endless differences, and often painfully difficult pursuits for common ground.

We found that overall, the youth deployed *cultural tools of individualism* in all their engagements, ranging from individual life plans or career strategies to hardliner collective action. This is not really a novelty: the thesis of intensifying individualization has been repeated in sociological *zeitdiagnose* since the 1980s, and the state of the art of youth research has acknowledged the importance of this feature in any description of youth generations for decades.

The novelty, instead, is this: in this book, we have taken individualism as the meta-toolkit that steers and patterns cultural action by way of providing tools for very different engagements. These varying engagements we call cultures of doing society.

Doing society in a spectrum of engagements

After the introductory chapter, the book can be roughly divided into three thematic parts. The first one, comprising Chapters 2, 3 and 4, concentrates on analyses of engagement in the formal end of the political, having to do with youth councils, e-democracy services and young candidates in municipal elections. The people we met in these chapters are mostly the kind who did exactly what they were 'supposed' to do: when offered a way or a format of participating, they took part, made their opinion known and, with notable exceptions, overall behaved in an adult-passing manner.

In Chapter 2, the young people thrust into the youth council participatory system were learning through a simulation what a democratic system might look like rather than through actual participation. This simulation meant a lot of meetings, as well as seats offered at the grown-ups' table, but actual power to participate in the decision making or agenda setting was missing. The young people who had been successfully recruited to participatory budgeting processes, in turn, found themselves as subjects of youth work rather than participants in a democratic process. Still, in Chapter 3, we found that for many young people who actually ended up as candidates in local elections, experiences such as these were hugely influential. Young candidates who had come through the participatory-industry path had learned valuable skills and gained self-confidence in those endless meetings. The same holds true for the broader group of youth organization veterans, even though the meetings might have been different in style and in tone. Some young candidates, in contrast, had taken the hobby-collector path to politics, party politics being (at least in the beginning) just another hobby to fill up their free time. In Chapter 4, young people used the e-democracy service in quite a limited capacity, commenting on sport facilities and material deficiency in their respective schools, and wishing for municipality-organized rap concerts in their semirural towns. These were, however, totally adequate ways of using the service given the way in which it was designed.

The culture of doing society connecting all these three chapters was marked by *techno-rationalist problem solving*. The participants' civic imagination focused on problem identification and solving, their engagements were oriented around a future-oriented plan and individual interests, and they used industrial justifications – referencing efficiency, expertise and technical-scientific solutions – as the dominant common good. It can be argued that this is also the way of doing society that the 'system' wants and expects, or at least the one that is the easiest to push through as acceptable. Youth councils end up promoting the individual careers and skills of future politicians who then put them to good use when standing up for election, and e-democracy services teach children to ask for a better form of municipal services.

The second part, comprising Chapters 5 and 6, turns to the opposite end of the spectrum of engagements. While the youth in the previous chapters participated, and even if everybody wasn't always exactly well behaved, they still played along, in contrast the marginalized youth and the (often quite right-wing) online imageboard lurkers were not doing anything right by the standards of a solution-oriented society. They most certainly were not learning public oratory and detailed planning of political operations to manoeuvre access to a better subcommittee, or thinking about how their career would be best advanced by taking a position in a party organization, like the young people in Chapters 2 and 3.

By studying young people in marginalized positions forging an 'imagined common' on the one hand, and youth engaging in anonymous online debates and looking to form a common in terms of what politics can be, on the other hand, we identified cultures of doing society that the extant social science concepts most obviously risk omitting or overlooking. For the marginalized young in Chapter 5, the hurtful experiences of being excluded translated into a variety of engagements. Some withdrew and dreamed of self-transformation: changing oneself into a 'respectable citizen' and becoming 'fitting' for society. Others were opting out and flipping the finger to 'the system', and thus resisting, both disruptively and actively, the excluding mechanisms. Finally, some challenged the valuation systems of the society through at least proto-political projects of mirroring the reasons of exclusion – such as mental ill health – back at society to push the blame onto the excluders. On the Ylilauta imageboard in Chapter 6, the norm-breaking, disruptive and slur-laden means of communicating were patterned into group styles of the participants' shared understandings of a fragile, fleeting and yet recognizable common.

Together, the culture of doing society for these two chapters has to do with *finding a place for the individual within society*. For the most part, withdrawal, or clearly marking oneself outside of society, connects quite separate cultural practices. For the marginalized young people in Chapter 5, the central question was that of recognition, which the online warriors in Chapter 6 sought less from the broader society and more from their online peer group. This seeking took forms of transgression and policing of community borders. The outward political expressions of such forms may be very different, but both are grounded in a civic justification of equal rights – of a place in society, or outside it, but nonetheless as individuals whose right to be and say is recognized. It should be noted that this is not to say that they were *civic* in their arguments – or civil, for that matter, which the young people, online especially, were often explicitly not – but that their patterned form of reaching towards the common was paved with intentions of forging a place for individual chances to talk, belong or dream *like anyone else*.

Of course, the overtly political, sometimes even philosophical nature of the debates on Ylilauta in Chapter 6 is light years away from the all-encompassing feeling of nonbelonging present among the marginalized young in Chapter 5. In Ylilauta, even if political conversation includes all kinds of themes and sometimes even quite sophisticated argumentation, the overall tendency is from moderate to extreme to fringe right, with some participants calling out a more recent rightward shift as memetic in-group preservation. This is fortified by their depicting 'Social Justice Warriors' as a common enemy. Or at least this was the common enemy in 2019, as by the time you are reading this, it might be something completely different. The young in Chapter 5, in contrast, had a less narrow view of the 'enemy', if they had a clear one at all, and a more serious and shareable overall diagnosis of the wrongs they kept facing in their engagements with the society.

Finally, in the third part, Chapters 7 and 8 address engagements that, by the look of them, are close to the kind traditionally defined as *collective action*. As suggested in the conclusion of Chapter 8, the tension between individualism and collectivism was sharp in these formulations of doing society and had major consequences for the emerging cultures, as well as the participants. Perhaps this resulted exactly from the pressure of 'looking like' collective action, in the eyes of outsiders and probably also many insiders. There also was, at least in passing, nostalgia and longing for a culture that would define and produce commitment. Yet, both in the Kallio movement and among the climate activists, instead of the membership and belonging structures of more traditional civic organizations, we encountered actors engaging individually. Doing society in these contexts was patterned around participants *doing* instead of being (members, for instance), and carrying the responsibility of their doings individually. The culture of doing society was substantially about *individualist problem solving by using the collective as an instrument*. In this culture, collectives are crucial for the form of engagement and civic imagination built *around* them, but they nonetheless are secondary to the tasks at hand. Performing these tasks included the use of public justification in abundance, but it was noteworthy that, again, as in the first part of the book, the dominating civic imaginations were more about solving problems, using expertise and being efficient, be it organizing a block party or saving the planet. Above all, it was much less about building stable collective structures, or even redoing institutional arrangements. Suffice to say that traditional social movement ideas of collective identities, or movements claiming participants as their own, were not really applicable at all.

Even if both the Kallio Block Party organizers and the Extinction Rebellion (XR) activists are using collective structures to individual goals, there are notable differences. For the Block Party organizers, individualism means wanting something for themselves. Their individualism was personalism, and it meant pursuing their own individual dreams. For XR activists, individualism means individual responsibility for the whole world and the crisis it is in. They blame themselves for all the shortcomings, of the movement, of governments and of humankind, and thus of the bleakness of the future. In both cases, nobody was a 'member' in the traditional sense. This is why the Kallio movement had trouble getting people to step up and volunteer, and the solution was sought by creating an appealing commitment culture. Conversely, in XR, trouble came in the form of burnout from the demanding, intense and individualized commitments, and solutions were sought by offering a regenerative culture of engagement in presence (see Brahy et al 2023) with meditation and mindfulness practices and globally modelled emotional debriefing sessions. However, neither of these solutions built community in a collective sense, and as the Kallio movement's failure in pursuing prefigurative politics showed, and the climate activists' solitary accounts and recurrent hope that the movement would cease to be (if and when it achieved its goals) gave away, the solutions did not really manage to soothe the tensions of individualism and collectivism in the respective cultures of doing society.

Furthermore, perceiving such a tension makes it possible to observe much less obvious connections than those between the Kallio movement and XR participants. One of these is the connection between the most traditionally 'active' and 'passive' young people in our data. Many marginalized young people in Chapter 5 describe society as something that they do not understand, accept or count themselves as being part of. This is echoed in the talks of the most committed XR activists, who forcibly keep themselves outside of society and push aside ideas of jobs, careers and travelling – all individual dreams and goals. The difference is important: the marginalized young mainly abandon the idea of taking part, but often dream of fitting in, while the XR activists do their voting, but abandon the normative materialities of a middle-class life. The common as a petit-bourgeois society feels distant to both, but from opposite perspectives. Dreams push the antipodes apart – for the (almost) full-time climate activists, the dreams of stable middle-class life with income and children recounted by Hanna in the Preface seem alien, something to be actively avoided. Nevertheless, it has to be said that this also holds true for the young people in Chapter 5 opting out of the whole system: their disillusionment with society is similar to that of the climate activists, even if it lacks their background analysis of crisis and emergency, and thus comes closer to an anarchistic perception of the system's insanity.

The cultures of doing society that we have distilled in this section by combining findings of the analyses in this book were characterized by *techno-rationalist problem solving*; *finding a place for the individual within society* and *individualist problem solving by using the collective as an instrument*. These three analytical densifications show principles of group formation and coordination, and the varying effect of an individualized, yet traditionally collectivist cultural value base that our analyses of young in the Finnish context were equipped with. They are certain ways of using culture to do society: many other paths are possible even within Finnish political culture, and have also been taken. Despite this, the three crystallizations do tell us something about reaching towards the common in current societies. They come close to what Ann Swidler (2023: 30) has recently called *collective action schema*, the 'background recipe for how a group is constituted and, thus, how it would coordinate joint action if no other organizational solution were operative' and 'resembling the traditional view of culture as enduring, deeply rooted collective values'. In the next section, we delve deeper into the cultural tools of individualism that enable such cultures of doing society.

The cultural tools of individualism

We have shown that while individualism permeates the collective action schema, it also in some shape or form defines all the fields of research in this book. Individualism is not the only story – there are organizations, social movements, groups, parties, collectives and so on – but, nonetheless, everything is somehow touched by individualism. Even in the most collectively structured contexts, the young people are doing society using the *cultural tools of individualism*.

What this means is that both the action and the meaning-making associated with it operate primarily on the basis of participating individuals, not on the basis of forming collectives. This is especially the case in Chapter 7 concerning the Kallio Block Party. Even though many of the problems that the movement faces are the classical social movement problems of assigning responsibility, recruiting volunteers and making sure everything is running smoothly, the whole collective is built on avoiding the collectivist structures that are the stock answer to these problems. Rather, the whole constellation aims at creating a culture of commitment, through which individuals would assume the maximum amount of responsibility.

In the climate movement, individual responsibility takes on even more dire, bordering on apocalyptic, forms. The young climate warriors feel personally responsible for avoiding the climate crisis to a degree that makes living a normal life seem like an impossible luxury. Even if they are not wrong to ring the alarm bell in this crisis, it can be argued that internalizing responsibility to such a degree as a twentysomething activist is not a sensible, let alone sustainable, solution. Within the climate movement, the collectivist practices of regenerative culture are aimed at making sure that all the individuals are fostered and can reflect on their emotions – yet the activists seem to end up alone with their heavy responsibilities and sacrifices.

In the formal modes of participation, the tools of individualism are the individual interests and plans that form the basis of many of the engagements, as well as the aforementioned techno-rational problem-solving mindset that eschews collectives both as objects and as solutions to problems. The cultural tools of individualism also shape the form of presenting ideas in e-democracy in a way that resembles a customer wishlist in a local grocery store: here's what the selection of local services is lacking, this would be a sensible thing to provide here, 'we would like this Finnish rap star to have an all-ages concert in this small town'. On some level, this is also an important facet of democracy, and hearing these kinds of grassroots needs is a crucial feature in participatory democracy.

In an online platform defined by anonymity, the users are creating community and ingroup-outgroup divisions through obscure memes and displays of extremity. There clearly is value in claiming a status as a member of the community, but at the same time, it is also quite unreachable, as a 'membership' in the veteran users' club can be revoked at any time. On Ylilauta, as well as, perhaps surprisingly, in the two movements (the Kallio movement and XR), community has the role of a resource, or an *instrument*, for the young people – which is not at all the same thing as being a member of a supporting community. Some Kallio Block Party organizers, some climate activists and also some of the marginalized youth are able to draw on a certain form of backing from the communities that provide a supporting structure or enable action. But even in these cases, the accounts are not full of (youthful) exuberance, or the giving and taking and responsibility sharing that defines a more thorough form of communal thinking. We wrote in the introduction of this book that Finns have traditionally 'spoken' collectivist structures as their mother tongue and claimed that they are now also fluent in individualism as a kind of a second language. Now in this concluding chapter, it might be more apt to say that collective structures are the written language – everybody with a minimum level of literacy knows it, many of the 'serious things' are done using it, and when pushed enough, even the staunchest individualist in the Kallio movement reaches for it in the form of a registered association. However, individualism is the casual spoken vernacular, with its various and ever-changing sociolects that are not always immediately clear to outside observers. The collective action schema then finds its expression in the cross-pressures of these two ideas.

Surprisingly, after all the well-documented changes in political processes, be it from Dalton (2004), Juris (2008), Bennet and Segerberg (2012), Luhtakallio and Meriluoto (2023) or from the chapters in this book, the collective actor that is in some ways looking the strongest even among young people is the political party. Naturally young politicians are individualistic and career-oriented in all kinds of ways, and we have presented their problem-oriented and individual-driven civic imagination at length in Chapter 3. But party members also experience collective wins and losses, take on the collective identities offered by the parties, are willing to prop up their comrades (from left to right), and speak of them not only as resources (although also that) but also as a genuine community. This is of course helped by the electoral system, where all the candidates benefit from the same votes – a first-past-the-post system, for example, provides quite different incentives. It is still nothing short of remarkable. It should be noted that this also positions the core politicians and party activists as a group quite far apart from 'the people', which especially in Finland represents a novel development.

From descriptive to constructive representation?

In Finland, political parties have traditionally been quite close to the organized civil society and, to a degree, this is still the case. Our young politicians describe a world where the same people come together through a plethora of democracy-education-tinted participatory projects and various nongovernmental organizations (NGOs), and end up in party organizations together. However, this connection is not what it used to be. Next, we look briefly at what the future of the relationship between the civil society and the institutional political sphere, and at the same time the broader strokes of Finnish political culture, might hold.

According to Risto Alapuro (2005), the strong organizational networks of civil society, which helped to create Finnish society as we now know it, have resulted in a political culture whose practices are grounded in mediation and mediating structures, and are mainly acted out through registered associations (see Chapter 7 for an overview of this history).

Hence, Alapuro explains, civil society has been the important guarantor of stability, in the sense of communicating the people's mindset to the government. In turn, this has gradually translated into a system that has granted the inclusion of civil society organization to decision-making bodies, and it has also ensured that political parties are strongly anchored in civil society groups.

This book suggests that in the Nordic societies, the collective action schema, and along with it the key characteristics of the Finnish political culture, are going through a major shift, from traditionally organization-focused culture to something that is built around individuals and their heightened capabilities (see also Eranti 2016).

Borrowing a term from Rosanvallon (1998), Risto Alapuro (2005: 388) diagnosed the strongly associational Finnish approach to representation and constitution of society as 'descriptive':

> [S]ociety is seen to consist of elementary units that are easy to locate and identify. The society seems transparent. To simplify, in the traditional Finnish approach, groups appear well-ordered, with predetermined interests and ambitions. It is as if a direct line went from objective group characteristics to organizations and further to the action uncontroversially taken in the name of the objectively defined groups.

What this means is that Finland used to have, and to an extent still has, an association for each imaginable issue. Indeed, many young people in this study have been active in these associations: in Chapter 3, many of the young politicians had a past or current membership in multiple NGOs, some of which were defining for their political activity. Associations also pop up in Chapter 5, where they provide a space of action for some of the marginalized young people, and as a tool and a resource (as well as a source of constant conflict) in Chapters 7 and 8. But the traditional Finnish associational life, with official memberships, statutes and annual meetings, is far-removed from the ways in which young people do society.

Based on the empirical results of this book, it seems that the Finnish political culture is progressing away from this kind of organized, descriptive culture and representation, towards a culture and representation based on individualistic tools of doing society. Here, it is also useful to reflect back on the survey results we presented in Chapter 1: 70 per cent of young people said that a good citizen acts themselves to make their own life better. Only voting in elections was a more popular choice. Moreover, traditional collective ways of using political power, such as joining a party and participating in civil society activities, activist groups or community organizations *all* scored behind the response option 'you don't have to do anything if you don't want to' (which was chosen by 11 per cent of respondents). So, in effect, all the youngsters have participated in one way or another, most often in rather traditional collective ways. Yet, at the same time, they think that a good citizen is primarily responsible themself for making their life better, and view collective ways of using power as something *more marginal* than the decision of tuning out completely.

The opposite of descriptive representation, which Alapuro (2005) takes from theorizing of French society, is constructive representation. In the case of 'constructive' representation, the 'people' and their will are continuously re-created and, as such, are not transparent or known to the governing system. As has been noted elsewhere (Luhtakallio 2012), individual citizens and activists in a situation of a constructive representation have, in a sense, a more direct connection to the state and society that is not mediated by the associational culture. 'Direct' should not be understood to mean 'more influential', as these modes of representation both have their respective pros and cons. Instead, direct versus mediated connection has important implications to the action repertoires and means of politicization that are culturally deemed to make sense (Luhtakallio 2012) – and thus have everything to do with the idea of cultural tools steering the actions of doing society that this book has put forward.

Of course, shifting away from a descriptive association-led political culture towards something more individualistic does not automatically lead to a French-style constructive representation. In an individualistic world where even the most collective-looking actors are 'private entities for climate justice' instead of members of a movement, the whole concept of belonging to society through representation inevitably changes. If in the constructive representation, at least as it has been defined in the case of France, the *people* is directly connected to the *polis*, without mediators, and thus its characteristics are obscured from the power holders, the cultural tools of individualism point to a direction in which the polis expands to endless engagements in a common, how ever minimally shared they may be. Yet, the constructive creativity, in its 'purest' form, has been seen to require a collective body – indeed, the revolutionary mass – that is somewhat hard to fit with the picture painted in this book of individuals to whom commitment is conditional and collective an instrument.

Studying young people is looking into the future, and this is where we can see a shift on its way. Their way of building the common is more *ad hoc*, more interest-based and more dependent on temporary, summoned representation (see Eranti 2018) than on organizations as articulations of deep societal cleavages. If the organized civil society used to be a source of stability, as Alapuro noted, more turbulent times may well be ahead. Still, this book gives no reason to predict a disruptive spike unforeseen from the part of Finnish civil society, or a collapse of institutional structures for that matter. Cultural change mostly operates through sedimentation (Ricoeur 1995) rather than earthquakes; institutions are protected by inertia and laws.

But, most importantly, while we set out at the beginning of this book to explore the future of democracy, we nonetheless never intended to finish with a set of political forecasts. Instead, we have analysed the engagements of young people that pattern into *cultures of doing society*. The way in which such an analysis matters to the future of democracy is different from election result predictions or economic-political foresights of the trends for the next quarter. With the determination to conduct a holistic analysis of political, proto-political or even apolitical participation without predetermining what groups or segments the participants belonged to, and what relation to the political, the society or civicness they had, we have carved out a new route to understanding culture through action.

We felt this new route was badly needed in order to better equip social scientists for the task of analyzing how societies are and may remain possible through people's efforts to build the common. The suggestion of doing society has been crafted by adhering to the cultural sociological understanding that any action leaves a trace, and that change comes about through new patterns steering practices to new directions, however invisible such reorientations may be to the people involved in the process (see Ricoeur 1971; Eliasoph 2011). With each such trace and new pattern, our being-in-the-world changes a little, and so does the only view of this world we can share: the common that we reach towards. That is where the future of democracy is *en route*, and that is where we can follow it and the trajectory it is about to take.

Dispelling myths about young people

This book has shown, in a variety of ways, the two faces of intensified individualism. On one side, we have met thriving young people absorbed in making and realizing their plans, and imagining, often with due enthusiasm, their path forward in society. On the other side, grim, disappointed and disillusioned future perspectives reign, and lonely and isolated youth feel angry and exhausted in the face of the demands of the world ahead of them or the weight of it on their shoulders.

With this book, we have joined a long tradition of studies arguing that young people are individualistic. It would be easy to read a moral judgement in the whole project, thinking that we yearn for more collectivist times. However, from a broader perspective, we feel that our empirical chapters also give us grounds to dispel a few myths that fly around whenever public spotlight turns towards the youth.

Young people are apathetic! The young we encountered in our studies were all pretty much strangers to the idea of young people being politically apathetic, because we did not depart from predefined definitions of politics, but worked with the young actors' own conception of politics. Their approach to doing society is manifold, sometimes more classically active than other times, but it is not neutral or non-existent. In our data, apathy, when it appeared, was rather an actively chosen strategy of resistance in certain marginalized circumstances than a fate that fell on some weak-willed creatures. As was reported earlier, in our survey, the two most frequently chosen options for what a good citizen does were voting and that you do not need to anything if you don't want to. This is a moral stake that is different from apathy in a traditional sense.

Participatory democracy saves democracy! Or participatory democracy is all a hoax! Critiques of participatory democracy are right – but, in a sense, so are the promoters. There is a long line of critique of the participatory industry that has formed since the decades of political philosophy and governance calls for wider participation as the remedy for the crisis of representative democracy worldwide (for example, Fraser 1990; Benhabib 1996; Young 2002; Eliasoph 2011; Baiocchi and Ganuza 2017). This book shows – with a kind of multiple exposure approach – that the critiques are all correct: participatory projects aimed at young people all too often result in disillusionment among the participants. The processes are not followed through, or they take too long, or there is simply no adequate planning about how participation is supposed to influence decision making. We found all this too. At the same time, the young in our research, engaging with different participatory devices, made manifold use of them. For some, this was a life-changing experience, providing camaraderie and potentially a career in politics, while for others, it often provided something meaningful to do, and sometimes even a bit of influence here and there.

The new climate movement is a herald of collectivity in the rise. Well, yes. And no. The social movement actors in our study used many recognizable cultural tools of collective action. However, their engagements were individualistic, often completely so.

Is this a book about the collective lost? Perhaps not, but it certainly tells the story of a *collective transformed*: thinking of the collective is, throughout this book, heavily plan-oriented. Doing society means reaching towards the common by engagements dominated by the liberal grammar. The contents of the common are not so much embedded in a common good that is strived for, and only at fleeting moments is the common an intimately shared commonplace, but that is perhaps always bound to be the case in complex, differentiated societies. Rather, the common that is and can be pursued is a minimum common denominator, a common plan that can include many different interests, a junction of temporary agreement of a common goal, and cross-feeding of individual interests.

The upside of this is that in principle, everybody's uniqueness can be respected, and interests can be treated in the manner of a marketplace of ideas, as equally important, yet morally empty, opinions. The downside – and perhaps symptomatically an issue about which the young in this book have not often talked to us – is that solving *conflicts* from this perspective is troublesome. Indeed, conflict is largely missing from the pages of this book (see Eranti and Meriluoto 2023). This is remarkable as it is a book about political engagements. Politics is often understood in terms of choices, problems to be solved or questions of efficiency. Thus, in the midst of the changing patterns we have identified, features that are constant also emerge: relying on industrial justifications and avoiding conflicts at the cost of politicization (see Luhtakallio 2012). They re-appear, perhaps not intact, but recognizable, within the cultures of doing society, forged into being by the individualistic engagements of the actors of the future of democracy.

APPENDIX

Mixed Distance Methods and Data

Tuukka Ylä-Anttila, Lotta Junnilainen and Taina Meriluoto

To oversimplify: with a given amount of time and resources, one can either study a few subjects in great detail or many subjects in broader strokes. Again simplifying, we can say that the first, 'small-n' strategy is typically taken by 'qualitative' or 'interpretive' research, such as ethnography, producing 'thick descriptions', deeper understandings, compelling interpretations and novel theories, whereas the second, 'large-n' strategy is more common in 'quantitative' work aiming for replicable and generalizable results and the systematic testing of precise hypotheses. The project presented in this book began with the idea of combining deep-diving ethnographic work, in which researchers may spend years with a small group of people they study, with 'big data' computational analysis, which in contrast can scrape the surface of very large datasets. The idea was to study ways of doing society both very thoroughly and very broadly.

Another way to think about this is the metaphor of observational distance. Whereas interpretive qualitative methods are sometimes described as close reading (where an abundance of meaning is derived from material), computational big data analysis can be described as 'distant reading', looking at an abundance of material from afar, so that details are imperceptible, but a wider-angle view is rendered: 'If we want to understand the system in its entirety, we must accept losing something' (Moretti 2013: 49). Whereas with text, observational distance is an apt metaphor, with ethnography, it becomes quite real: ethnographers are indeed much *closer*, physically as well as socially, to their subjects than big data analysts looking at patterns emerging from texts written by distant humans. But the advantage that big data analysts have is the ability to look at, however superficially, texts produced by thousands of subjects. Our aim was to get the best of both worlds – what could be called *mixed-distance methods*.

To plan field cases, we used a two-dimensional theoretical space with an axis from informal to formal engagement and another one from latent to manifest engagement, creating a 2x2 table. Informal latent means nonparticipation, formal latent engagement could be seen in empowerment projects in which institutions try to engage people, manifest informal engagement could be described as activism, and manifest formal engagement corresponds to institutional 'politics' as typically recognized. Seen in this way, politics is only one of four possible 'modes of engagement'. We planned field cases by employing at least two differing analytical viewing distances for each of the four quadrants, for a total of eight cases of different engagements at different distances.

Bent Flyvbjerg (2011: 302–303) argues that much of the empirical knowledge about the world has been gained through case studies, underlining that knowledge in the social sciences is always situational and case-specific. Case studies do not necessarily verify assumptions, but can offer new insights and a more detailed understanding of the complexities of human interaction. Such knowledge cannot always be generalized through hypotheses or theory, but can be transferred to similar cases or used as examples (Flyvbjerg 2011: 305). Accordingly, a strategically well-chosen case is one which can be generalized based on the assumption that whatever is found in this specific case should apply to others. These principles guided our case selection.

Since we were about to study very different data of different people using different methods, the theoretical framework of cultural sociological tools and new pragmatist thinking – which we here codify as focusing on *doing society* laid out in Chapter 1 of this book – was to act as a device binding the various approaches together. In the research project that transpired, some choices of fields, subjects and data had to be modified, and not all quadrants were studied using both distant and close methods. Also, we made the decision to prioritize the closer-distance, qualitative work in this book, and also to take a cultural sociology approach to the big data work (see, for example, Mohr et al 2020) rather than a more traditional quantitative hypothesis-testing approach. Nevertheless, all qualitative work was informed by the quantitative analyses we conducted, which helped in terms of selecting and getting to know the fields, having an idea of what is important before diving in more deeply.

The chronological order in which analyses should be conducted, of course, depends on the role each analysis should play in the whole project. One possibility would be to first look closely at small data to come up with a theory (induction), before zooming out to view big data to test the generalizability of that theory (deduction). Another would be sampling: first looking at big data to select interesting parts of those data and then to study more carefully using qualitative data – this is an approach we employed in many parts of this work. But in practice, sociological research, especially multisited group work, rarely follows such neatly prefigured idealizations of the research process. What unfolded during this work was more of an *abductive* process (see Tavory and Timmermans 2014): piecing together the evidence here and there, going back and forth between perspectives and conceptual development, understanding a bit more with each step and by each surprise that the empirical fields provided. Crucially, each different methodological viewpoint informed the work done in each step forward.

Altogether, the project data consist of over 200 interviews, four ethnographic field projects, tens of thousands of pages of text analysed from different distances, a demonstration survey among the Fridays for Future (FFF) participants (for details, see de Moor et al 2020), as well as a survey with 1,247 young respondents.

Getting close: ethnography and the focus on patterned (inter)action

The various ethnographic projects in this book all aim at understanding and explaining situated, patterned actions of young people participating in society. Ethnography, a method of immersing oneself into people's daily routines and systematically recording social processes as they unfold in real time, is well suited for exploring mundane, everyday action. At the same time, it makes it possible to pay attention to how these actions are not haphazard, but culturally patterned. Following everyday actions and interactions with a pragmatist and cultural sociological lens allowed us to notice how different cultures of doing society shaped young people's actions and, conversely, how their everyday actions shaped the cultural tools of doing society.

As we entered the world of young people we studied, whether in youth council meetings, youth houses, climate strikes or online forums, we followed, observed and participated in their routines, seeking to understand life as it is lived. In so doing, we were able to understand how young people participate in doing society in different areas of life, in extremely varying ways – sometimes in a conscious, wilful manner as they (sometimes) participated in democratic processes, but also imperceptibly, more as a side effect of ongoing activities. Whereas with more distant methods it would have been hard to grasp these less apparent and less articulated forms of action, ethnography that is based on 'being there' in order to observe people acting (Jerolmack and Khan 2018) enabled us to recognize and become attuned to the less explicit and apparent forms of doing society. Rather than following the established ideas of what doing society is or should be, we embraced the discovery-oriented nature of the ethnographic method and volitionally followed 'surprise data, things [we] didn't ask about but were told anyway' (Becker 1996: 56).

Multisited ethnography with a relatively open design allowed us to broaden our gaze from the 'usual suspects', and the classical modes of societal participation to asking how everyone – in one way or another – *does society*. Not designing our field sites and research foci solely based on the existing literature on societal participation led us to new discoveries concerning where, how and by whom society is being done. This also led us to challenge some of the conceptualizations of civic action and participation, as we learned, for example, that not all ways of doing society can be described as 'civic', and some forms of doing society are better described as nonparticipation. Crucially, we did not commit to any predetermined normative theory on how societal participation *ought to* look like, but instead went on to enquire how the actors themselves valued their action or inaction.

It is of course difficult to know about people's practices without talking to them about the meanings these practices have for them. While our theoretical approach is focused on both action and meaning, we put great emphasis on in-depth interviewing and collecting data about cultural repertoires, imagined futures and meanings of actions. We wanted to understand how the actors themselves made sense of their actions or inactions, how they assigned value to them, what they imagined as possible and what, conversely, entirely out of their reach. Asking questions and listening (see Lamont and Swidler 2014) helped us to direct our ethnographic gaze at what we call the three ways of doing society: imagining, engaging and acting. We enquired how the youth envision society, both now and in the future, how these imaginations shape their current actions, and how they build commonalities, with whom and with which tools. The tools for doing this ranged from just asking the young people about their visions of society, what they thought is good life and how they defined politics, to observing how they asked for floor in meetings, who they invited to planning sessions, and who stepped up and took responsibility in crucial moments and how.

In order to make ethnographic observation usable and generalizable, the interpretation of the results was done abductively, with an explicit objective of theory construction. All the fields were discussed together with the whole group, both in data sessions as well as sessions on theoretical development.

In addition to participant observation, we also used other methods of qualitative data collection. For Chapter 3, we interviewed 32 young candidates. We also employed qualitative text-reading techniques with the more distanced data sets.

Zooming out: big data, surveys and large-n text analysis

We employed several methods for zooming out from ethnographic and interview-based fieldwork. We collected hundreds of ideas from an e-democracy website and conducted category-driven theory-based content analysis to provide a broader look at the cultural tools used therein. We utilized a demonstration survey we participated in conducting within the climate movement (de Moor et al 2020) to better understand participant dynamics among the climate activists and Kallio Block Party participants.

We conducted a representative random-sample mail survey of people aged between 15 and 25 in the Helsinki metropolitan region (N=1,247), the results of which informed the conclusions drawn from each field case. For example, the survey let us know that roughly a quarter of Finnish 15–25 year olds had used Ylilauta, the 4chan-insipired imageboard studied in Chapter 6, and that the respondents that had done so were dominantly male, before launching deeper qualitative work thereon.

For the Ylilauta data of about 800,000 messages, we employed topic modelling (Blei et al 2003; see, for example, diMaggio et al 2013; Evans 2014) as well as a word embeddings-based neural network classifier (Ylä-Anttila et al 2020). Computational approaches have often emphasized induction, in which patterns are expected to arise from the data with as few theoretical preconceptions as possible, while sometimes simultaneously making aggressive claims about causality (Babones 2016). We attempted to reconcile some of these issues with our approach, complementing text mining with deep-diving qualitative work both before and after.

As we have argued elsewhere (Ylä-Anttila et al 2021), topic modelling has noticeable points of convergence with certain versions of frame analysis. If a frame is defined so that it 'links two concepts, so that after exposure to this linkage, the intended audience now accepts the concepts' connection' (Nisbet 2009: 17), these linkages can be found by an algorithm that detects which terms 'tend to occur in documents together more frequently than one would expect by chance' (diMaggio et al 2013: 578). Ongoing habitual usage of certain words together is a sign that those words have meaning *in relation to each other*, forming a cluster of words that is then interpreted as a frame.

Text mining models are necessarily reductions of the complexity of human interaction. But by observing patterns and changes in these reductions, we may observe variations in meaning-making habits – that is, culture.

Methods and data notes for individual chapters

Chapter 2: participatory projects

This chapter is based on the ethnographic participant observation of two institutional youth participation initiatives in the Helsinki metropolitan region conducted by Georg Boldt from 2015 to 2018: a youth council and participatory budgeting with young people. The fieldwork sites were chosen to study the democratic merits of institutional youth participation by focusing on methods of participation, patterns of interaction and the use of political power. A multisited research design was developed to enable an interpretation of the significance of local variations of a translocal policy (Marcus 1995; Hannerz 2015).

In accordance with our case selection principles about choosing cases that likely inform us of other cases, a well-established 'textbook' example of a youth council was chosen. In the participatory budgeting case, contrasting districts were selected: one well-to-do and the other strongly segregated and marginalized.

A research permit was obtained from the city of Helsinki's youth department. Youth council meetings are public. Nevertheless, the researcher (Boldt) conducting this fieldwork still reached out to the chairperson and secretary-general before attending his first meeting. They invited him to meetings and other events, and added him to their instant messaging groups. Boldt also carried out numerous one-on-one interviews with council members as well as those who had dropped out. The youth council fieldwork included one full mandate period, as well as the end of the preceding mandate and the start of the subsequent period. The participatory budgeting process was observed for three consecutive cycles. During the fieldwork, Boldt participated in games and activities, but refrained from participating in political discussions or influencing decisions.

Throughout the fieldwork period, the process of seeking informed consent was continuous and reflexive (Hoong Sing 2005). At the roll call at the start of each monthly assembly, the chairperson stated Boldt's name and reason for being present, along with those of other guests. In this way, everyone was reminded of his role at the meeting. At participatory budgeting events, he introduced himself at the beginning and offered handouts providing more information about his research, together with his contact details. Over the years, he discussed his research and interpretations with participants, and at his last youth council assembly in 2017, he gave a presentation on his impressions, which seemed to be well received by most council members.

Boldt's subjective position as a researcher was also shaped by his past involvement in youth politics. This was the basis not only for his interest in the research topic, but also for his understanding that participatory structures often fail. This made him a critical advocate of participation, motivated not only to understand why institutional youth participation works or does not work, but also to improve it by showing how cases differ from each other and what the various participatory methods and settings achieve. This emancipatory, embodied and critical stance is necessary since institutional youth participation tends to be planned, implemented and reported by local authorities. Accordingly, in order to understand the limitations of participatory vehicles, one has to study them from the viewpoint of their participants (Rolin 1999).

Chapter 3: aspiring politicians

To find young people manifestly engaged in formal politics, we decided to interview first-time candidates in the Helsinki metropolitan region city council elections of 2017 right before election day. We searched for first-time candidates under the age of 25 in the Voting Advice Application of YLE, the Finnish national broadcaster, and randomly chose 25 candidates for interview, while ensuring representation of all parties and a reasonable balance of genders. This was done to ensure that we would capture as broad a range of potential backgrounds and ways of doing society as possible. We planned a list of semistructured interview questions in planning meetings involving the whole research team. In a few cases, we wanted to include specific candidates who were already familiar to us from other fields, to increase the dialogue between datasets; in some of those cases, the interviewees were over 25, but still under 30. Each researcher in the team then conducted several interviews, adding up to 32 in total. Each interviewer made logbook entries about each interview for the other researchers to review, and we also discussed how the interviews were going in several team meetings as the interviewing project went on. Interviews, which lasted between 25 and 120 minutes, were recorded as audio and then transcribed verbatim.

Chapter 4: e-democracy

The Nuortenideat.fi service had 459 ideas or suggestions submitted to it at the time when we gathered our materials (20 January 2017). Most of these were in Finnish, with a small number of them also in Swedish. All ideas were scraped for the analysis using a python script written by the authors, together with the comments they had received. However, we excluded the official responses the ideas had received. While these official responses are an interesting data in their own right, they were not essential for the analysis focused on studying young people's ways of doing society.

While going through the materials, we discovered that, in addition to the actual ideas submitted by young people, the service is used in many cities as a channel for gathering feedback from young people concerning, for example, local bus routes. This is understandable, as the service is promoted to young people (those under 29) and professionals working with young people. We have removed these kinds of facilitated 'feedback ideas' from our data corpus. We also removed ideas in which the person submitting them expressed clearly that they were older than the actual target age. The final dataset we used consisted of 428 submitted ideas, which varied from a few sentences to about one page in length. Of these, 63 ideas were extremely scant, less than one sentence in length.

The ideas were analysed using public justification analysis (Ylä-Anttila and Luhtakallio 2016; Luhtakallio and Ylä-Anttila 2023), paying attention to grammars of commonality (following Eranti 2017 procedures) and in the categories of civic imagination (Baiocchi et al 2014). We also did a broader content analysis to record the primary 'issue' presented in the idea, similar to political claims analysis (Koopmans and Statham 1999) and the scope or range of the ideas.

Chapter 5: stigmatized youth

Chapter 5 is based on ethnographic research on two separate but coalescing field sites. In 2012–2016 and 2018–2022, we carried out two ethnographic research projects among young people at the margins of society.

The first project was conducted by Junnilainen in two stigmatized urban neighbourhoods in Finland with a focus on urban inequality and place-based stigma (see Junnilainen 2019, 2020, 2022). Over a period of four years, Junnilainen participated in the everyday lives of the neighbourhoods and conducted around 60 interviews with local inhabitants and public officials. The analysis of this chapter particularly draws on the data that were collected in youth houses, local schools, libraries and other places, where Junnilainen intensively followed the local youth, participating in their everyday routines and detecting how and why they acted, thought and felt the way they did (see Wacquant 2003).

The second project was conducted by Meriluoto among youth with stigmatizing and marginalizing experiences. Over four years, Meriluoto participated in the everyday activities of a group of homelessness activists and another group of young mental health activists, with a focus on their visual political action (for example, Meriluoto 2023; Luhtakallio, et al 2024). She also conducted fieldwork in a rehabilitation centre for young people recovering from addiction for three months in early 2020. She followed the groups and their consenting individual participants with the snap-along ethnographic method both online and offline (Luhtakallio and Meriluoto 2022). As part of the fieldwork, she conducted 32 interviews with the youth.

Chapter 6: anonymous imageboard

Our work on the anonymous online Ylilauta imageboard was originally conducted by a team of three: two cultural/political sociologists (Veikko Eranti and Tuukka Ylä-Anttila) and one computational linguist (Sam Hardwick), all of whom had longstanding cultural familiarity with such online communities. For data, we collected over 800,000 messages on Ylilauta posted in two time windows – 2012–2014 and 2018–2019 – since our initial interest was whether Ylilauta had become more politicized in recent years.

For quantification, we obviously also needed a working definition of 'political' that could be operationalized, but we had a distaste for defining it beforehand, since the definitions of Ylilauta users might well diverge from our own. In team discussions planning the study, we eventually tasked Hardwick with training a convolutional neural network based language model on Ylilauta's 'Politics' sub-board to learn the linguistic features that are categorized as political by Ylilauta users themselves, and a scoring model to rate how linguistically similar messages on other sub-boards to those on the 'Politics' sub-board were (this is based on a probability the model assigns to a message being from 'Politics' as opposed to the other sub-boards). Before using the model, we validated it qualitatively by assessing a random sample of 400 messages from four score categories (100 each) and noted after blind coding that in fact the model's scoring of messages corresponded quite closely to our conception of what politics on Ylilauta would look like.

This enabled two things: first, quantifying politics on Ylilauta as a whole and on the various sub-boards; and, second, inspired by our theoretical background, locating discussions in which something we could call 'doing society' arises in ostensibly nonsocietal discussions, which could then be further assessed qualitatively. Comparing the old and new corpora, we found that Ylilauta had indeed become more political over time. These results were published in Ylä-Anttila et al (2020), together with a topic model assessing the prevalent political themes and a qualitative text analysis of selected 'political' messages.

For the work in this book, Eranti and Ylä-Anttila extended their previous article, armed with our previous quantitative and qualitative results, now diving deeper into the culture of Ylilauta and what it tells us about ways of 'doing society'. Here, the previous computational work about the amount and themes of political and proto-political content allowed us to select materials for qualitative work in a theoretically relevant way and to focus on what matters.

Chapter 7: street party – urban individualism and sense of community

Jokela gathered the fieldwork data on Kallio movement during 2017–2019 by attending the movement meetings, following discussions in Facebook groups and by conducting in-depth interviews with ten Kallio movement participants. Especially compared to more radical groups such as the Extinction Rebellion (XR), it was easy to gain access to study the movement since the Kallio movement does not engage in civic disobedience. In addition, the movement members were used to being approached by students doing their theses in, for instance, sociology, architecture or urban planning. The meetings Jokela attended were mostly Kallio Block Party meetings that focused on the practical arrangements of the festival. In the meetings, she usually acted as the secretary, but also took up practical tasks with other participants, such as filing an online event application, meeting with the City of Helsinki traffic department about the closing of streets during the festival, or running errands at the Kallio Block Party backstage. All participants are anonymized.

Chapter 8: climate activists

The chapter is based on 17 interviews with 15 young climate activists, aged between 14 and 30. The interviewees had been engaged in climate strikes organized by the FFF and/or in XR, and they were chosen to represent the younger generation of the climate mobilization. Nine interviewees were part of the Finnish chapter of XR, and the interviews were conducted by Kettunen in 2021, interviewing two of them twice in different thematic interviews. The interviewees were recruited as part of Kettunen's separate ethnographic project (see Malafaia et al 2024).

Jokela conducted six interviews in 2019 with young people taking part in climate strikes, who were recruited by attending the protests in which they took part. During the FFF protests of that year, Jokela and Luhtakallio also took part in an internationally comparative protest survey project on the climate movement (de Moor et al 2020).

The analysis focuses more on the XR activists, yet interpretations emerging from the interviews with climate strikers have been included when appropriate. In addition, at least two of the climate strikers later joined XR, making the distinction between the activists' affiliations less than watertight. This also reflects the terrain of the current climate activism that consists of unofficial movements and campaigns rather than rigid organizations with a clear membership base.

Research ethics

Ethnographic research that includes young people, some of whom are in vulnerable and marginal positions, imposes high ethical demands regarding how the research is conducted. We took special care in explaining the research design, purpose and ethical guidelines to all research participants prior to their involvement in the study and informed them of their rights and the safeguards in place. We obtained research permits wherever necessary, notably in the cases of institutional youth participation of Chapter 2, and of the youth we met at the rehabilitation centre in Chapter 5. Interviewees were asked to fill and sign a form with background information, contact details and consent – those who were underage were asked to provide us with the consent of a guardian. All interviews that we have reported on in this book have been consented to our use by the interviewees and pseudonymized to protect their identities. In Chapter 3, we also considered the display of party affiliations and specific positions in youth organizations of the interviewees: we omitted information of party affiliation where we estimated that naming this would compromise the interviewees' anonymity, and we also left out all mentions of positions held by the interviewees in specific organizations, such as chairperson and vice-chairperson positions, as well as the exact names of the organizations whenever these seemed to give away the identities of those interviewed.

For ethnographic and interview data collection in particular, we followed the ethics codes of the American Anthropological Association (AAA 2012), based on the grounding principle of causing no harm to any of the research participants, and of exercising continuous ethical assessment throughout the research process. All ethnographic work has commenced with a careful explanation of the overall project design, objectives and practices, followed by a discussion on the research participants' rights and the safeguards to protect them.

For the data collection on the online fora, we followed the ethics code of the British Psychological Society's guidelines for internet-mediated research (BPS 2021). We did not use consent (as identified in the General Data Protection Regulation [GDPR]) as the legitimation basis for processing personal data. Instead, the legitimation was based on research for general interest as identified in the GDPR, as well as the Finnish data protection legislation. Further, the project uses texts submitted on the youthideas.fi service, as well as Ylilauta imageboard, stripped from their original contexts and with no metadata or user information included. Scraped text data were stored in secure servers provided by CSC – IT Centre for Science, a centre of expertise in information technology owned by the Finnish state and higher education institutions, and only for the time period necessary for the processing of the analyses.

The risk of vulnerable individuals' and groups' stigmatization has been prevented by strict pseudonymization techniques used throughout the data collection, analysis and reporting phases, and organizational and technical measures adopted to prevent illegitimate access to data.

Our research work has in its integrity been carried out according to the general guidelines of the Finnish Advisory Board on Research Integrity (TENK 2012), the guidelines on data security of the Universities of Helsinki and Tampere, and the Finnish legislation, as well as the European GDPR.

Notes

Chapter 1
1. 'Citizen' in this book refers to a person acting in a society and, empirically, people residing, on a more or less stable basis, in the context country of our study – it takes no stance on formal citizenship status.
2. The main data collection for this project was carried out between 2015 and 2019, thus leaving the COVID-19 crisis mostly beyond our scope.

Chapter 2
1. See Chapter 5 for a description of how elitist, state-led participation leads to complete resignation and alienation.
2. This is in slight contrast to the survey results in this project, where the top choices for what a good citizen does were voting, acting yourself to make your own life better, taking care of your immediate surroundings and helping your neighbours.
3. This populist right-wing party was in government at the time. See Ylä-Anttila (2017) for a discussion of how this party positioned itself in relation to other political actors.
4. Attempts to utilize charismatic authority are relatively common. Nevertheless, they are generally unsuccessful unless used in combination with other sources of authority.

Chapter 3
1. For example, in countries with a first-past-the-post system, the number of candidates is radically smaller, and in closed-list proportional systems, party organs have tighter control over the list, especially in the places where there is a realistic chance of getting elected. This seriously limits the number of potential young candidates.
2. Perhaps more specific to Australian context, reconciliation and indigenous issues were also mentioned by 9 per cent.
3. The interviewees represent a variety of genders and also ethnic backgrounds. However, in addition to using pseudonyms when quoting the interviewees, we have made the choice to limit descriptions of them to the alleged gender communicated by the pseudonym. The reason for this is the potential recognizability of the candidates, especially those from small parties and/or with distinct ethnic background (a vast majority of the candidates were White, so noting any other ethnicity would risk revealing the identity of the research participant). Apart from the random sampling, two of the candidates were chosen because of they were already known from previous fieldwork presented in Chapter 2.
4. This interviewee's party affiliation has been omitted for the sake of anonymity.
5. The concept of a hobby varies between cultures – in the Finnish context, hobbies are an important part of people's (especially youth's) wellbeing and 'a good life'. A hobby in this context refers to a leisure activity that is usually organized by an NGO or municipality or

a private company. It can be and often is educative, but primarily should be fun. Typical youth hobbies in the Finnish context include different kinds of group and individual sports, playing musical instruments, participating in tutored art classes, theatre workshops, handicraft courses, girl and boy scouts, and so on.

6   This was, notably, before the party leadership of now former Prime Minister Sanna Marin.

Chapter 4

1   At the time of writing in the autumn of 2023, the service had been discontinued and replaced by a broader democratia.fi feedback-gathering channel.
2   By 'deliberation', we refer to the democratic practices based on citizens' discussions and judgements.
3   Here the age of the data most likely shows itself a bit. As the data in this chapter is between 2015 and January 2017, one can quite safely assume that newer, post-#Metoo (which started in earnest in October 2017) data would have included stronger feminist tones as well as trans and broader social justice themes. However, it is notable that in the fieldwork for Chapter 2, collected during roughly the same time, gender-neutral bathrooms for schools as well as other similar themes did come up in the fieldwork. Also notable is that our survey (see the Appendix) did show a hegemonical position for pro-LGBTQIA+ themes among the young people.

Chapter 6

1   As such, the term 'imageboard' is somewhat misleading now that we live in the era of social media, when image-based or even video-based online communication is considered the norm. This was not the case when imageboards were born – imageboards are called imageboards to separate them from textboards, simple text forums with no image-posting features.
2   Both 4chan and Ylilauta in fact have explicit posted rules as well. In the case of Ylilauta, at the time of writing (2 April 2024), these explicitly prohibit material that is illegal, promotes violence, 'harassment, stalking, [and] "doxing"' as well as all nudity and pornography.
3   Translating the colloquial slang of Ylilauta from Finnish to English is difficult, but in the examples here, we have tried to keep the tone of the posts rather than translate everything literally. For example, here, the word translated as 'cancer' was 'mädätys', which literally means to (actively) rot or decay, as in 'too much sugar will rot your teeth', a term favoured by the Finnish far right to refer to promoting multiculturalism seen as damaging to society. 'Hippie' was 'takku'; the word literally means 'tangle', 'knot' or 'dreadlock', and on Ylilauta refers to 'anarchists' or 'social justice warriors', named after Takku.net, a radical-left website.

Chapter 7

1   Established in 1919, following Finnish independence in 1917 and the Law on Associations, the registration was paradoxically meant to safeguard people's freedom of association. '[A]ll voluntary associations wishing to obtain a status as a juridical person, had to get their organization rules approved by the authorities and also be enrolled on an official register' (Stenius 2010: 73–74). In Finland, associations have historically been closely linked to the state since their existence is verified by a statist organization (the Finnish Patent and Registration Office), and because local associations have historically been part of national umbrella organizations (Siisiäinen and Kankainen 2009: 94; Sivesind and Selle 2010: 95), that are again in connection to the 'statist planning and implementation machinery' (Nieminen 2006: 150–151).
2   See Chapters 1 or 4 for a fuller explication.

3 '[T]he Finnish term for 'association' – 'yhdistys' – means 'a uniting' and has a sense of joining together entities that then become one. It stresses more the collectivity resulting from joining together than the individuality of those who join together to form an 'association' (Alapuro 2005: 382).
4 See Chapter 2 for how this interpretation plays out in a formal participation context.
5 The movement usually applied, and received, funding from the City of Helsinki each year. It would also make sponsorship deals to cover some of the bills. However, in the spirit of legislation for associations, the KBP was not supposed to make a profit and when the organizing effort began in the spring, there was practically no money to be used in advance.
6 According to Antti, a member of the Kallio movement since the beginning, it was so important for the newly formed movement to steer clear of institutionalized politics that over the years, the movement truly had become nonpolitical.
7 Ultimately, being noncommercial meant *looking* like a noncommercial event. By saying that the KBP is, and should be, noncommercial, what was meant was that it should evoke the cultural images of a noncommercial event and, in the end, this discussion over commerciality boiled down to the question of *visible* sponsor logos in the festival area.
8 The five values that gathered the most votes were 'equality'; 'taking over urban space and more freedom from bureaucracy'; 'non-commerciality', 'fair play and sense of community' and finally 'talkoo spirit and "DIY"'. The values that that were left out for not getting enough votes were 'openness and transparency', 'ideological non-alignment', 'ecology and responsibility', '"anything is possible" attitude' and 'doing things, not opposing'. A total of 149 votes were cast, which was a good turnout in a Facebook group with approximately 170 members.
9 I have categorized the open-ended replies to this question in eight categories, listed here according to their popularity: egalitarianism; sustainability; sense of community and local solidarity; individualism and liberalism; participation and active citizenship; right to the city; anti-capitalism; and urbanism and urban culture.

Chapter 8

1 The Finnish chapter calls itself *Elokapina*, which means, by and large, the rebellion of living. For the sake of clarity and readability, we use the English name of the movement and specify when we are talking about the international XR.
2 Some of the activists interviewed here were mainly active in climate strikes organized by Fridays for Future (FFF). We also made a survey in FFF protests (Wahlström et al 2019). The FFF movement started in August 2018 as a grassroots movement demanding more efficient climate action from politicians by means of school strikes on Fridays (Ernman et al 2020). However, the analysis focuses on XR.
3 www.extinctionrebellion.co.uk
4 Some of the interviews were conducted during the COVID-19 pandemic, which might have affected the informants' moods, since now there was a new threat on top of the climate crisis.

References

AAA (2012) *Code of Ethics*. Available from: https://archaeologicalethics.org/code-of-ethics/american-anthropological-association-aaa-ethics-blog-principles-of-professional-responsibility/ [Accessed 16 April 2024].

Adams, S., Blokker, P., Doyle, N., Krummel, J. and Smith J. (2015) 'Social imaginaries in debate', *Social Imaginaries*, 1(1): 15–52.

Adut, Ari (2018) *Reign of Appearances: The Misery and Splendor of the Public Sphere*. Cambridge University Press.

Aichholzer, G. and Rose, G. (2020) 'Experience with digital tools in different types of e-participation', *European E-democracy in Practice*: 93–140.

Alapuro, R. (1994) *Suomen synty paikallisena ilmiönä 1890–1933*. Tammi.

Alapuro, R. (2005) 'Associations and contention in France and Finland: Constructing the society and describing the society', *Scandinavian Political Studies*, 28(4): 377–399.

Alapuro, R. (2019) *State and Revolution in Finland*. Haymarket Books.

Alapuro, R. and Stenius, K. (1987) 'Kansanliikkeet loivat kansakunnan' in R. Alapuro, I. Liikanen, K. Smeds and H. Stenius (eds) *Kansa liikkeessä*. Kirjayhtymä, pp 7–52.

Alexander, J., Lund, A. and Voyer, A. (eds) (2019) *The Nordic Civil Sphere*. Polity Press.

Almond, G.A. and Verba, S. (1963) *The Civic Culture: Political Attitudes and Democracy in Five Nations*. Princeton University Press.

Alteri, L., Leccardi, C. and Raffini, L. (2016) 'Youth and the reinvention of politics: New forms of participation in the age of individualization and presentification', *Partecipazione e conflitto*, 9(3): 717–747.

Anderson, E. (1999) *Code of the Street: Decency, Violence, and the Moral Life of the Inner City*. W.W. Norton.

Archer, M.S. and Maccarini, A. (eds) (2013) *Engaging with the World: Agency, Institutions, Historical Formations*. Routledge.

Augsberger A., Collins, M.E., Gecker, W. and Dougher, M. (2018) 'Youth civic engagement: Do youth councils reduce or reinforce social inequality?', *Journal of Adolescent Research*, 33(2): 1–22.

Auray, N. (2007) 'Folksonomy: The new way to serendipity', *Communications & Strategies*, 65.

Autio, K., Hiillos, L., Mattila, P. and Keskinen, V. (2008) 'Hesan nuorten ääni: kuuluuko se?' in P. Bäcklund (ed.) *Tutkimuskatsauksia 7: Helsinkiläisten käsityksiä osallisuudesta*. Helsingin kaupungin tietokeskus, pp 24–38.

Babones, S. (2016) 'Interpretive quantitative methods for the social sciences', *Sociology*, 50(3): 453–469.

Bäcklund, P. (2007) *Tietämisen politiikka: Kokemuksellinen tieto kunnan hallinnassa*. Helsingin kaupungin tietokeskus.

Bail, C.A., Argyle, L.P., Brown, T.W., Bumpus, J.P., Chen, H., Hunzaker, M.B.F., Lee, J., Mann, M., Merhout, F. and Volfovsky, A. (2018) 'Exposure to opposing views on social media can increase political polarization', *Proceedings of the National Academy of Sciences*, 115(37): 9216–9221.

Baiocchi, G. and Ganuza, E. (2017) *Popular Democracy: The Paradox of Participation*. Stanford University Press.

Baiocchi, G., Bennett, E., Cordner, A., Klein, P.T. and Savell, S. (2013) 'The civic imagination: Political culture in contemporary American cities', *Annual Meeting of the American Political Science Association*, 1 August.

Baiocchi, G., Bennett, E.A., Cordner, A., Klein, P.T. and Savell, S. (2014) *The Civic Imagination: Making a Difference in American Political Life*. Routledge.

Bang, H. (2004) 'Culture governance: Governing self-reflexive modernity', *Public Administration*, 82(1): 157–190.

Barber, T. (2009) 'Participation, citizenship, and well-being: Engaging with young people making a difference', *Young*, 17(1): 25–40.

Barnes, L. and Hall, P.A. (2013) 'Neoliberalism and social resilience in the developed democracies' in P.A. Hall and L. Lamont (eds) *Social Resilience in the Neoliberal Era*. Cambridge University Press, pp 209–238.

Beck, U. and Beck-Gernsheim, E. (2002) *Individualization: Institutionalized Individualism and Its Social and Political Consequences*. SAGE.

Becker, H. (1996) 'The epistemology of qualitative research' in R. Jessor, A. Colby and R.A. Shweder (eds) *Ethnography and Human Development: Context and Meaning in Social Inquiry*. University of Chicago Press, pp 53–71.

Beierle, T.C. (1999) 'Using social goals to evaluate public participation in environmental decisions', *Policy Studies Review*, 16(3–4): 75–103.

Bellah, R.N. et al (1996 [1985]) *Habits of the Heart, with a New Preface: Individualism and Commitment in American Life*. University of California Press.

Belschner, J. (2023) Too young to win? Cross-national evidence on young candidates' electoral performance. *SSRN*.

Benford, R.D. and Snow, D.A. (2000) 'Framing processes and social movements: An overview and assessment', *Annual Review of Sociology*, 26: 611–639.

Benhabib, S. (ed.) (1996) *Democracy and Difference: Contesting the Boundaries of the Political*. Princeton University Press.

Bennett, E.A., Cordner, A., Klein, P.T., Savell, S. and Baiocchi, G. (2013) 'Disavowing politics: Civic engagement in an era of political skepticism', *American Journal of Sociology*, 119(2): 518–548.

Bennett, W.L. and Segerberg, A. (2012) 'The logic of connective action: Digital media and the personalization of contentious politics', *Information, Communication & Society*, 15(5): 739–768.

Bennett, W.L. and Segerberg, A. (2013) *The Logic of Connective Action: Digital Media and the Personalization of Contentious Politics*. Cambridge University Press.

Berger, M. (2015) 'The politics of copresence: An ecological approach to resistance in top-down participation', *European Journal of Cultural and Political Sociology*, 2(1): 1–22.

Bertram, C. (2018) 'Jean-Jacques Rousseau', in E.N. Zalta (ed.) *The Stanford Encyclopedia of Philosophy*. Available from: https://plato.stanford.edu/archives/fall2018/entries/rousseau/ [Accessed 5 February 2019].

Blei, D.M., Ng, A.Y. and Jordan, M.I. (2003) 'Latent Dirichlet allocation'. *Journal of Machine Learning Research*, 3: 993–1022.

Blok, A., Meilvang, M.L. and Carlsen, H. (2018) 'Methods of engagement: On civic participation formats as composition devices in urban planning', *European Journal of Cultural and Political Sociology*, 5(1–2): 12–41.

Blokland, T. (2008) '"You got to remember you live in public housing": Place-making in an American housing project', *Housing, Theory and Society*, 25(1): 31–46.

Blühdorn, I. and Deflorian, M. (2021) 'Politicisation beyond post-politics: New social activism and the reconfiguration of political discourse', *Social Movement Studies*, 20(3): 259–275.

Blumer, H. (1958) 'Race prejudice as a sense of group position', *Pacific Sociological Review*, 1(1): 3–7.

Bohman, J. (1997) 'Deliberative democracy and effective social freedom: Capabilities, resources, and opportunities' in J. Bohman and W. Rehg (eds) *Essays on Reason and Politics: Deliberative Democracy*. MIT Press, pp 321–348.

Boldt, G. (2018) 'Condescension or co-decisions: A case of institutional youth participation', *Young*, 26(2): 108–125.

Boldt, G. (2021) 'Citizens in training: How institutional youth participation produces bystanders and active citizens in Finland'. Doctoral dissertation, Tampere University.

Bolin, N., Backlund, A. and Jungar, A.C. (2023) 'Attracting tomorrow's leaders: Who joins political youth organisations for material reasons?', *Party Politics*, 29(3): 527–539.

Boltanski, L. (2011) *On Critique: A Sociology of Emancipation*. Polity Press.

Boltanski, L. and Thévenot, L. (1999) 'The sociology of critical capacity', *European Journal of Social Theory*, 2(3): 359–377.

Boltanski, L. and Thévenot, L. (2006) *On Justification: Economies of Worth*. Princeton University Press.

Borg, S., Kestilä-Kekkonen, E. and Wass, H. (2020) 'Politiikan ilmastonmuutos Vaalitutkimus 2019 Oikeusministeriön julkaisuja', *Selvityksiä ja ohjeita* 5. Available from: http://urn.fi/URN:ISBN:978-952-259-838-7 [Accessed 20 March 2024].

Borland, M., Hill, M., Laybourn, A. and Stafford, A. (2001) *Improving Consultation with Children and Young People in Relevant Aspects of Policy-Making and Legislation in Scotland*. Scottish Parliament.

BPS (2021) *Ethics Guidelines for Internet-Mediated Research*. Available from: https://www.bps.org.uk/guideline/ethics-guidelines-internet-mediated-research [Accessed 16 April 2024].

Brahy, R., Pattaroni, L. and Hoffman, A.S. (2023) 'Commoning the touristic city', *Ambiance, Tourism and the City*, 113.

Breeze, M., Gorringe, H., Jamieson, L. and Rosie, M. (2017) 'Becoming independent: Political participation and youth transitions in the Scottish referendum', *British Journal of Sociology*, 68(4): 754–774.

Bruter, M. and Harrison, S. (2009) 'Tomorrow's leaders? Understanding the involvement of young party members in six European democracies', *Comparative Political Studies*, 42(10): 1259–1290.

Busse, B., Hashem-Wangler, A. and Tholen, J. (2015) 'Two worlds of participation: young people and politics in Germany', *Sociological Review*, 63(S2): 118–140.

Cammaerts, B., Bruter, M., Banaji, S., Harrison, S. and Anstead, N. (2016) *Youth Participation in Democratic Life: Stories of Hope and Disillusion*. Palgrave Macmillan.

Carrel, M. (2015) 'Politicization and publicization: The fragile effects of deliberation in working-class districts', *European Journal of Cultural and Political Sociology*, 2(3–4): 189–210.

Chilton, S. (1988) 'Defining political culture', *Western Political Quarterly*, 41(3): 419–445.

Chou, M., Pruitt, L. and Dean, L. (2021) 'Too young to run? Young political candidates and the 2020 Victorian local government elections', *Australian Journal of Political Science*, 56(4): 428–444.

Cohen, J. (1997) 'Deliberation and democratic legitimacy' in J. Bohman and W. Rehg (eds) *Deliberative Democracy*. MIT Press.

Colley, T. and Moore, M. (2020) 'The challenges of studying 4chan and the alt-right: "Come on in the water's fine"', *New Media & Society*, 24(1): 5–30.

Costa, L., Voronka, J., Landry, D., Reid, J., Mcfarlane, B., Reville, D. and Church, K. (2012) 'Recovering our stories: A small act of resistance', *Studies in Social Justice*, 6: 85–101.

Council of Europe (2004) *Recommendation of the Committee of Ministers to Member States on the Participation of Young People in Local and Regional Life*. Available from: https://search.coe.int/cm/Pages/result_details.aspx?ObjectId=09000016805dbd33 [Accessed 1 April 2019].

Council of Europe (2015) *Revised Charter on the Participation of Young People in Local and Regional Life*. Council of Europe.

Craddock, E. (2019) 'What is the point of anti-austerity activism? Exploring the motivating and sustaining emotional forces of political participation', *Interface: A Journal for and about Social Movements*, 11(1): 62–88.

Dalton, R.J. (2004) *Democratic Challenges, Democratic Choices: The Erosion of Political Support in Advanced Industrial Democracies*. Oxford University Press.

Dalton, R.J. (2008) *The Good Citizen: How a Younger Generation Is Reshaping American Politics*. CQ Press.

Davies, W. (2016) *The Happiness Industry: How the Government and Big Business Sold Us Wellbeing*. Verso.

De Moor, J. (2017) 'Lifestyle politics and the concept of political participation', *Acta Politica*, 52: 179–197.

De Moor, J., Uba, K., Wahlström, M., Wennerhag, M. and de Vydt, M. (2020) 'Protest for a future II: Composition, mobilization and motives of the participants in Fridays For Future climate protests on 20–27 September, 2019, in 19 cities around the world'. Available from: https://www.researchgate.net/publication/339443851_Protest_for_a_future_II_Composition_mobilization_and_motives_of_the_participants_in_Fridays_For_Future_climate_protests_on_20-27_September_2019_in_19_cities_around_the_world [Accessed 27 January 2024].

De Moor, J., de Vydt, M., Uba, K. and Wahlström, M. (2021) 'New kids on the block: Taking stock of the recent cycle of climate activism', *Social Movement Studies*, 20(5): 619–625.

Deseriis, M. (2015) 'Anonymous, the transducer' in M. Deseriis (ed.) *Improper Names: Collective Pseudonyms from the Luddites to Anonymous*. University of Minnesota Press, pp 165–273.

DiMaggio, P., Nag, M. and Blei, D.M. (2013) 'Exploiting affinities between topic modeling and the sociological perspective on culture: Application to newspaper coverage of U.S. government arts funding', *Poetics*, 41(6), 570–606.

Eatwell, R. and Goodwin, M. (2018) *National Populism: The Revolt against Liberal Democracy*. Pelican.

Eliasoph, N. (1997) 'Close to home: The work of avoiding politics', *Theory and Society*, 26(5): 605–647.

Eliasoph, N. (1998) *Avoiding Politics: How Americans Produce Apathy in Everyday Life*. Cambridge University Press.

Eliasoph, N. (2011) *Making Volunteers: Civic Life after Welfare's End*. Princeton University Press.

Eliasoph, N. and Lichterman, P. (2003) 'Culture in interaction', *American Journal of Sociology*, 108(4): 735–794.

Elokapina (2020) *About Us*. Available from: https://elokapina.fi/about-us/ [Accessed 6 September 2020].

Enroth, H. and Henriksson, M. (2019) 'The civil sphere and the welfare state', in J.C. Alexander, A. Lund and A. Voyer (eds) *The Nordic Civil Sphere*. Polity Press.

Eranti, V. (2014) 'Oma etu ja yhteinen hyvä paikallisessa kiistassa tilasta', *Sosiologia*, 51(1): 21–38.

Eranti, V. (2016) 'Individuals doing politics: Urban participation, social media campaigning and online nano-politics'. Doctoral dissertation, Helsingin yliopisto.

Eranti, V. (2017) 'Re-visiting NIMBY: From conflicting interests to conflicting valuations', *Sociological Review*, 65(2): 285–301.

Eranti, V. (2018) 'Engagements, grammars, and the public: From liberal grammar to individual interests', *European Journal of Cultural and Political Sociology*, 5(1–2): 42–65.

Eranti, V. and Lonkila, M. (2015) 'Social significance of Facebook like button', *First Monday*, 20(6).

Eranti, V. and Meriluoto, T. (2023) 'Plurality in urban politics: Conflict and commonality in Mouffe and Thévenot', *International Journal of Urban and Regional Research*, 47: 693–709.

Eranti, V., Luhtakallio, E. and Blok, A. (2024) 'New social pragmatism: Revisiting the conceptual scope of participation'.

Ercan, S.A. (2014) 'Deliberative democracy' in D. Phillips (ed.) *Encyclopedia of Educational Theory and Philosophy*. SAGE, pp 214–216.

Ernman, M., Thunberg, G., Thunberg, S. and Ernman, B. (2020) *Our House Is on Fire: Scenes of a Family and Planet in Crisis*. Penguin.

Erpyleva, S. and Luhtakallio, E. (2023) '"The climate is changing, and the President is not": How the Russian climate activists avoid politics and fight with the regime', *Europe-Asia Studies*.

Eskelinen, T., Gretschel, A., Kiilakoski, T., Kiili, J., Korpinen, S., Lundbom, P., Matthies, A.L., Mäntylä, N., Niemi, R., Nivala, E., Ryynänen, A. and Tasanko, P. (2015) 'Lapset ja nuoret subjekteina kunnallisessa päätöksenteossa' in A. Gretschel and T. Kiilakoski (eds) *Demokratiaoppitunti: Lasten ja nuorten kunta 2010-luvun alussa*. Nuorisotutkimusseura.

European Commission (2001) *European Commission White Paper: A New Impetus for European Youth*. Commission of the European Communities.

Evans, M.S. (2014) 'A computational approach to qualitative analysis in large textual datasets'. *PLoS ONE*, 9(2): 1–10.

Extinction Rebellion (2020) *About Us*. Available from: https://extinctionrebellion.uk/the-truth/about-us/ [Accessed 6 September 2020].

Feldman-Wojtachnia, E., Gretschel, A., Helmisaari, V., Kiilakoski, T., Matthies, A-L., Meinhold-Henschel, S., Roth, R. and Tasanko, P. (2010) *Youth Participation in Finland and in Germany: Status Analysis and Data Based Recommendations*. Finnish Youth Research Network.

Ferree, M.M., Gamson, W.A., Gerhards, J. and Rucht, D. (2002) 'Four models of the public sphere in modern democracies', *Theory and Society*, 31(3): 289–324.

Finn, D. (2014) 'DIY urbanism: Implications for cities', *Journal of Urbanism*, 7(4): 381–398.

Fjellman, E. and Rosén Sundström, M. (2021) 'Making a (political) career: Young party members and career-related incentives for party membership', *Scandinavian Political Studies*, 44(4): 369–391.

Flyvbjerg, B. (2011) 'Case study' in N.K. Denzin and Y.S. Lincoln (eds) *The SAGE Handbook of Qualitative Research*. SAGE.

France, A. (2016) *Understanding Youth in the Global Economic Crisis*. Policy Press.

Fraser, N. (1990) 'Rethinking the public sphere: A contribution to the critique of actually existing democracy', *Social Text*, 25/26, pp 56–80.

Fraser, N. (1997) *Justice Interruptus. Critical Reflections on the 'Postsocialist' Condition*. Routledge.

Fraser, N. (2000). 'Rethinking recognition', *New Left Review*, 3: 107–120.

Fung, A. (2004) 'Deliberation's darker side: six questions for Iris Marion Young and Jane Mansbridge', *National Civic Review*, 93(4): 47–54.

Fung, A. (2006) 'Varieties of participation in complex governance', *Public Administration Review*, 66(1): 66–75.

Fung, A. and Wright, E.O. (2003) *Deepening Democracy: Institutional Innovations in Empowered Participatory Governance*. Verso.

Furlong, A. and Cartmel, F. (2006) *Young People and Social Change*. McGraw-Hill.

Gerbaudo, P. (2012) *Tweets and the Streets: Social Media and Contemporary Activism*. Pluto Press.

Gibson, J. (1979) *The Ecological Approach to Visual Perception*. Houghton Mifflin.

Giddens, A. (1991) *Modernity and Self-Identity: Self and Society in the Late Modern Age*. Stanford University Press.

Giugni, M. and Grasso, M. (2021) *Youth and Politics in Times of Increasing Inequalities*. Springer International Publishing.

Goffman, E. (1986) *Frame Analysis: An Essay on the Organization of Experience*. Northeastern University Press.

Gretschel, A. and Kiilakoski, T. (eds) (2015) *Demokratiaoppitunti: Lasten ja nuorten kunta 2010-luvun alussa*. Nuorisotutkimusseura.

Grönlund, K. and Wass, H. (2016) 'Poliittisen osallistumisen eriytyminen: Eduskuntavaalitutkimus 2015', *Oikeusministeriön julkaisu*. Available from: http://urn.fi/URN:ISBN:978-952-259-517-1 [Accessed 20 March 2024].

Habermas, J. (1984) *The Theory of Communicative Action, Volume 1: Reason and the Rationalization of Society*. Beacon Press.

Hannerz, U. (2015) 'Being there … and there … and there! Reflections on multi-site ethnography', *Ethnography* 4(2): 201–216.

Hansen, C. (2019) *Solidarity in Diversity: Activism as a Pathway of Migrant Emplacement in Malmö*. Doctoral thesis, Malmö University.

Harinen, P. (2000) *Valmiiseen tulleet*. Finnish Youth Research Network.

Harris, A. (2015) 'Transitions, cultures, and citizenship: Interrogating and integrating youth studies in new times' in D. Woodman and A. Bennett (eds) *Youth Cultures, Transitions, and Generations: Bridging the Gap in Youth Research*. Palgrave Macmillan, pp 84–98.

Harris, M. (1976) 'History and significance of the emic/etic distinction', *Annual Review of Anthropology*, 5(1): 329–350.

Hatakka, N. (2017) 'When logics of party politics and online activism collide: The populist Finns Party's identity under negotiation', *New Media & Society*, 19(12): 2022–2038.

Haugseth, J.F. and Smeplass, E. (2023) 'The Greta Thunberg effect: A study of Norwegian youth's reflexivity on climate change', *Sociology*, 57(4): 921–939.

Helliwell, J.F., Layard, R., Sachs, J.D., Aknin, L.B., de Neve, J.-E. and Wang, S. (eds) (2023) *World Happiness Report 2023* (11th edn). Sustainable Development Solutions Network.

Hernberg, H. (2013) *Helsinki beyond Dreams: Actions Towards a Creative and Sustainable Hometown*. Urban Dream Management.

Highfield T. (2016) *Social Media and Everyday Politics*. Polity.

Hill, M., Davis, J., Prout, A. and Tisdall, K. (2004) 'Moving the participation agenda forward', *Children & Society*, 18(2): 77–96.

Hine, G.E., Onaolapo, J., de Cristofaro, E., Kourtellis, N., Leontiadis, I., Samaras, R., Stringhini, G. and Blackburn, J. (2017) 'Kek, Cucks, and God Emperor Trump: A measurement study of 4chan's politically incorrect forum and its effects on the web', *Proceedings of the 11th International AAAI Conference on Web and Social Media*. Available from: http://arxiv.org/abs/1610.03452 [Accessed 20 March 2024].

Honkatukia, P. and Rättilä, T. (2023) *Young People as Agents of Sustainable Society: Reclaiming the Future*. Taylor & Francis.

Hooghe, M., Stolle, D. and Stouthuysen, P. (2004) 'Head start in politics: The recruitment function of youth organizations of political parties in Belgium (Flanders)', *Party Politics*, 10(2): 193–212.

Hoong Sing, C. (2005) 'Seeking informed consent: Reflections on research practice', *Sociology* 39(2): 277–294.

Huttunen, J. (2021) 'Young rebels who do not want a revolution: The non-participatory preferences of Fridays for Future activists in Finland', *Frontiers in Political Science*, 3.

Ikola, V. (2018) 'Maija Li Raudaskoski löysi teininä oman paikkansa naisvihaa lietsovasta nettiyhteisöstä, kunnes sai tarpeekseen – Nyt hän kertoo, miksi kuvalaudat ovat vaarallisia', *Helsingin Sanomat*, 17 September. Available from: https://www.hs.fi/nyt/art-2000005831074.html [Accessed 20 March 2024].

Inglehart, R. (1997) *Modernization and Postmodernization: Cultural, Economic, and Political Change in 43 Societies*. Princeton University Press.

Inglis, D. and Thorpe, C. (2023) 'Beyond the "inimitable" Goffman: From "social theory" to social theorizing in a Goffmanesque manner', *Frontiers in Sociology*, 8: 1171087.

Irvin, R.A. and Stansbury, J. (2004) 'Citizen participation in decision making: Is it worth the effort?', *Public Administration Review*, 64(1): 55–65.

Irwin, S. (2015) 'Class and comparison', *British Journal of Sociology*, 66(2): 259–281.

Isin, E.F. (2008) 'Theorizing acts of citizenship' in E.F. Isin and G.M. Nielsen (eds) *Acts of Citizenship*. Zed Books, pp 15–43.

Iveson, K. (2013) 'Cities within the city: Do it yourself urbanism and the right to the city', *International Journal of Urban and Regional Research*, 37(3): 941–946.

Jerolmack, C. and Khan, S. (2018) 'Introduction: An analytic approach to ethnography' in C. Jerolmack and S. Khan (eds) *Approaches to Ethnography: Analysis and Representation in Participant Observation*. Oxford University Press.

Johnston, H., Laraña, E. and Gusfield, J.R. (1994) 'Identities, grievances and new social movements', in E. Laraña, H. Johnston and J.R. Gusfield (eds) *New Social Movements: From Ideology to Identity*. Temple University Press, pp 3–35.

Jokela, M. (2017) 'Kaupungin rajat. Sosiaalikeskus Satama, romanit ja nuorisopolitiikka' [City Limits: Social Centre Satama, the Roma and Youth Politics], *Sosiologia*, 1(54): 63–78.

Jokela, M. (2024) *Performing Civic Action: Networked Activism in Helsinki 2017– 2019*. Doctoral dissertation, Tampere University.

Joshi, D.K. (2013) 'The representation of younger age cohorts in Asian parliaments: Do electoral systems make a difference?', *Representation*, 49(1): 1–16.

Junnilainen, L. (2019) *Lähiökylä: Tutkimus yhteisöllisyydestä ja eriarvoisuudesta*. Vastapaino.

Junnilainen, L. (2020) 'Place narratives and the experience of class: Comparing collective destigmatization strategies in two social housing neighborhoods', *Social Inclusion*, 8(1): 44–54.

Junnilainen, L. (2022) 'Turning newcomers into locals: Kinship practices and belonging in low-income neighborhoods in Finland', *Ethnography*. https://doi.org/14661381221124511

Junttila-Vitikka, P. and Peitso, V. (2016) *Sinä olet demokratiakasvattaja – opas demokratiakasvatukseen.* Oulun kaupunki, Koordinaatti – Nuorten tieto- ja neuvontatyön kehittämiskeskus. Available from: http://www.koordinaatti.fi/sites/default/files/opas-demokratiakasvatukseen_1.pdf [Accessed 25 November 2019].

Juris, J. (2008) *Networking Futures: The Movements against Corporate Globalization.* Duke University Press.

Juusola, H. and Varsaluoma, J. (2023) 'Stakeholders' perception on youths' e-participation in Finland', *Journal of Applied Youth Studies*: 1–19.

Kavada, A. (2015) 'Creating the collective: Social media, the Occupy Movement and its constitution as a collective actor', *Information, Communication and Society*, 18(8): 872–886.

Kennedy, E.H., Johnston, J. and Parkins, J.R. (2018) 'Small-p politics: How pleasurable, convivial and pragmatic political ideals influence engagement in eat-local initiatives', *British Journal of Sociology*, 69: 670–690.

Keskinen, S. (2013) 'Antifeminism and white identity politics: Political antagonisms in radical right-wing populist and anti-immigration rhetoric in Finland', *Nordic Journal of Migration Research*, 3(4): 225–232.

Keskinen, S., Skaptadóttir, U.D. and Toivanen, M. (2019) 'Narrations of homogeneity, waning welfare states, and the politics of solidarity' in *Undoing Homogeneity in the Nordic Region.* Routledge, pp 1–17.

Kettunen, P. (2001) 'The Nordic welfare state in Finland', *Scandinavian Journal of History*, 26 (3): 225–247.

Kettunen, P. (2004) 'The Nordic model and consensual competitiveness in Finland' in A.-M. Castrén, M. Lonkila and M. Peltonen (eds) *Between Sociology and History: Essays on Microhistory, Collective Action, and Nation-Building.* SKS / Finnish Literature Society, pp 289–309.

Kiilakoski, T. (2020) *Perspectives on Youth Participation: Partnership between the European Commission and the Council of Europe in the Field of Youth.* Available from: https://pjpeu.coe.int/documents/42128013/59895423/Kiilakoski_Participation_Analytical_Paper_final%252005-05.pdf/b7b77c27-5bc3-5a90-594b-a18d253b7e67 [Accessed 19 November 2020].

Knops, L. (2021) 'Stuck between the modern and the terrestrial: The indignation of the youth for climate movement'. *Political Research Exchange*, 3(1): 1868946.

Koopmans, R. and Statham, P. (1999) 'Political claims analysis: Integrating protest event and political discourse approaches', *Mobilization: An International Quarterly*, 4(2): 203–221.

Kukkonen, A., Stoddart, M.C.J. and Ylä-Anttila, T. (2020) 'Actors and justifications in media debates on Arctic climate change in Finland and Canada: A network approach', *Acta Sociologica*, 64(1): 103–117.

Kumar, S. (Ed.). (2014). *Indian Youth and Electoral Politics: An Emerging Engagement.* SAGE.

Kuokkanen, K. and Palonen, E. (2018) 'Post-political development and emancipation: Urban participatory projects in Helsinki' in S. Knierbein and T. Viderman (eds) *Public Space Unbound: Urban Emancipation and the Post-political Condition*. Routledge, pp 99–112.

Laclau, E. (2007) *On Populist Reason*. Verso.

Laine, S. (2012) *Young Actors in Transnational Agoras: Multi-sited Ethnography of Cosmopolitan Micropolitical Orientations*. Finnish Youth Research Network.

Lamont, M. (2012) 'Toward a comparative sociology of valuation and evaluation', *Annual Review of Sociology*, 38: 201–221.

Lamont, M. (2018) 'Addressing recognition gaps: Destigmatization and the reduction of inequality', *American Sociological Review*, 83(3): 419–444.

Lamont, M. (2023) *Seeing Others: How Recognition Works – and How It Can Heal a Divided World*. Simon & Schuster.

Lamont, M. and Swidler A. (2014) 'Methodological pluralism and the possibilities and limits of interviewing', *Qualitative Sociology* 37(2): 153–171.

Lamont, M., Beljean, S. and Clair, M. (2014) 'What is missing? Cultural processes and causal pathways to inequality', *Socio-Economic Review*, 12(3): 573–608.

Lamont, M., Silva, G.M., Welburn, J., Guetzkow, J., Mizrachi, N., Herzog, L. and Reis, E. (2016) *Getting Respect: Responding to Stigma and Discrimination in the United States, Brazil, and Israel*. Princeton University Press.

Lannegrand-Willems, L., Chevrier, B., Perchec, C. and Carrizales, A. (2018) 'How is civic engagement related to personal identity and social identity in late adolescents and emerging adults? A person-oriented approach', *Journal of Youth and Adolescence*, 47: 731–748.

Lewis, R. (2020) '"This is what the news won't show you": YouTube creators and the reactionary politics of micro-celebrity', *Television & New Media*, 21(2): 201–217.

Lichterman, P. (1996) *The Search for Political Community: American Activists Reinventing Commitment*. Cambridge University Press.

Lichterman, P. (2005) *Elusive Togetherness: Church Groups Trying to Bridge America's Divisions*. Princeton University Press.

Lichterman, P. (2020) *How Civic Action Works: Fighting for Housing in Los Angeles*. Princeton University Press.

Lichterman, P. and Cefaï, D. (2006) 'The idea of political culture' in R.E. Goodin and C. Tilly (eds) *The Oxford Handbook of Contextual Political Analysis*. Oxford University Press, pp 392–414.

Lichterman, P. and Eliasoph, N. (2014) 'Civic action', *American Journal of Sociology*, 120(3): 798–863.

Loader, B., Vromen, A. and Xenos, M.A. (2014) 'The networked young citizen: Social media, political participation and civic engagement', *Information, Communication & Society*, 17(2): 143–150.

Luhtakallio, E. (2012) *Practicing Democracy: Local Activism and Politics in France and Finland*. Palgrave Macmillan.

Luhtakallio, E. (2019) 'Group formation, styles, and grammars of commonality in local activism', *British Journal of Sociology*, 70(4): 1159–1178.

Luhtakallio, E. (2020) 'Politicization: Conflict, public, and performance', American Sociological Association's Conference: Power, Inequality, and Resistance at Work, San Francisco, 8 August.

Luhtakallio, E. and Meriluoto, T. (2020) 'Elokapinan aktio näyttää miten kuvat politisoivat uusilla tavoilla' *Ilmiö-media*, blog, 8 October. Available from: https://ilmiomedia.fi/artikkelit/elokapinan-aktio-nayttaa-miten-kuvat-politisoivat-uusilla-tavoilla/ [Accessed 16 April 2024].

Luhtakallio, E. and Meriluoto, T. (2022) 'Snap-along ethnography: Studying visual politicization in the social media age'. *Ethnography*. https://doi.org/10.1177/14661381221115

Luhtakallio, E. and Meriluoto, T. (2023) 'Fame democracy? Social media and visuality-based transformation of the public sphere' *Distinktion: Journal of Social Theory*.

Luhtakallio, E. and Tavory, I. (2018) 'Patterns of engagement: Identities and social movement organizations in Finland and Malawi', *Theory and Society*, 47(2): 151–174.

Luhtakallio, E. and Ylä-Anttila, T. (2011) 'Julkisen oikeuttamisen analyysi sosiologisena tutkimusmenetelmänä', *Sosiologia*, 48(1): 34–51.

Luhtakallio, E. and Ylä-Anttila, T. (2023) 'Justifications analysis' in R. Diaz-Bone and G. de Larquier (eds) *Handbook of Economics and Sociology of Conventions*, Springer, published online in July 2023.

Luhtakallio, E., Meriluoto, T. and Malafaia, C. (2024) 'Visual politicization and youth challenges to an unequal public sphere: Conceptual and methodological perspectives' in J. Conner (ed.) *The Handbook on Youth Activism*. Edward Elgar, 140–153.

Mäenpää, P. (1991) *Kallion keskiluokkaistuminen 1980-luvulla: työläisyhteiskunnan tuho?* [The Gentrification of Kallio in the 1980s: The Destruction of Working Class Community?]. Helsingin kaupungin kaupunkisuunnitteluvirasto [City of Helsinki Urban Planning Bureau].

Mäenpää, P. and Faehnle, M. (2021) *Neljäs sektori: Kuinka kaupunkiaktivismi haastaa hallinnon, muuttaa markkinat ja laajentaa demokratiaa*. Vastapaino.

Malafaia, C., Kettunen, J. and Luhtakallio, E. (2024) 'Visual bodies, ritualised performances: An offline-online analysis of Extinction Rebellion's protests in Finland and Portugal', *Visual Studies*: 1–14.

Marcus, G.E. (1995) 'Ethnography in/of the world system: The emergence of multi-sited ethnography', *Annual Review of Anthropology* 24: 95–117.

Marwick, A.E. and Caplan, R. (2018) 'Drinking male tears: Language, the manosphere, and networked harassment', *Feminist Media Studies*, 18(4): 543–559.

Matthews, H. and Limb, M. (2003) 'Another white elephant? Youth councils as democratic structures', *Space and Polity*, 7(2): 173–192.

Melucci, A. (1994) 'A strange kind of newness. What's "new" in new social movements?', in H. Johnston, E. Laraña and J.R. Gusfield (eds) *New Social Movements. From Ideology to Identity*. Temple University Press.

Meriluoto, T. (2018) 'Turning experience into expertise: Technologies of the self in Finnish participatory social policy', *Critical Policy Studies*, 12(3): 294–313.

Meriluoto, T. (2023) 'The self in selfies: Conceptualizing the selfie-coordination of marginalized youth with sociology of engagements', *British Journal of Sociology*, 74(4): 638–656.

Micheletti, M. (2003) *Political Virtue and Shopping: Individuals, Consumerism, and Collective Action*. Palgrave.

Milan, S. (2019) 'The materiality of clouds' in M. Mortensen, C. Neumayer and T. Poell (eds) *Social Media Materialities and Protest*. Routledge.

Mohr, J.W., Bail, C.A., Frye, M., Lena, J.C., Lizardo, O., McDonnell, T.E., Mische, A., Tavory, I. and Wherry, F.F. (2020) *Measuring Culture*. Columbia University Press.

Moisio, S. and Leppänen, L. (2007) 'Towards a Nordic competition state? Politico-economic transformation of statehood in Finland, 1965–2005', *Fennia-International Journal of Geography*, 185(2): 63–87.

Moody, M. and L. Thévenot (2000) 'Comparing models of strategy, interests, and the public good in French and American environmental disputes', in M. Lamont and L. Thévenot (eds) *Rethinking Comparative Cultural Sociology: Repertoires of Evaluation in France and the United States*. Cambridge University Press, pp 273–306.

Moretti, F. (2013) *Distant Reading*. Verso.

Morrow, V. (2001) 'Using qualitative methods to elicit young people's perspectives on their environments: Some ideas for community health initiatives', *Health Education Research*, 16(3): 255–268.

Mouffe, C. (2005) *On the Political*. Routledge.

Mounk, Y. (2018) *The People vs. Democracy: Why Our Freedom Is in Danger and How to Save It*. Harvard University Press.

Nagle, A. (2017) *Kill All Normies: Online Culture Wars from 4chan and Tumblr to Trump and the Alt-Right*. Zero Books.

Navarro, V.A. (2002) 'Critique of social capital', *International Journal of Health Services*, 32(3): 423–432.

Neveu, C. (2003) *Citoyenneté et espace public: Habitants, jeunes et citoyens dans une ville du Nord*. Presses Universitaires de Septentrion.

Nieminen, H. (2006) *Kansa seisoi loitompana. Kansallisen julkisuuden rakentuminen Suomessa 1809–1917*. ['People Stood Apart': The Founding of the National Public Sphere in Finland 1809–1917]. Vastapaino.

Nisbet, M.C. (2009) 'Communicating climate change: Why frames matter for public engagement', *Environment: Science and Policy for Sustainable Development*, 51(2): 12–23.

Nissenbaum, A. and Shifman, L. (2017) 'Internet memes as contested cultural capital: The case of 4chan's /b/ board', *New Media and Society*, 19(4): 483–501.

Norgaard, K.M. (2006) 'People want to protect themselves a little bit: Emotions, denial and social movement nonparticipation', *Sociological Inquiry*, 76(3): 372–396.

Nykänen, T., Kukko, J-E and Koikkalainen, P. (2023) *Tottelematon kansa: poliittisen vastarinnan muuttuvat muodot*. Tampere: Vastapaino.

Ødegård, G. (2007) 'Political socialization and influence at the mercy of politicians: A study of a local participation project amongst young people in Norway', *Young*, 15(3): 273–297.

Paakkunainen, K. (2004) *Nuorten ääni ja kunnantalon heikko kaiku: Nuoret kunnallisessa demokratiassa ja paikallisissa vaikuttajaryhmissä*. Edita.

Pateman, C. (1970) *Participation and Democratic Theory*. Cambridge University Press.

Pateman, C. (2012) 'Participatory democracy revisited', *Perspectives on Politics*, 10(1): 7–19.

Pekkarinen, E. and Myllyniemi, S. (eds) (2018) *Vaikutusvaltaa Euroopan laidalla: Nuorisobarometri 2018*. Valtion nuorisoneuvosto.

Phillips, W. (2013) 'The house that Fox built: Anonymous, spectacle, and cycles of amplification', *Television and New Media*, 14(6): 494–509.

Phillips, W. (2016) *This Is Why We Can't Have Nice Things: Mapping the Relationship between Online Trolling and Mainstream Culture*. MIT Press.

Phillips, W. (2019) 'It wasn't just the trolls: Early internet culture, "fun", and the fires of exclusionary laughter', *Social Media + Society*, 5(3): 1–4.

Pickard, S. and Bessant, J. (eds) (2018) *Young People Re-generating Politics in Times of Crises*. Springer International Publishing.

Pike, K.L. (1967) *Etic and Emic Standpoints for the Description of Behaviour*. Princeton University Press.

Purhonen, S. (2016) 'Generations on paper: Bourdieu and the critique of "generationalism"', *Social Science Information*, 55(1): 94–114.

Putnam, R.D. (2000) *Bowling Alone: The Collapse and Revival of American Community*. Simon & Schuster.

Pyyhtinen, O. and Lehtonen, T.-K. (2023) 'The gift of waste: The diversity of gift practices among dumpster divers', *Anthropological Theory*, 23(2): 209–231.

Ricoeur, P. (1971) 'The model of the text: Meaningful action considered as a text', *Social Research*, 529–562.

Ricoeur P. (1995) *Le Juste*. Editions Esprit.

Rikala, S. (2020) 'Agency among young people in marginalised positions: Towards a better understanding of mental health problems', *Journal of Youth Studies*, 23(8): 1022–1038.

Rissanen, E., Kuvaja-Köllner, V., Elonheimo, H., Sillanmäki, L., Sourander, A. and Kankaanpää, E. (2022) 'The long-term cost of childhood conduct problems: Finnish Nationwide 1981 Birth Cohort Study', *Journal of Child Psychology and Psychiatry*, 63(6): 683–692.

Roberts, S. and Evans, S. (2012) 'Aspirations and imagined futures: The im/possibilities for Britain's young working class' in W. Atkinson, S. Roberts and M. Savage (eds) *Class Inequality in Austerity Britain*. Palgrave Macmillan, pp 70–89.

Rolin, K. (1999) 'Humanistisen ja yhteiskuntatieteellisen tutkimuksen perinteet' in J. Hallamaa, V. Launis, S. Lötjönen and I. Sorvali (eds) *Etiikkaa ihmistieteille*. Suomalaisen kirjallisuuden seura.

Rosanvallon, P. (1998) *Le peuple introuvable. Histoire de la représentation démocratique en France*. Gallimard.

Rosanvallon, P. (2006) *La Contre-Démocratie. La politique à l'âge de la défiance*. Seuil.

Rosanvallon, P. (2008) *La légitimié démocratique. Impartialité, réflexivité, proximité*. Seuil.

Rosanvallon, P. (2011) *La société des égaux: Collecion 'Les livres du nouveau monde'*. Seuil.

Rousseau, J.-J. (1998) *Yhteiskuntasopimuksesta, eli valtio-oikeuden johtavat aatteet (Du contrat social ou principes du droit politique)*. Translated by J.V. Lehtonen. Karisto.

Rubin, B. (2007) 'There's still not justice: Youth civic identity development amid distinct school and community contexts', *Teachers College Record*, 109: 449–481.

Ruuti Munstadi (2015) 'RuutiBudjetti pähkinänkuoressa'. Available from: https://youtu.be/2AiFOFt3Qvc [Accessed 20 March 2024].

Sauerborn, E. (2022) 'The politicisation of secular mindfulness – Extinction Rebellion's emotive protest practices', *European Journal of Cultural and Political Sociology*, 9(4): 451–474.

Savage, M. (2015) *Social Class in the 21st Century*. Penguin.

Savage, M., Bagnall, G. and Longhurst, B. (2001) 'Ordinary, ambivalent and defensive: Class identities in the northwest of England', *Sociology*, 35(4): 875–892.

Sayer, A. (2005) 'Class, moral worth and recognition', *Sociology*, 39(5): 947–963.

Schudson, M. (1998) *The Good Citizen: A History of American Civic Life*. Free Press.

Scott, J.C. (1990) *Domination and the Arts of Resistance: Hidden Transcripts*. Yale University Press.

Selle, P. (1996) 'Norsk (skandinavisk) frivilligdom i endring' in E.T. Rasmussen and I. Koch-Nielsen (eds) *Den tredje sektor under forandring*. Socialforsknings- instituttet, pp 69–83.

Sevi, S. (2021) 'Do young voters vote for young leaders?', *Electoral Studies*, 69: 102200.

Shifman, L. (2013) *Memes in Digital Culture*. MIT Press.

Siisiäinen, M. (1998) 'Uusien ja vanhojen liikkeiden keinovalikoimat' [Old and new movements' repertoires of action], in K. Ilmonen and M. Siisiäinen (eds) *Uudet ja vanhat liikkeet* [Old and New Movements]. Vastapaino, pp 219–243.

Siisiäinen, M. and Kankainen, T. (2009) 'Järjestötoiminnan kehitys ja tulevaisuudennäkymät Suomessa', *Oikeusministeriön julkaisuja*, 5: 91–138.

Silber, I.F. (2003) 'Pragmatic sociology as cultural sociology: Beyond repertoire theory?', *European Journal of Social Theory*, 6(4): 427–449.

Siltala, A. (2020) '"Lurkkaa lisää": Etnografinen tutkielma yksilöllisyydestä Anonyymissä kuvalautakulttuurissa'. Master's thesis, Tampere University.

Silva, J.M. (2013) *Coming up Short: Working-Class Adulthood in an Age of Uncertainty*. Oxford University Press.

Siurala, L. and Turkia, H. (2012) 'Celebrating pluralism: Beyond established forms of youth participation', in P. Loncle, M. Cuconato, V. Muniglia and A. Walther (eds) *Youth Participation in Europe: Beyond Discourses, Practices and Realities*. Policy Press, pp 76–92.

Sivesind, K.H. and P. Selle (2010) 'Civil society in the Nordic countries: Between displacement and vitality', in R. Alapuro and H. Stenius (eds) *Nordic Associations in a European Perspective*. Nomos, pp 89–120.

Skeggs, B. (1997) *Formations of Class & Gender: Becoming Respectable*. SAGE.

Skeggs, B. (2001) 'The toilet paper: Femininity, class and misrecognition', *Women's Studies International Forum*, 24(3–4): 295–307.

Statistics Finland (2018) 'Finland among the best in the world'. Available from: https://www.stat.fi/tup/satavuotias-suomi/suomi-maailman-karjessa_en.html [Accessed 20 March 2024].

Statistics Finland (2023) 'Voting according to age group and gender in parliamentary elections'. Available from: https://pxdata.stat.fi/PxWeb/pxweb/en/StatFin/StatFin__evaa/ [Accessed 20 March 2024].

Stenius, H. (2003) 'Kansalainen', in M. Hyvärinen, J. Kurunmäki, K. Palonen, T. Pulkkinen and H. Stenius (eds) *Käsitteet liikkeessä: Suomen poliittisen kulttuurin käsitehistoria*. Vastapaino, pp 309–362.

Stenius, H. (2010) 'Nordic associational life in European and inter-Nordic perspectives', in R. Alapuro and H. Stenius (eds) *Nordic Associations in a Comparative Perspective*. Nomos, pp 29–88.

Stockemer, D. and Sundström, A. (2021) 'Quotas, the electoral system type and the election of young women', *Social Politics: International Studies in Gender, State & Society*, 28(4): 1025–1045.

Sundback, A. (2004) 'Glappet mellan de aktiva och dem som de representerar', in K. Paakkunainen (ed.) *Nuorten ääni ja kunnantalon heikko kaiku: Nuoret kunnallisessa demokratiassa ja paikallisissa vaikuttajaryhmissä*. Edita, pp 145–157.

Suomen Nuorisovaltuustojen Liitto (2020) *Nuvalaisen käsikirja*. Suomen Nuorisovaltuustojen Liitto ry. Available from: http://www.nuva.fi/s/nuvalaisen_kasikirja_3painos_verkkoon.pdf [Accessed 19 November 2020].

Suoninen, A., Kupari, P. and Törmäkangas, K. (2010) *Nuorten yhteiskunnalliset tiedot, osallistuminen ja asenteet: Kansainvälisen ICCS 2009 tutkimuksen päätulokset*. Jyväskylän yliopistopaino.

Swidler, A. (1986) 'Culture in action: Symbols and strategies', *American Sociological Review*, 51(2): 273–286.

Swidler, A. (2001) *Talk of love: How Culture Matters*. University of Chicago Press.

Swidler, A. (2023) 'Life's work: History, biography, and ideas', *Annual Review of Sociology*, 49: 21–37.

Taft, J.K. and Gordon, H.R. (2013) 'Youth activists, youth councils, and constrained democracy', *Education, Citizenship and Social Justice*, 8(1): 87–100.

Talpin, J. (2011) *Schools of Democracy: How Ordinary Citizens (Sometimes) Become Competent in Participatory Budgeting Institutions*. ECPR Press.

Tavory, I. and Timmermans, S. (2014) *Abductive Analysis: Theorizing Qualitative Research*. University of Chicago Press.

TENK (2012) *Responsible Conduct of Research and Procedures for Handling Allegations of Misconduct in Finland*. Available from: http://www.tenk.fi/sites/tenk.fi/files/HTK_ohje_2012.pdf [Accessed 20 March 2024].

Thévenot, L. (2006) *L'action au pluriel: Sociologie des régimes d'engagement*. La Découverte.

Thévenot, L. (2007) 'The plurality of cognitive formats and engagements: Moving between the familiar and the public', *European Journal of Social Theory*, 10(3): 409–423.

Thévenot, L. (2011) 'Oikeuttavuuden rajat: Yhteiselämää koossapitävät sidokset ja niiden väärinkäyttö', *Sosiologia*, 48(1): 7–21.

Thévenot, L. (2014) 'Voicing concern and difference: From public spaces to common-place', *European Journal of Cultural and Political Sociology*, 1(1): 7–34.

Thévenot, L. (2015) 'Bounded justifiability: Making commonality on the basis of binding engagements' in P. Dumouchel and R. Gotoh (eds) *Social Bonds as Freedom: Revisiting the Dichotomy of the Universal and the Particular*. Berghahn Books, pp 82–108.

Thévenot, L. (2020) 'How does politics take closeness into account? Returns from Russia', *International Journal of Politics, Culture, and Society*, 33: 221–250.

Tiidenberg, K. and Allaste, A.-A. (2020) 'LGBT activism in Estonia: Identities, enactment and perceptions of LGBT people', *Sexualities*, 23(3): 307–324.

Tilly, C. (2006) *Regimes and Repertoires*. University of Chicago Press.

Tognato, C. (2019) 'Commentary: The civil state in the Nordic region, and beyond', in J.C. Alexander, A. Lund and A. Voyer (eds) *The Nordic Civil Sphere*. Polity Press.

Toikkanen, P. (2020) *Tulevaisuuden näkymät järjestöissä*. Osana Yhteistä Ratkaisua oy. Available from: https://drive.google.com/uc?export=download&id=1HQRcd-IDofV_gbNLsK0e-P4uw6j6ltB5 [Accessed 20 March 2024].

Tomperi, T. and Piattoeva, N. (2005) 'Demokraattisten juurten kasvattaminen' in T. Kiilakoski, T. Tomperi and M. Vuorikoski (eds) *Kenen kasvatus? Kriittinen pedagogiikka ja toisinkasvatuksen mahdollisuus*. Vastapaino.

Trammell, M. (2014) 'User investment and behaviour policing on 4chan', *First Monday*, 19(2–3): 1–11.

Tuters, M. and Hagen, S. (2020) '(((They))) rule: Memetic antagonism and nebulous othering on 4chan', *New Media & Society*, 22(12): 2218–2237.

Tyler, I. and Slater T. (2018) 'Rethinking the sociology of stigma', *Sociological Review*, 66(4): 721–743.

Typpö, J. and Pullinen, J. (2016) 'Sanna-Mari Paakki aloitti kampanjan tissien puolesta ja joutui Ylilaudalta nousseen vihakampanjan kohteeksi – ja se kertoo siitä, mikä internetiä nyt riivaa kaikkialla', *Helsingin Sanomat*, 29 November. Available from: https://www.hs.fi/nyt/art-2000004885975.html [Accessed 20 March 2024].

Uldam, J. and Kaun, A. (2019) 'Theorizing civic engagement and social media: The case of the "refugee crisis" and volunteer organizing in Sweden', in M. Mortensen, C. Neumayer and T. Poell (eds) *Social Media Materialities and Protest: Critical Reflections*. Routledge, pp 110–115.

Uusitalo, R. (1979) *Nuoret, nuorisoryhmät ja yhteiskunta: Tietoja nuorten ryhmistä 1950–, 1960– ja 1970-luvuilta*. Helsingin yliopiston sosiologian laitos, Working papers n:o 10.

Väänänen, N. and Liukko, J. (2023) 'Justifying a financially and socially sustainable pension reform: A comparative study of Finland and France', *International Journal of Sociology and Social Policy*, 43(5/6): 507–520.

Vainikka, E. (2018) 'The anti-social network: Precarious life in online conversations of the socially withdrawn', *European Journal of Cultural Studies*, 23(4): 596–610.

Wahlström, M., Kocyba, P., de Vydt, M. and de Moor, J. (2019) *Protest for a Future: Composition, Mobilization and Motives of the Participants in Fridays for Future Climate Protests on 15 March, 2019 in 13 European Cities*. Available from: https://www.researchgate.net/publication/334745801_Protest_for_a_future_Composition_mobilization_and_motives_of_the_participants_in_Fridays_For_Future_climate_protests_on_15_March_2019_in_13_European_cities [Accessed 15 March 2024].

Warren, M. (1999) 'What is political?', *Journal of Theoretical Politics*, 11(2): 207–231.

Watts, R. (2019) 'New politics: The anonymous politics of 4chan, outrage and the new public sphere' in P. Kelly, P. Campbell, L. Harrison and C. Hickey (eds) *Young People and the Politics of Outrage and Hope*. Brill, pp 73–89.

Wacquant L. (2003) 'Ethnografeast: A progress report on the practice and promise of ethnography'. *Ethnography*, 4(1): 5–14.

Walther, A., Batsleer, J., Loncle, P. and Pohl, A. (eds) (2019) *Young People and the Struggle for Participation: Contested Practices, Power and Pedagogies in Public Spaces*. Routledge.

Weber, M. (2009) *Tiede ja politiikka: Kutsumus ja ammatti*. Vastapaino.

Weber, R. (2020) 'Why do young people join parties? The influence of individual resources on motivation', *Party Politics*, 26(4): 496–509.

Weijo, H.A., Martin, D.M. and Arnould, E.J. (2018) 'Consumer movements and collective creativity: The case of restaurant day', *Journal of Consumer Research*, 45(2): 251–274.

Westwell, E. and Bunting, J. (2020) 'The regenerative culture of Extinction Rebellion: Self-care, people care, planet care', *Environmental Politics*, 29(3): 546–551.

Wilkinson, R.D. and Pickett, K. (2009) *The Spirit Level: Why More Equal Societies Almost Always Do Better*. Bloomsbury Publishing.

Wollebæk, D. and Selle, P. (2002) 'Does participation in voluntary associations contribute to social capital? The impact of intensity, scope, and type', *Nonprofit and Voluntary Sector Quarterly*, 31: 32–61.

Wollabæk, D. and Selle, P. (2003) 'Participation and social capital formation: Norway in a comparative perspective', *Scandinavian Political Studies*, 26(1): 67–91.

Wollebæk, D., Ibsen, B. and Siisiäinen, M. (2010) 'Voluntary associations at the local level in three Nordic countries', in R. Alapuro and H. Stenius (eds) *Nordic Associations in a European Perspective*. Nomos, pp 121–150.

Woodman, D. and Wyn, J. (2014) *Youth and Generation: Rethinking Change and Inequality in the Lives of Young People*. SAGE.

Wright, E. (2019) *How to Be an Anti-capitalist for the 21st Century*. Verso.

Yates, L. (2015) 'Rethinking prefiguration: Alternatives, micropolitics and goals in social movements', *Social Movement Studies*, 14(1): 1–21.

Young, I. (2002) *Inclusion and Democracy*. Oxford University Press.

Ylä-Anttila, T. (2017) 'Familiarity as a tool of populism: Political appropriation of shared experiences and the case of Suvivirsi', *Acta Sociologica*, 60(4): 342–357.

Ylä-Anttila, T. (2018) 'Populist knowledge: "Post-truth" repertoires of contesting epistemic authorities', *European Journal of Cultural and Political Sociology*, 5(4): 356–388.

Ylä-Anttila, T. (2020) 'Social media and the emergence, establishment and transformation of the right-wing populist Finns Party', *Populism*, 3(1): 121–139.

Ylä-Anttila, T. and Luhtakallio, E. (2016) 'Justifications analysis: Understanding moral evaluations in public debates', *Sociological Research Online*, 21(4): 1–15.

Ylä-Anttila, T., Bauvois, G. and Pyrhönen, N. (2019) 'Politicization of migration in the countermedia style: A computational and qualitative analysis of populist discourse', *Discourse, Context & Media*, 32(4): 1–8.

Ylä-Anttila, T., Eranti, V. and Hardwick, S. (2020) 'Going overboard: How ironic group style becomes political on an anonymous imageboard', *Social Media + Society*, 6(4): 1–11.

Ylä-Anttila, T., Eranti, V. and Kukkonen, A. (2021) 'Topic modeling for frame analysis: A study of media debates on climate change in India and USA'. *Global Media and Communication*.

YLE (2019) Tältä näyttää nuorisovaalien valitsema eduskunta – eniten paikkoja haalivat vihreät ja perussuomalaiset. Available from: https://yle.fi/a/3-10728219 [Accessed 5 April 2024].

Ziblatt, S. and Lewitsky, D. (2018) *How Democracies Die*. Crown Publishing.

Zivi, K. (2012) *Making Rights Claims: A Practice of Democratic Citizenship*. Oxford University Press.

Index

A

abduction 61, 173–175, 202
accountability 42, 45
activism, activist 1–15, 20–25, 40, 48, 51, 56–7, 59, 61–2, 91, 100–103, 106–7, 111–112, 117, 120, 122, 124, 124–9, 138–159, 162–3, 165, 166–8, 173, 175
 climate activism 139, 140, 151, 154, 155, 156, 181
 urban activism 124, 125
 see also Kallio movement
affordance 18, 108–112, 120, 136
Alapuro, R. 14–15, 121, 166–168, 185n3
anonymity 106, 108, 109, 111, 115, 117, 165
anti-feminism 106, 107, 115, 116
atomized individuals 100

B

Baiocchi, G-P. 9, 13, 28, 51, 61, 69, 71, 73, 80–81, 83, 86–87, 92, 120, 125–126, 142, 155–156, 170, 178
Bellah, R. 12–13, 21–22
belonging 2–3, 6, 24, 37, 47, 67, 88–9, 106, 109–10, 118–9, 122, 124, 126–9, 137, 142–3, 146–7, 158, 162, 168
Bennett, E. A. 2, 87, 92
Bennett, W. L. 13, 119–120, 134, 166
Boltanski, L. 5, 7–8, 73, 83
burnout 146, 148–9, 152, 163

C

candidacy 49, 52, 55, 56, 57, 58, 64, 66
candidate 23, 49, 50, 51, 56, 59, 61, 62–3, 64, 65, 66–7, 81, 155–6, 160
ceremonial keying 39
citizenship 12, 21, 25, 30, 44, 71, 85, 107, 119, 183, 185n9
 active citizenship 2, 29, 72, 125
civic action 9–10, 11, 12, 33, 37, 118, 121, 127, 137, 143, 178
civic imagination 3, 6–7, 9, 23, 25, 51, 60–1, 64, 66, 69, 72–3, 77–8, 80, 82–3, 86–7, 124, 126, 133–4, 136, 138, 141–142, 156–7, 160–2, 166

civil disobedience 125, 138, 139, 145, 146, 147–8, 153, 154, 157
civil society 7, 10, 14–15, 17–8, 21–2, 73, 105, 127, 166
class 12, 14, 74, 86, 89, 97, 120, 122–3, 163
climate change, climate crisis 19, 51, 139, 140–2, 148, 151–6
collective 2, 7, 8, 12, 14, 21, 24, 42, 45, 64, 67, 102–3, 122, 128, 140, 142, 143, 144–6, 157, 162–6, 168, 170
collective action 27, 35, 84, 118, 120, 133, 137, 159, 162, 164
collectivism 1, 4, 11, 13, 14, 17, 22–3, 25, 104, 119, 138, 157–8, 162–3
common, the 1–4, 7, 10–12, 18, 22, 25, 46–7, 52, 66, 159, 161–4, 168–170
common good 7, 8, 41, 44, 58, 69, 72–3, 78–9, 81–5, 118–9, 121–2, 125–6, 131, 133, 137, 157, 161, 170
computational (text analysis) 23–4, 115, 172, 176
connective action 120, 134
constructive representation 167–8
councilor 37, 53, 61
cultural tools, toolkit 3, 5–6, 8–9, 13, 17–20, 23–25, 68, 87, 105, 107–8, 117, 168, 170, 173–5
 cultural tools of individualism 159, 164–5, 168
culture, the 5–6, 8–9, 29, 105, 115, 164, 167, 169, 176
 commitment culture 118, 119, 122, 128, 130, 163, 164
 cultural norms 30, 86, 89, 120
 cultural practices 51, 89, 107, 109, 110, 117, 159, 161
 subculture 99, 105–7, 110, 114, 117

D

debriefing 140, 145, 146, 148, 163
deliberation 28, 31, 72, 74, 82, 84, 136, 159, 184n2
democracy 1–2, 4–5, 11, 14, 16, 18, 20, 25, 27–30, 32–3, 40, 46, 69–72, 77–8, 83, 94, 155, 165, 168–9, 171

206

INDEX

participatory democracy 4, 9, 26, 28, 29, 32, 41, 49, 71, 165, 170
representative democracy 4, 26–8, 29, 31–3, 40, 155, 170
democracy education 21, 55, 70, 81, 84, 166
descriptive representation 14, 166–8
disadvantaged youth 85, 86, 103, 104
DIY urbanism 121, 185n8
doing society 1–4, 5, 6, 8–9, 11, 13, 17, 19, 22, 24–5, 50–2, 58, 65–7, 71, 82–7, 95, 98, 102, 108, 115–9, 122, 138, 140–1, 152, 156–7, 159, 161, 162, 164, 169, 170, 173, 174–5
  cultures of doing society 1, 2, 8, 9, 10, 143, 155, 157–8, 160, 161, 162, 164, 168, 171, 174
dreams 1–2, 8, 41–3, 54, 65, 67, 84, 93, 104, 131, 150–2, 156, 162–3

E

e-democracy 24, 68, 81, 83, 160–1, 165, 175
elections 17, 21, 27, 32, 34, 35, 37, 43, 48–51, 53, 57–9, 61, 63–6, 70, 92, 94, 98, 107, 160–1, 167, 177
electoral system 49, 50, 166
Eliasoph, N. 2–3, 5, 7, 9, 27, 29, 42, 46, 92, 107, 109–112, 120, 169–170
enemy 112, 114–6, 162
engagement 2–3, 4, 6, 9, 11, 12, 13, 18, 21, 23, 25, 27–32, 36, 40, 43, 49, 51, 56–60, 66–7, 73, 86–7, 91–2, 138, 141, 152, 156, 159–163, 168, 170–3
  engaging in a plan 52, 64, 66, 122, 140
  engaging in exploration 52, 58–9, 66
  modes of engagement 4–5, 173
ethnography 6–7, 21, 23, 24, 32, 61, 69, 85, 110, 118, 172, 174–5, 179, 181, 182
everyday action, practices 3, 8, 21, 25, 89, 121, 127, 140, 174, 179
exclusion 17, 23–24, 88, 89, 91, 94, 111, 161
exhaustion 148–9, 150, 152
Extinction Rebellion (XR) 24, 138–158, 163, 180

F

far-right 53, 60, 107, 114, 115, 117
feminism 79, 82, 116
Finland 1, 11, 13, 15–17, 22, 30, 33, 46, 49, 107, 119–121, 166
  see also political culture, Finnish
Finnish Youth Barometer 31
Finns party 17, 37, 51, 53–54, 60, 112
frame analysis 35, 176
Fraser, N. 86, 101, 170
free speech 115–116, 125
Fung, A. 27–28, 30, 41–42, 71–72

G

Ganuza, E. 13, 28, 170
Goffman, E. 7, 39, 44

grammars of 'commonality in the plural' 5, 7–8, 72, 82, 145, 170, 178
Greens, Green Party 17, 53–55, 64, 127
group styles 3, 6–8, 24, 29, 42, 109–112, 116, 161

H

hobby 33, 52, 58–60, 66, 75, 141, 160, 183n5
hyperbole 114, 116

I

imageboard 13, 23, 80, 105–112, 116–117, 161, 176, 179
  see also Ylilauta
immigration 17, 22, 79, 81, 106, 115
individualism 11, 12, 19, 21, 22, 87, 97–8, 119–20, 121–2, 126–7, 130, 132, 133, 136–7, 144, 160, 163–165
individualization 11–12, 19–20, 119
induction 173, 176
International Civic and Citizenship Study 31
irony 106, 111–14

J

Juris, J. 13, 166
justification theory, justifications 7–8, 62, 73, 79–80, 82–4, 139, 154, 161–162, 171, 178

K

Kallio movement 24, 118–19, 122–9, 133–7, 140, 145, 156–8, 158, 163, 180

L

Lamont, M. 86, 88–89, 104, 116
left-wing, leftist 56, 58, 62, 82, 142, 154
leisure 58, 59, 70, 75, 183n5
Lichterman, P. 3, 7, 9, 13, 29, 42, 69, 107, 109–112, 119–120, 122, 127–128, 130, 137, 139–140, 143–145, 157

M

marginalization 8, 10, 22, 24, 28, 86, 90, 106, 117, 169, 179
marginalized youth 10, 23, 84, 88–9, 105, 152, 155, 161–3, 165, 167, 177
meme, memetic 13, 105, 109, 112–5, 117, 120, 162, 165
minority 48, 86, 87, 101, 112
minors 28, 31, 32
mixed methods 114, 172
municipal council 33–4, 49, 55, 61

N

National Coalition 35, 59–60, 63, 95
NGO 53, 56, 69, 78, 124, 150, 166–7, 198n5
Nordic countries 4, 11, 13–18, 22, 121, 166–7
normie 110, 112, 114–6

O

Official, public 30, 33, 40, 43, 44, 69, 70, 76, 82, 90, 100, 126, 179

P

participation 6, 20–1, 22, 30
  in Finland 21–2, 32
  political 9, 11, 17, 31, 49, 92, 94, 100, 102, 104
participatory budgeting 21, 23, 26, 28, 30–33, 40–48, 52–53, 55–56, 74, 79, 83–84, 160, 176–177
  in Helsinki 32, 40–1, 47, 48
  see also RuutiBudjetti
party members 36, 50, 166
personalism 119, 122, 130, 137, 143, 163
personalized commitment 122, 128, 130, 133
political (the) 2–3, 8, 10, 30, 119, 121, 134, 137, 160, 169
  action 2, 5–6, 10, 14, 23, 25, 39, 49, 52, 61, 87, 100, 103, 140, 159, 179
  career (in politics) 35, 50, 63, 64, 66, 71, 170
  culture 5, 11, 13, 14–15, 17, 22, 32, 69, 71, 73, 81, 83, 106–108, 120, 166, 168
    Finnish 15, 17, 62, 69, 73, 83, 164, 166, 167
  engagement 2, 4, 9, 11, 23, 43, 51–52, 58, 138, 170
  participation 9, 11, 17–18, 20–21, 23, 31, 49, 102, 104, 155, 159
  passivity 86, 92–95
  repertoire 30, 36
politician 1, 8, 16, 30, 50–51, 55, 59–61, 80, 83, 111, 125, 141, 153, 155–157, 161, 166–167, 185n2
politicization 82, 105, 107, 112, 115, 117, 168, 171
politics
  climate 25, 139, 141–143, 153–154, 156–158
  contentious (forms of) 20, 30
  doing 12, 29, 30, 114, 116
  formal 35, 58, 121
  institutional (forms of), institutionalized 20, 87, 91–92, 94–95, 103, 119, 125–126, 133, 152–155, 157, 173, 185n6
  path to 56–58
  party 10, 25, 35, 49, 51, 53, 55–56, 66, 86, 113, 115, 124, 125, 133, 160
  personalized 24, 122, 127–8, 140, 143–145, 157
  prefigurative 126, 133, 135–136, 140, 147, 152, 157, 163
  student 53, 56, 63–64
Porsgrunn model 31
power 7, 21, 30, 34, 36, 38–39, 41, 61, 62, 64–65, 67, 71, 72, 75, 81, 83–84, 116, 124, 125, 145, 160, 167–168, 176

practice 25, 27, 28, 30, 31, 34, 109, 125, 145, 154
pragmatist 3–4, 107, 122, 172–173
prefiguration 134, 137, 140–142, 158
private interest 69, 73, 80–84
privilege 7, 124
problem solving 3, 7, 9–10, 64, 67, 73, 78, 80, 82–83, 124, 142, 160, 162, 164–165
procedure 27–28, 32–34, 38–39, 46–47
protest 24, 33, 113, 114, 140, 146, 181
public transportation 75–77, 81, 136

Q

qualitative 20, 66, 105, 172–173, 175–176, 180
quantitative 172–173, 180

R

recognition 28, 86–87, 89, 91, 95, 97, 99–104, 161
regenerative culture 145–146, 148, 163, 165
representation 14, 28, 31, 44, 49, 51, 126, 167–168, 178
resistance 14, 21, 24, 44, 169
respect 36, 41, 44, 45, 91, 95, 101
right-wing 10, 17, 51, 56, 58, 105–107, 112–115, 117, 161, 183n3
Rosanvallon, P. 5, 167
RuutiBudjetti 40
rural 76, 77

S

Savage, M. 12, 89
scene style 6–9, 42, 44
school 27, 28, 32, 35, 37, 39, 41–43, 48, 54, 57, 59, 60, 69, 74, 75, 77–82, 84, 90, 91, 155
  school council 20–21, 36, 53
  school strike 13, 185n2
  school vote 41–43, 45, 47
Sedergerg, A. 13, 119–120, 134, 166
self-interest 11, 41, 45, 57–58, 131–132
self-transformation 87, 95, 97–99, 102–103, 161
self-worth 97, 104
Social Democrat; Social Democratic Party 60, 62, 65
social justice 61, 109, 111–112, 116, 162–163, 184n3
social movement 1, 10, 17, 22, 25, 56–58, 66, 81, 120–121, 138, 140, 163–164, 170
social movement studies 4, 8
sports 43, 59, 75–76, 80, 82, 160
Stenius, H. 14–15, 127, 129, 184n1
stigma 102–3, 179
stigmatization 86, 88, 89, 91, 100, 104, 182
survey 18, 20–23, 31, 50–51, 62, 70, 105, 118, 136, 167, 169, 174–176
Swedish People's Party 63
Swidler, A. 3, 5, 107, 164, 175

INDEX

T

Thévenot, L. 2, 4–5, 7–8, 52, 57, 64, 69, 73, 120, 122, 132, 139–140, 145, 151
transgression 111, 161
trolling 25, 106, 113–14

V

voting 12, 17, 21, 27, 29, 31, 34, 45, 49, 50, 70, 87, 91–94, 98, 136, 153, 155, 163, 167, 169, 183n2

W

wellbeing 140, 148, 153

Y

Ylilauta 24, 105–117, 156, 161–162, 165, 176, 179–180, 182, 184n2, 184n3
youth council 23, 26–28, 29–40, 46–48, 52–54, 60, 160, 174, 176–177
youth organization 50, 52–53, 56–60, 66, 133
  as a path to politics 56–58
youth participation 8, 20, 23, 26, 28, 29–34, 40, 46–48, 54–55, 71, 91, 176–177, 181
  see also youth council; participatory budgeting in Helsinki
youth studies 4, 18–19, 50